Lecture Notes in Computer Science 9017

Commenced Publication in 1973
Founding and Former Series Editors:
Gerhard Goos, Juris Hartmanis, and Jan van Leeuwen

More information about this series at http://www.springer.com/series/7407

Luís Miguel Pinho · Wolfgang Karl
Albert Cohen · Uwe Brinkschulte (Eds.)

Architecture of Computing Systems – ARCS 2015

28th International Conference
Porto, Portugal, March 24–27, 2015
Proceedings

 Springer

Editors
Luís Miguel Pinho
CISTER/INESC TEC, ISEP Research Center
Porto
Portugal

Wolfgang Karl
Karlsruher Institut für Technologie
Karlsruhe
Germany

Albert Cohen
Inria and École Normale Supérieure
Paris
France

Uwe Brinkschulte
Goethe University Fachbereich Informatik und
    Mathematik
Frankfurt am Main
Germany

ISSN 0302-9743
Lecture Notes in Computer Science
ISBN 978-3-319-16085-6
DOI 10.1007/978-3-319-16086-3

ISSN 1611-3349   (electronic)

ISBN 978-3-319-16086-3   (eBook)

Library of Congress Control Number: Applied for

LNCS Sublibrary: SL1 – Theoretical Computer Science and General Issues

Printed on acid-free paper

Springer International Publishing AG Switzerland is part of Springer Science+Business Media
(www.springer.com)

Preface

The 28th International Conference on Architecture of Computing Systems (ARCS 2015) was hosted by the CISTER Research Center at Instituto Superior de Engenharia do Porto, Portugal, from March 24 to 27, 2015 and continues the long-standing ARCS tradition of reporting top-notch results in computer architecture and related areas. It was organized by the special interest group on 'Architecture of Computing Systems' of the GI (Gesellschaft für Informatik e. V.) and ITG (Informationstechnische Gesellschaft im VDE), with GI having the financial responsibility for the 2015 edition. The conference was also supported by IFIP (International Federation of Information Processing).

The special focus of ARCS 2015 was on "Reconciling Parallelism and Predictability in Mixed-Critical Systems." This reflects the ongoing convergence between computational, control, and communication systems in many application areas and markets. The increasingly data-intensive and computational nature of Cyber-Physical Systems is now pushing for embedded control systems to run on complex parallel hardware. System designers are squeezed between the hammer of dependability, performance, power and energy efficiency, and the anvil of cost. The latter is typically associated with programmability issues, validation and verification, deployment, maintenance, complexity, portability, etc. Traditional, low-level approaches to parallel software development are already plagued by data races, non-reproducible bugs, time unpredictability, non-composability, and unscalable verification. Solutions exist to raise the abstraction level, to develop dependable, reusable, and efficient parallel implementations, and to build computer architectures with predictability, fault tolerance, and dependability in mind. The Internet of Things also pushes for reconciling computation and control in computing systems. The convergence of challenges, technology, and markets for high-performance consumer and mobile devices has already taken place. The ubiquity of safety, security, and dependability requirements meets cost efficiency concerns. Long-term research is needed, as well as research evaluating the maturity of existing system design methods, programming languages and tools, software stacks, computer architectures, and validation approaches. This conference put a particular focus on these research issues.

The conference attracted 45 submissions from 22 countries. Each paper was assigned to at least three Program Committee Members for reviewing. The Committee selected 19 submissions for publication with authors from 11 countries. These papers were organized into six sessions covering topics on hardware, design, applicatrions, trust and privacy, and real-time issues. A session was dedicated to the three best paper candidates of the conference. Three invited talks on "The Evolution of Computer Architectures: A View from the European Commission" by Sandro D'Elia, European Commission Unit "Complex Systems & Advanced Computing," Belgium, "Architectures for Mixed-Criticality Systems based on Networked Multi-Core Chips" by Roman Obermaisser, University of Siegen, Germany, and "Time Predictability in High-Performance Mixed-Criticality Multicore Systems" by Francisco Cazorla,

Barcelona Supercomputing Center, Spain, completed the strong technical program. Four workshops focusing on specific sub-topics of ARCS were organized in conjunction with the main conference, one on Dependability and Fault Tolerance, one on Multi-Objective Many-Core Design, one on Self-Optimization in Organic and Autonomic Computing Systems, as well as one on Complex Problems over High Performance Computing Architectures. The conference week also featured two tutorials, on CUDA tuning and new GPU trends, and on the Myriad2 architecture, programming and computer vision applications.

We would like to thank the many individuals who contributed to the success of the conference, in particular the members of the Program Committee as well as the additional external reviewers, for the time and effort they put into reviewing the submissions carefully and selecting a high-quality program. Many thanks also to all authors for submitting their work. The workshops and tutorials were organized and coordinated by João Cardoso, and the poster session was organized by Florian Kluge and Patrick Meumeu Yomsi. The proceedings were compiled by Thilo Pionteck, industry liaison performed by Sascha Uhrig and David Pereira, and conference publicity by Vincent Nélis. The local arrangements were coordinated by Luis Ferreira. Our gratitude goes to all of them as well as to all other people, in particular the team at CISTER, which helped in the organization of ARCS 2015.

January 2015

Luís Miguel Pinho
Wolfgang Karl
Albert Cohen
Uwe Brinkschulte

Organization

General Co-Chairs

Luís Miguel Pinho   CISTER/INESC TEC, ISEP, Portugal
Wolfgang Karl   Karlsruhe Institute of Technology, Germany

Program Co-chairs

Albert Cohen   Inria, France
Uwe Brinkschulte   Universität Frankfurt, Germany

Publication Chair

Thilo Pionteck   Universität zu Lübeck, Germany

Industrial Liaison Co-chairs

Sascha Uhrig   Technische Universität Dortmund, Germany
David Pereira   CISTER/INESC TEC, ISEP, Portugal

Workshop and Tutorial Chair

João M. P. Cardoso   University of Porto/INESC TEC, Portugal

Poster Co-chairs

Florian Kluge   University of Augsburg, Germany
Patrick Meumeu Yomsi   CISTER/INESC TEC, ISEP, Portugal

Publicity Chair

Vincent Nelis   CISTER/INESC TEC, ISEP, Portugal

Local Organization Chair

Luis Lino Ferreira   CISTER/INESC TEC, ISEP, Portugal

Program Committee

Michael Beigl	Karlsruhe Institute of Technology, Germany
Mladen Berekovic	Technische Universität Braunschweig, Germany
Simon Bliudze	École Polytechnique Fédérale de Lausanne, Switzerland
Florian Brandner	École Nationale Supérieure de Techniques Avancées, France
Jürgen Brehm	Leibniz Universität Hannover, Germany
Uwe Brinkschulte	Universität Frankfurt am Main, Germany
David Broman	KTH Royal Institute of Technology, Sweden, and University of California, Berkeley, USA
João M.P. Cardoso	University of Porto/INESC TEC, Portugal
Luigi Carro	Universidade Federal do Rio Grande do Sul, Brazil
Albert Cohen	Inria, France
Koen De Bosschere	Ghent University, Belgium
Nikitas Dimopoulos	University of Victoria, Canada
Ahmed El-Mahdy	Egypt-Japan University of Science and Technology, Egypt
Fabrizio Ferrandi	Politecnico di Milano, Italy
Dietmar Fey	Friedrich-Alexander-Universität Erlangen-Nürnberg, Germany
Pierfrancesco Foglia	Università di Pisa, Italy
William Fornaciari	Politecnico di Milano, Italy
Björn Franke	University of Edinburgh, UK
Roberto Giorgi	Università di Siena, Italy
Daniel Gracia Pérez	Thales Research and Technology, France
Jan Haase	University of the Federal Armed Forces Hamburg, Germany
Jörg Henkel	Karlsruhe Institute of Technology, Germany
Andreas Herkersdorf	Technische Universität München, Germany
Christian Hochberger	Technische Universität Darmstadt, Germany
Jörg Hähner	Universität Augsburg, Germany
Michael Hübner	Ruhr University Bochum, Germany
Gert Jervan	Tallinn University of Technology, Estonia
Ben Juurlink	Technische Universität Berlin, Germany
Wolfgang Karl	Karlsruhe Institute of Technology, Germany
Christos Kartsaklis	Oak Ridge National Laboratory, USA
Jörg Keller	Fernuniversität in Hagen, Germany
Raimund Kirner	University of Hertfordshire, UK
Andreas Koch	Technische Universität Darmstadt, Germany
Hana Kubátová	Czech Technical University in Prague, Czech Republic
Olaf Landsiedel	Chalmers University of Technology, Sweden
Paul Lukowicz	Universität Passau, Germany

Erik Maehle	Universität zu Lübeck, Germany
Christian Müller-Schloer	Leibniz Universität Hannover, Germany
Alex Orailoglu	University of California, San Diego, USA
Carlos Eduardo Pereira	Universidade Federal do Rio Grande do Sul, Brazil
Thilo Pionteck	Universität zu Lübeck, Germany
Pascal Sainrat	Université Toulouse III, France
Toshinori Sato	Fukuoka University, Japan
Martin Schulz	Lawrence Livermore National Laboratory, USA
Karsten Schwan	Georgia Institute of Technology, USA
Leonel Sousa	Universidade de Lisboa, Portugal
Rainer Spallek	Technische Universität Dresden, Germany
Olaf Spinczyk	Technische Universität Dortmund, Germany
Benno Stabernack	Fraunhofer Institut für Nachrichtentechnik, Germany
Walter Stechele	Technische Universität München, Germany
Djamshid Tavangarian	Universität Rostock, Germany
Jürgen Teich	Friedrich-Alexander-Universität Erlangen-Nürnberg, Germany
Eduardo Tovar	CISTER/INESC TEC, ISEP, Portugal
Pedro Trancoso	University of Cyprus, Cyprus
Carsten Trinitis	Technische Universität München, Germany
Martin Törngren	KTH Royal Institute of Technology, Sweden
Sascha Uhrig	Technische Universität Dortmund, Germany
Theo Ungerer	Universität Augsburg, Germany
Hans Vandierendonck	Queen's University Belfast, UK
Stephane Vialle	CentraleSupelec and UMI GT-CNRS 2958, France
Lucian Vintan	"Lucian Blaga" University of Sibiu, Romania
Klaus Waldschmidt	Universität Frankfurt am Main, Germany
Stephan Wong	Delft University of Technology, The Netherlands

Additional Reviewers

Ardeshiricham, Armaiti
Backasch, Rico
Blochwitz, Christopher
Bradatsch, Christian
Comprés Ureña, Isaías A.
Eckert, Marcel
Engel, Andreas
Feng, Lei
Gangadharan, Deepak
Gottschling, Philip
Grudnitsky, Artjom
Guo, Qi
Haas, Florian

Habermann, Philipp
Hassan, Ahmad
Hempel, Gerald
Hu, Sensen
Huthmann, Jens
Iacovelli, Saverio
Jordan, Alexander
Kantert, Jan
Maia, Cláudio
Meyer, Dominik
Mische, Jörg
Naji, Amine
Nogueira, Luís

Pohl, Angela
Preußer, Thomas
Pyka, Arthur
Sanz Marco, Vicent
Schirmeier, Horst
Shuka, Romeo
Smirnov, Fedor

Spiegelberg, Henning
Westman, Jonas
Yomsi, Patrick
Zabel, Martin
Zhang, Xinhai
Zolda, Michael

Invited Talks

Dr. Sandro D'Elia, European Commission Unit "Complex Systems and Advanced Computing"

The Evolution of Computer Architectures: A view from the European Commission

Abstract of Talk: The changes in technology and market conditions have brought, in recent years, a significant evolution in the computer architectures. Multi-core chips force programmers to think parallel in any application domain, heterogeneous systems integrating different specialised processors are now the rule also in consumer markets, and energy efficiency is an issue across the entire computing spectrum from the wearable device to the high performance cluster. These trends pose significant issues: software development is a bottleneck because efficient programming for parallel and heterogeneous architectures is difficult, and application development remains a labour-intensive and expensive activity; non-deterministic timing in multicore chips poses a huge problem whenever a guaranteed response time is needed; software is typically not aware of the energy it uses, and therefore does not use hardware efficiently. Security is a cross-cutting problem, which in some cases is addressed through hardware-enforced "secure zones". This presentation discusses the recent evolution in computing architectures focusing on examples from European research and innovation projects, with a look forward to some promising innovations in the field like bio-inspired, probabilistic and approximate computing.

Dr. Sandro D'Elia is Project Officer at the European Commission Unit A/3 "Complex Systems & Advanced Computing". He spent a significant part of his career as IT project manager, first in the private sector and then in the IT service of the European Commission. In 2009 he moved to a position of research project officer. His role is evaluating, negotiating, controlling and supporting research and innovation projects financed by the European Commission, contributing to the drafting of the research and innovation work programme, and contributing to European policies on software, cyber-physical systems and advanced computing.

Prof. Dr. Roman Obermaisser, University of Siegen

Architectures for Mixed-Criticality Systems Based on Networked Multi-Core Chips

Abstract of Talk: Mixed-criticality architectures with support for modular certification make the integration of application subsystems with different safety assurance levels both technically and economically feasible. Strict segregation of these subsystems is a key requirement to avoid fault propagation and unintended side-effects due to integration. Also, mixed-criticality architectures must deal with the heterogeneity of subsystems that differ not only in their criticality, but also in the underlying computational models and the timing requirements. Non safety-critical subsystems often demand adaptability and support for dynamic system structures, while certification standards impose static configurations for safety-critical subsystems. Several aspects such as time and space partitioning, heterogeneous computational models and adaptability were individually addressed at different integration levels including distributed systems, the chip-level and software execution environments. However, a holistic architecture for the seamless mixed-criticality integration encompassing distributed systems, multi-core chips, operating systems and hypervisors is an open research problem. This presentation discusses the state-of-the-art of mixed-criticality systems and presents research challenges towards a hierarchical mixed-criticality platform with support for strict segregation of subsystems, heterogeneity and adaptability.

Prof. Dr. Roman Obermaisser is full professor at the Division for Embedded Systems at University of Siegen in Germany. He has studied computer sciences at Vienna University of Technology and received the Master's degree in 2001. In February 2004, Roman Obermaisser has finished his doctoral studies in Computer Science with Prof. Hermann Kopetz at Vienna University of Technology as research advisor. In July 2009, Roman Obermaisser has received the habilitation ("Venia docendi") certificate for Technical Computer Science. His research work focuses on system architectures for distributed embedded real-time systems. He is the author of numerous conference and journal publications. He also wrote books on cross-domain system architectures for embedded systems, event-triggered and time-triggered control paradigms and time-triggered communication protocols. He has also participated in several EU research projects (e.g. DECOS, NextTTA, universAAL) and was the coordinator of the European research projects GENESYS and ACROSS. At present Roman Obermaisser coordinates the European research project DREAMS that will establish a mixed-criticality architecture for networked multi-core chips.

Dr. Francisco Cazorla, Barcelona Supercomputing Center

Time Predictability in High-Performance Mixed-Criticality Multicore Systems

Abstract of Talk: While the search for high-performance will continue to be one of the main driving factors in computer design and development, there is an increasing need for time predictability across computing domains including high-performance (data-centre and supercomputers), handheld and embedded devices. The trend towards using computer systems to increasingly control essential aspects of human beings and the increasing connectivity across devices will naturally lead to situations in which applications - partially executed in handheld and datacentre computers, directly connect with more embedded critical systems such as cars or medical devices. The problem lies in the fact that high-performance is usually achieved by deploying aggressive hardware features (speculation, caches, heterogeneous designs) that negatively impact time predictability. The challenge lies on finding hardware/software designs that balance high-performance and time-predictability as needed by the application environment. In this talk I will focus on the increasing needs of time predictability in computing systems. I will present some of the main challenges in the design of multicores and manycores, widely deployed in the different computer domains, to provide increasing degrees of time predictability without significantly degrading average performance. I will present the work done in my research group in two different directions to reach this goal, namely, probabilistic multicore systems and the analysis of COTS multicore processors.

Dr. Francisco J. Cazorla is a researcher at the National Spanish Research Council (CSIC) and the leader of the CAOS research group (Computer Architecture - Operating System) at the Barcelona Supercomputing Centre (www.bsc.es/ caos). His research area covers the design for both high-performance and real-time systems. He has led several research projects funded by industry including several processor vendor companies (IBM, Sun microsystems) and the European Space Agency. He has also participated in European FP6 (SARC) and FP7 Projects (MERASA, parMERASA). He led the FP7 PROARTIS project and currently leads the FP7 PROXIMA project. He has co-authored over 70 papers in international refereed conferences and has several patents on the area.

Contents

Hardware

Parallel-Operation-Oriented Optically Reconfigurable Gate Array

Takumi Fujimori and Minoru Watanabe[⊠]

Electrical and Electronic Engineering, Shizuoka University, 3-5-1 Johoku,
Hamamatsu, Shizuoka 432-8561, Japan
tmwatan@ipc.shizuoka.ac.jp

Abstract. Recently, studies exploring acceleration of software operations on a processor have been undertaken aggressively using field programmable gate arrays (FPGAs). However, currently available FPGA
architectures present waste occurring with parallel operation in terms
of configuration memory because the same configuration context corresponding to same-function modules must be programmed onto numerous configuration memory parts. Therefore, a parallel-operation-oriented
FPGA with a single shared configuration memory for some programmable gate arrays has been proposed. Here, the architecture is applied
for optically reconfigurable gate arrays (ORGA). To date, the ORGA
architecture has demonstrated that a high-speed dynamic reconfiguration capability can increase the performance of its programmable gate
array drastically. Software operations can be accelerated using an ORGA.
This paper therefore presents a proposal for combinational architecture
of the parallel-operation oriented FPGA architecture and a high-speed
reconfiguration ORGA. The architecture is called a parallel-operation-
oriented ORGA architecture. For this study, a parallel-operation-oriented
ORGA with four programmable gate arrays sharing a common configuration photodiode-array has been designed using $0.18\,\mu$m CMOS process
technology. This study clarified the benefits of the parallel-operation-
oriented ORGA in comparison with an FPGA having the same gate
array structure, produced using the same process technology.

1 Introduction

Recently, studies of acceleration of software operations on a processor have been
executed aggressively using general-purpose computing on graphics processing
units (GPGPUs) [1]–[3] and using field programmable gate arrays (FPGAs)
[4]–[6]. Particularly, along with the increasing size of FPGAs, many FPGA
hardware acceleration results have been reported. According to several reports,
FPGA acceleration is suitable for fluid analysis, electromagnetic field analysis,
image processing operation, game solvers, and so on. The importance of FPGA
hardware acceleration of software operations therefore appears to be increasing.

Actually, FPGA programmability can be achieved based on a look-up table
(LUT) and switching matrix (SM) architecture. For that architecture, FPGA
performance is always inferior to that of custom VLSIs since a circuit implemented onto a LUT is always slower than the corresponding custom logic circuit

© Springer International Publishing Switzerland 2015
L.M. Pinho et al. (Eds): ARCS 2015, LNCS 9017, pp. 3–14, 2015.
DOI: 10.1007/978-3-319-16086-3_1

Fig. 1. Photograph of an optically reconfigurable gate array (ORGA) with 16 configuration contexts

and because the path delay of SMs on FPGA is greater than that of simple metal wires on custom VLSIs. When implementing processors, the clock frequency of the soft core processor on FPGA is always about a tenth of the frequency of custom processors having the same process technology as that of the FPGA [7][8][9].

Nevertheless, many high-performance FPGA implementations that are superior to the performance of the latest processors and the latest GPGPUs on personal computers have been reported. In such cases, the architecture invariably uses a massively parallel operation. Although the clock frequency of a single unit on an FPGA is lower than that of Intel's processors, the total performance of the parallel operation overcomes the processors. Therefore, when an FPGA is used as a hardware accelerator the architecture must become a parallel operation.

However, a main concern of a parallel operation on FPGA is that the same configuration context corresponding to the same-function modules must be programmed onto many parts of the configuration memory. Currently available FPGAs are designed as general-purpose programmable gate arrays so that all logic blocks, switching matrices, and so on can be programmed individually. Such an architecture is wasteful when functioning under parallel operation.

A better structure in the case of implementing a number of identical circuits onto LUTs and SMs is to share a common configuration memory for a parallel operation. Consequently, the amount of configuration memory can be decreased so that a larger programmable gate array can be realized on a die of the same size. Therefore, a parallel-operation-oriented FPGA that has a single shared configuration memory for some programmable gate arrays has been proposed [10]. The gate density can be increased by sharing configuration memory compared with general-purpose FPGAs.

Here, the parallel-operation-oriented FPGA architecture is applied for optically reconfigurable gate arrays (ORGAs). An ORGA consists of a holographic memory, a laser array, and an optically programmable gate array, as shown in Fig. 1 [11]–[15]. The ORGA can have over 256 reconfiguration contexts inside a holographic memory, which can be implemented dynamically onto an optically programmable gate array at every 10 ns. To date, ORGA architecture has

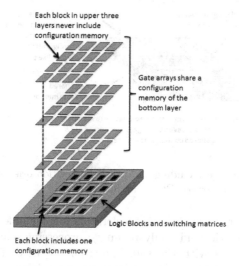

Each block in upper three layers never include configuration memory

Gate arrays share a configuration memory of the bottom layer

Logic Blocks and switching matrices

Each block includes one configuration memory

Fig. 2. Parallel-operation-oriented FPGA architecture including four common programmable gate arrays in which four parallel operations can be implemented

demonstrated that such high-speed dynamic reconfiguration capability can increase the performance of its programmable gate array drastically. Using the high-speed dynamic reconfiguration, simple circuits with a few functions can be implemented onto a programmable gate array. Change of the function can be accomplished using high-speed dynamic reconfiguration. Simple function requires only a small implementation area so that a large parallel computation can be realized. Therefore, a software operation can be accelerated drastically by exploiting the high-speed dynamic reconfiguration of ORGAs. Moreover, if the parallel-operation-oriented FPGA architecture is applied to ORGA, then the acceleration power or the number of parallel operation units is increased extremely.

This report therefore presents a proposal for a combined architecture of the parallel-operation oriented FPGA architecture and a high-speed reconfiguration ORGA. The architecture, called a parallel-operation-oriented ORGA architecture, includes a shared common configuration architecture. For this study, a parallel-operation-oriented ORGA with four programmable gate arrays sharing a common configuration photodiode-array has been designed using 0.18 μm CMOS process technology. The benefits of the parallel-operation-oriented ORGA were clarified in comparison with an FPGA having the same gate array structure and the same process technology.

2   Parallel-Operation-Oriented ORGA Architecture

2.1   Parallel-Operation-Oriented FPGA Architecture

Under current general-purpose FPGA architectures, each logic block, switching matrix, I/O block, block RAM, and so on includes a configuration memory

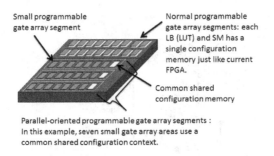

Small programmable
gate array segment

Normal programmable
gate array segments: each
LB (LUT) and SM has a
single configuration
memory just like current
FPGA.

Common shared
configuration memory

Parallel-oriented programmable gate array segments :
In this example, seven small gate array areas use a
common shared configuration context.

Fig. 3. Hybrid architecture including the parallel-operation-oriented FPGA architecture and current general-purpose FPGA architecture

individually. However, in an FPGA accelerator, for example, in uses for fluid analysis, electromagnetic field analysis, image processing operation, and game solvers, numerous units with the same function are used. In this case, each function should use a shared configuration memory to increase the gate density of a programmable gate array. Therefore, a parallel-operation-oriented FPGA architecture with a common shared configuration memory has been proposed as shown in Fig. 2.

Figure 2 presents one example of a parallel-operation-oriented FPGA architecture including four common programmable gate arrays in which four parallel operations can be implemented. Of course, the number of common programmable gate arrays depends on the target application. For example, a game solver invariably uses numerous common evaluation modules. In this case, a programmable gate array partly including 10 common programmable gate array areas might be suitable for the application. As a result, the amount of configuration memory inside an FPGA can be decreased so that the gate array density can be increased.

Figure 3 shows that the parallel-operation-oriented FPGA architecture should be used along with a current general-purpose FPGA architecture. A suitable implementation is that a part is designed as parallel-operation-oriented FPGA architecture. The remainder should be current general-purpose FPGA architecture. Therefore, a system includes both a parallel operation part and a dedicated operation part. The ratio of a parallel operation part to a dedicated operation part also depends on the target application.

2.2   Parallel-Operation-Oriented ORGA Architecture

To date, ORGA architecture has demonstrated that a high-speed dynamic reconfiguration capability can increase its programmable gate array performance drastically. If a high-speed reconfiguration is possible on a programmable gate array, then a single-function unit can be implemented. Multi-functionality can be achieved by reconfiguring the hardware itself. Such single-function unit works at the highest clock frequency. Numerous units can be implemented onto a small implementation area compared with a general-purpose multi-function unit with numerous functions because the complexity and size of units is smaller and

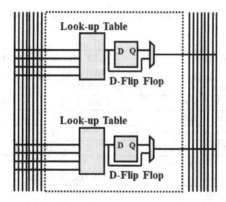

Fig. 4. Construction of a logic block

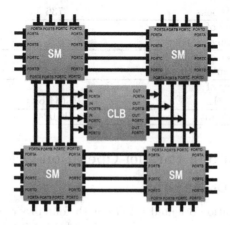

Fig. 5. Connection of logic blocks and switching matrices

simpler than those of multi-function units. Therefore, the performance can be increased compared with static uses of current FPGAs.

Moreover, an ORGA can support a high-speed dynamic reconfiguration. Its reconfiguration period is less than 10 ns. The number of reconfiguration contexts is at least 256. In the future, the number of configuration contexts on an ORGA will be increased to a million configuration contexts. For the goal of realizing numerous reconfiguration contexts, studies of new ORGAs have been progressing. Therefore, ORGA is extremely useful to accelerate a software operation on a processor. Additionally, the parallel-operation-oriented FPGA architecture is useful to increase the number of parallel operations on a gate array or the gate density of an ORGA under a parallel operation can be increased. In this study, a parallel-operation-oriented ORGA with four programmable gate arrays sharing a common configuration photodiode-array has been designed using 0.18 μm CMOS process technology.

Table 1. Specifications of a parallel-operation-oriented optically reconfigurable gate array

Technology	0.18 μm double-poly 5-metal CMOS process
Chip size	$5.0 \times 5.0\ mm^2$
Supply Voltage	Core 1.8V, I/O 3.3V
Photodiode size	$4.40 \times 4.45\ \mu m^2$
Photodiode response time	< 5 ns
Sensitivity	2.12×10^{-14} J
Distance between Photodiodes	h.=30.08, v.= 20.16 $[\mu m]$
Number of Photodiodes	25,056
Number of Logic Blocks	736
Number of Switching Matrices	828
Number of Wires in a Routing Channel	8
Number of I/O blocks	16 (64 bit)
Gate Count	25,024

3   VLSI Design of a Parallel-Operation-Oriented ORGA

3.1   Entire VLSI Design

Here, a parallel-operation-oriented ORGA with four programmable gate array sharing a configuration architecture was designed using 0.18 μm standard complementary metal oxide semiconductor (CMOS) process technology. The ORGA-VLSI specifications are shown in Table 1. In an ORGA, a configuration context is provided optically from a holographic memory. Therefore, an ORGA has numerous photodiodes to detect the configuration context, as shown in Table 1. The number of photodiodes corresponds to the number of configuration bits. In this design, 25,056 photodiodes were implemented for programming a programmable gate array. All blocks of the programmable gate array can be reconfigured at once. In this design, the ORGA has four programmable gate array planes which share the single configuration photodiode architecture of the 25,056 photodiodes. Each programmable gate array plane has 184 optically reconfigurable logic blocks and 207 optically reconfigurable switching matrices. The programmable gate array works along with the same configuration information based on a single photodiode configuration system.

3.2   Optically Reconfigurable Logic Block

Figure 4 shows that each logic block on a programmable gate array plane has two four-input look-up tables (LUTs) and two delay-type flip flops. An optically

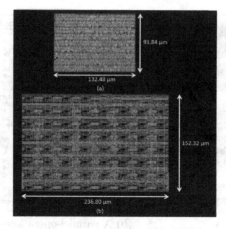

Fig. 6. CAD Layouts of logic blocks of (a) a comparison target design of a current general-purpose FPGA including a single programmable gate array and (b) a parallel-operation-oriented ORGA including four banks sharing a common configuration photodiode

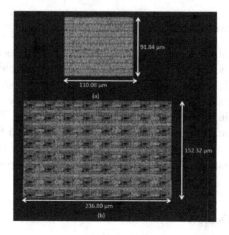

Fig. 7. CAD Layout of a switching matrix of (a) a comparison target design of a current general-purpose FPGA including a single programmable gate array and (b) a parallel-operation-oriented ORGA including four banks sharing a common configuration photodiode

reconfigurable logic block cell has four logic blocks. The four logic blocks share the same configuration context so that they can be reconfigured using 60 photodiodes. The CAD layout of the optically reconfigurable logic block is portrayed in Fig. 6(b). Therefore, all four logic blocks can be reconfigured at once and can function as the same circuit, although the input signals for logic blocks mutually differ. Figure 5 shows that the optically reconfigurable logic block cell has four output ports and four input ports for four programmable gate array planes.

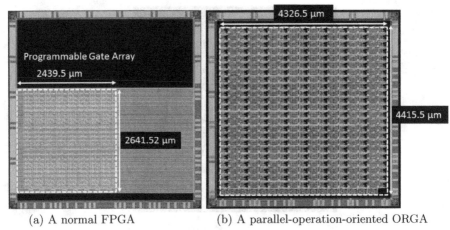

(a) A normal FPGA   (b) A parallel-operation-oriented ORGA

Fig. 8. CAD Layouts of (a) a comparison design of a current general-purpose FPGA and (b) a parallel-operation-oriented ORGA including four programmable gate arrays sharing a common configuration context

3.3   Optically Reconfigurable Switching Matrix

In addition, the optically reconfigurable switching matrix was designed as having four direction connections. Each switching matrix is connected for each direction to another one with eight wires. An optically reconfigurable switching matrix has 64 photodiodes for configuration procedures. The CAD layout of the optically reconfigurable switching matrix cell is portrayed in Fig. 7(b). The optically reconfigurable switching matrix cell has four switching matrices for four programmable gate arrays. Therefore, as shown in Fig. 5, each direction of the optically reconfigurable switching matrix cell has four ports for four programmable gate array planes.

3.4   Gate Array Design

Each photodiode was designed to be $4.40 \times 4.45 \mu$m. The photodiode sensitivity was estimated experimentally as 2.12×10^{-14} J. Even if reconfiguration can be executed constantly at 100 MHz, the necessary optical power for the configuration procedure is about 26.6 mW. Therefore, the configuration power consumption of the ORGA-VLSI can be estimated as low. Each logic block is surrounded by four switching matrices connecting eight wiring channels as an island style gate array. Since a parallel-operation-oriented ORGA has four of the same programmable gate arrays sharing a configuration architecture, in all, it has 736 logic blocks and 828 switching matrices. In this design, the number of I/O bits was limited to 64 bits because of chip package issues. The gate count reaches 25,024 gates. The CAD layout of the programmable gate array is presented in Fig. 8. The chip size is 5 mm × 5 mm. All gate array parts were designed using standard cells, except for a photodiode cell. The photodiode cell was designed

Table 2. Results of gate density comparisons

Type	Current FPGA	Parallel-operation-oriented ORGA
Number of functions	Single function (368 LUTs)	4 functions (1,472 LUTs)
Size of a Logic Block	$132.48 \times 91.84 \ \mu m^2$	$236.80 \times 152.32 \ \mu m^2$
Size of a Switching Matrix	$110.08 \times 91.84 \ \mu m^2$	$236.80 \times 152.32 \ \mu m^2$
Size of an I/O Block without PAD	$106.88 \times 91.84 \ \mu m^2$	$236.80 \times 152.32 \ \mu m^2$
Size of a gate array (184 LBs and 207 SMs)	$6,443,988 \ \mu m^2$	$19,103,661 \ \mu m^2$
Number of LUTs / mm^2	57.1	77.1

Table 3. Results of comparing the operating clock frequency of a seven-stage ring oscillator

Type	Current FPGA	Parallel-operation-oriented ORGA
Number of functions	Single function	4 functions
Operating clock frequency	43.71 MHz	72.78 MHz
Gate array performance / second · mm^2	2.50×10^9 LUT operations / sec. · mm^2	5.61×10^9 LUT operations / sec. · mm^2
Performance ratio	1	2.24

Table 4. Results of comparing the leakage power consumption

Type	Current FPGA	Parallel-operation-oriented ORGA
Number of functions	Single function	4 functions
Leakage Power	$6.14 \ \mu W$	$7.38 \ \mu W$

as full-custom. The gate array design was synthesized using a logic synthesis tool (Design Compiler: Synopsys Inc.). In addition, as a place and route tool, IC compiler (Synopsys Inc.) was used. Voltages of the core and I/O are 1.8 V and 3.3 V, respectively. Currently, to facilitate optical experiments, the ORGA photodiode size and space between the photodiodes were designed as large. Therefore, since the ORGA-VLSI design has spaces and the density of the logic cells is not maximum, the cell sizes of the logic block and the switching matrix of the ORGA-VLSI were larger than those of the comparison-target FPGA.

3.5   Comparison Target Design

Additionally, here, as a comparison target, a normal FPGA was also designed with the same 0.18 μm standard CMOS process technology. The FPGA has a single programmable gate array, which is the same structure as the ORGA design and the configuration memory above. Since the FPGA has only one programmable gate array plane, the gate array has 184 logic blocks and 207 switching matrices. Of course, the logic block structure and switching matrix structure are also the same. The CAD layouts of a logic block and a switching matrix are shown respectively in Fig. 6(a) and Fig. 7(a).

4 Evaluation Results

4.1 Gate Density

The implementation results of the parallel-operation-oriented ORGA and the comparison target FPGA are presented in Table 2. Figures 6, 7, and 8 show that the implementation area of the ORGA-VLSI is larger than that of the comparison target FPGA. The gate array's implementation area of the parallel-operation-oriented ORGA is 19,103,661 μm^2. However, the ORGA-VLSI includes four-times the gate array or four planes of programmable gate arrays. Therefore, a single programmable gate array corresponding to the comparison target FPGA has been implemented on only 4,775,915 μm^2. The implementation area is smaller than 6,443,988 μm^2 of the comparison target FPGA. Estimating the gate density, the number of LUTs / mm^2 of the parallel-operation-oriented ORGA and the comparison target FPGA are 77.1 and 57.1, respectively, because the programmable gate arrays of the parallel-operation-oriented ORGA and the comparison target FPGA respectively have 1,472 LUTs and 368 LUTs. Therefore, the gate density of the parallel-operation-oriented ORGA is higher than that of the comparison target FPGA, meaning that the ORGA-VLSI can execute larger operations than the comparison target FPGA.

4.2 Propagation Delay

Next, the operation clock frequencies of the parallel-operation-oriented ORGA and the comparison target FPGA were measured as results show in Table 3. The results are based on IC compiler generated SDF information and the corresponding HDL simulation. Here, a seven-stage ring oscillator has been implemented onto both ORGA-VLSI and FPGA. The operating clock frequencies of the parallel-operation-oriented ORGA and the comparison target FPGA were 72.78 MHz and 43.71 MHz. The results show that the operation on an ORGA can be done faster than on the comparison target FPGA. Currently, the comparison target FPGA was designed to be as small as possible. Therefore, although FPGA is small, the gate array performance is lower. Of course, the performance of the comparison target FPGA can be improved through future development. However, even if the performance of an ORGA becomes lower than that of current FPGA design, a parallel-operation-oriented ORGA has advantages under parallel operation because the number of programmable gate array planes can be increased easily. Anyway, the performance of the parallel-operation-oriented ORGA is higher than that of current FPGAs. The total performance per square millimeter of the parallel-operation-oriented ORGA was 2.24 times higher than that of the comparison-target FPGA. In another example, the 4-bit multiplier circuit works at 80.13 MHz. The working speed can be regarded as sufficient under the current 0.18 μm standard CMOS process technology.

4.3 Power Consumption Estimation

The leakage power consumption generated by the IC compiler is presented in Table 4. The leakage power consumption of the parallel-operation-oriented

ORGA is slightly higher than that of the comparison target FPGA. However, the leakage power consumption per single programmable gate array is decreased drastically compared with the comparison target FPGA because the ORGA-VLSI includes four programmable gate arrays. Considering a single programmable gate array, the leakage power consumption is estimated as 1.85 μW. Therefore, the leakage power consumption per programmable gate array of the parallel-operation-oriented ORGA is sufficiently smaller than the comparison target FPGA. The major component of the latest VLSI's power consumption is leakage power consumption. The result implies that when the ORGA-VLSI chooses the latest VLSI technology in the future, the power consumption of the parallel-operation-oriented ORGA is sufficiently lower than that of currently available FPGAs.

5   Conclusion

An accelerator using an FPGA must always use a massively parallel operation to constitute a high-performance system. The configuration memory of currently available FPGA architecture is wasted under parallel operation because the same configuration context corresponding to same-function modules must be programmed onto numerous parts of the configuration memory. Therefore, a parallel-operation-oriented FPGA with a single shared configuration memory has been proposed for some programmable gate arrays.

On the other hand, ORGA architecture has demonstrated that its high-speed dynamic reconfiguration capability can increase the number of parallel operations on its programmable gate array drastically. If both architectures could be implemented onto a single system, then numerous parallel operations would be realized.

This report has presented a proposal of a parallel-operation-oriented ORGA architecture including a shared common configuration photodiode architecture. In addition, a parallel-operation-oriented ORGA was designed using the same 0.18 μm process technology. Results show that the parallel-operation-oriented ORGA architecture presents benefits in terms of performance and power consumption related to the leak current, compared with current general-purpose FPGAs, which was also designed with the same 0.18 μm process technology and the same FPGA architecture. The performance per unit area of the parallel-operation-oriented ORGA is 2.24 times higher than that of a comparison-target FPGA. When using a parallel operation on an ORGA, the architecture is well-suited to realizing a high-performance system. The parallel-operation-oriented ORGA architecture is also well-suited to future three-dimensional VLSI technologies.

Acknowledgments. This research was partly supported by Nuclear Safety Research & Development Center of the Chubu Electric Power Corporation. The VLSI chip in this study was fabricated in the chip fabrication program of VLSI Design and Education Center (VDEC), the University of Tokyo in collaboration with Rohm Co. Ltd. and Toppan Printing Co. Ltd.

References

1. Archirapatkave, V., Sumilo, H., See, S.C.W., Achalakul, T.: GPGPU acceleration algorithm for medical image reconstruction. In: IEEE International Symposium on Parallel and Distributed Processing with Applications, pp. 41–46 (2011)
2. Unno, M., Inoue, Y., Asar, H.: GPGPU-FDTD method for 2-dimensional electromagnetic field simulation and its estimation. In: IEEE Conference on Electrical Performance of Electronic Packaging and Systems, pp. 239–242 (2009)
3. Lezar, E., Jakobus, U.: GPU-acceleration of the FEKO electromagnetic solution kernel. In: International Conference on Electromagnetics in Advanced Applications, pp. 814–817 (2013)
4. Sano, K., Hatsuda, Y., Yamamoto, S.: Multi-FPGA Accelerator for Scalable Stencil Computation with Constant Memory Bandwidth. IEEE Transactions on Parallel and Distributed Systems **25**(3), 695–705 (2014)
5. Saidani, T., Atri, M., Said, Y., Tourki, R.: Real time FPGA acceleration for discrete wavelet transform of the 5/3 filter for JPEG 2000. In: International Conference on Sciences of Electronics, Technologies of Information and Telecommunications, pp. 393–399 (2012)
6. Durbano, J.P., Ortiz, F.E.: FPGA-based acceleration of the 3D finite-difference time-domain method. In: IEEE Symposium on Field-Programmable Custom Computing Machines, pp. 156–163 (2004)
7. Sheldon, D., Kumar, R., Lysecky, R., Vahid, F., Tullsen, D.: Application-specific customization of parameterized FPGA soft-core processors. In: IEEE/ACM International Conference on Computer-Aided Design, pp. 261–268 (2006)
8. Zhen, Z., Guilin, T., Dong, Z., Zhiping, H.: Design and realization of the hardware platform based on the Nios soft-core processor. In: International Conference on Electronic Measurement and Instruments, pp. 4–865-4-869 (2007)
9. Hubner, M., Paulsson, K., Becker, J.: Parallel and flexible multiprocessor system-on-chip for adaptive automotive applications based on Xilinx MicroBlaze soft-cores. In: IEEE International Parallel and Distributed Processing Symposium, p. 149a (2005)
10. Watanabe, M.: A parallel-operation-oriented FPGA architecture. In: International Symposium on Highly Efficient Accelerators and Reconfigurable Technologies, pp. 123–126 (2014)
11. Kubota, S., Watanabe, M.: A four-context programmable optically reconfigurable gate array with a reflective silver-halide holographic memory. IEEE Photonics Journal **3**(4), 665–675 (2011)
12. Nakajima, M., Watanabe, M.: Fast optical reconfiguration of a nine-context DORGA using a speed adjustment control. ACM Transaction on Reconfigurable Technology and Systems **4**(2), 1–21 (2011). Article 15
13. Seto, D., Nakajima, M., Watanabe, M.: Dynamic optically reconfigurable gate array very large-scale integration with partial reconfiguration capability. Applied Optics **49**(36), 6986–6994 (2010)
14. Morita, H., Watanabe, M.: Microelectromechanical Configuration of an Optically Reconfigurable Gate Array. IEEE Journal of Quantum Electronics **46**(9), 1288–1294 (2010)
15. Nakajima, M., Watanabe, M.: A four-context optically differential reconfigurable gate array. IEEE/OSA Journal of Lightwave Technology **27**(20), 4460–4470 (2009)

SgInt: Safeguarding Interrupts for Hardware-Based I/O Virtualization for Mixed-Criticality Embedded Real-Time Systems Using Non Transparent Bridges

Daniel Münch[1]([✉]), Michael Paulitsch[1], Oliver Hanka[1],
and Andreas Herkersdorf[2]

[1] Airbus Group Innovation, Munich, Germany
{Daniel.Muench,Michael.Paulitsch,Oliver.Hanka}@airbus.com
[2] Institute for Integrated Systems, TU München, Munich, Germany
herkersdorf@tum.de

Abstract. Safety critical systems and in particular higher functional integrated systems like mixed-criticality systems in avionics require a safeguarding that functionalities cannot interfere with each other. A notably underestimated issue are I/O devices and their (message-signaled) interrupts. Message-signaled interrupts are the omnipresent type of interrupts in modern serial high-speed I/O subsystems. These interrupts can be considered as small DMA write packets. If there is no safeguarding for interrupts, an I/O device associated with a distinct functionality can trigger any interrupt or manipulate any control register like triggering reset of all processing cores to provoke a complete system failure. This is a particular issue for available embedded processor architectures, since they do not provide adequate means for interrupt separation like an IOMMU with a granularity sufficient for interrupts.

This paper presents the *SgInt concept* to enable the safeguarding of interrupts for hardware-based I/O virtualization for safety-critical and mixed-criticality embedded real-time systems using non-transparent bridges in single (multi-core) processor systems and multi (multi-core) processor systems. The advantage of this SgInt concept is that it is an general and reusable interrupt separation solution which is scalable from a single (multi-core) processor to a multi (multi-core) processor system and builds on available COTS chip solutions. It allows to upgrade spatial separation for interrupts to available processors having no means for interrupt separation. A practical evaluation shows that the SgInt concept provides the required spatial separation and even slightly outperforms state-of-the-art doorbell interrupt handling in transfer time and transfer rate (by about 0.04 %).

1 Introduction

Driven by the demand for more and more functionality, there is a trend in avionics similar to other field of electronics to a higher functional integration. To save space, weight and power, functionalities are integrated onto one computing

© Springer International Publishing Switzerland 2015
L.M. Pinho et al. (Eds): ARCS 2015, LNCS 9017, pp. 15–27, 2015.
DOI: 10.1007/978-3-319-16086-3_2

platform. This trend is pushed further by integrating functionalities of different criticality levels onto the same platform to so called mixed-criticality systems.

Functionalities of different criticality levels on one shared (multi-core) platform require that these functionalities cannot interfere with each other or with the entire system. To manage this interference issue, temporal separation and spatial separation are essential to grant a safe and secure system operation. The Input/Output (I/O) subsystem is a central part, because almost every function needs I/O for its operation. Since I/O is an often underestimated problem, this paper focuses on I/O. Temporal separation means having separation in the time domain. For example, it is guaranteed that an I/O device has a granted transfer rate or maximum transfer time [1]. Spatial separation means having separation in the address space domain. For example, it is assured that an I/O device only writes into a distinct address range or memory area belonging to a distinct functionality or application [2]. A particularly underestimated issue in I/O handling are (message-signaled) interrupts. Message-signaled interrupts are the ubiquitous type of interrupts in modern memory-mapped I/O subsystems and can be considered as small Direct Memory Access (DMA) write packets (e.g. with only 4 Byte payload). If there is no spatial separation for interrupts, an erroneous I/O device can trigger any interrupt of the system-on-chip of the processor or manipulate any memory-mapped control register like triggering reset of all processing cores. Such a situation could lead to a complete system failure [2] [3]. Therefore, it is common in today's avionics and similar highly safety-critical systems to effectively turn off all interrupts and handle I/O via polling. This is a very resource-consuming and ineffective, but a safe approach to solve the problem. Further constraints are the use of Commercial Of–The–Shelf (COTS) components, low complexity, determinism and predictability (cf. Section 3).

The challenge is that available embedded processor architectures do not offer spatial separation means for interrupts like an Input/Output Memory Management Unit (IOMMU) with sufficiently fine granularity (cf. Section 3 and [2]). Server or high-end workstation processor architectures providing such means (cf. Section 2 and [4] [5]) are not usable for embedded real-time systems because of size, weight, power, cooling, harsh environmental conditions, certification considerations, etc. Further constraints are the use of Commercial Off–The–Shelf (COTS) components. This is essential to keep costs low for products with low piece numbers / volume like aircraft. A fully customized design of a processor chip or system-on-chip is economically infeasible. For these reasons, this paper does not discuss the design of interrupt controllers or IOMMUs. Instead, it focuses on an approach to extend available embedded COTS processors or system-on-chip by additional means to provide spatial separation for interrupts with the least possible impact on performance.

The contribution of the Safeguarding Interrupts (SgInt) concept of this paper is an efficient, high-performance and safe interrupt handling approach for highly safety-critical systems. It enables spatial separation at interrupt level in systems that does not have already built-in means. This concept is a reusable and general solution, which is scalable from a single (multi-core) processor to a multi

(multi-core) processor system and builds on available COTS chip solutions. The SgInt concept uses a source / origin ID check in the Non-Transparent Bridge (NTB) with an exclusive address range within the NTB aperture for interrupts of one distinct I/O device in combination with a dedicated alias page in the processor only containing the interrupt triggering register as mapping target. Furthermore, the paper contributes a implementation and an application of the SgInt concept in context of hardware-based I/O virtualization (cf. Section 2). The result of the presented practical evaluation is that the performance in terms of transfer time and transfer rate of the SgInt concept is by about 0.04% better than state-of-the-art doorbell interrupt handling.

To our best knowledge, we are the first to discuss an interrupt separation solution for single (multi-core) processor systems and multi (multi-core) processor systems in mixed-criticality embedded real-time systems that do not provide adequate means for interrupt separation.

2 Related Work

The application context of this paper is hardware-based I/O virtualization (cf. [1,2,6]). This is the hardware-managed sharing of I/O in virtualized embedded systems. Virualized embedded systems are systems where multiple virtual machines or application partitions are running on a shared computing platform managed by virtual machine manager or hypervisor. The key point is that the sharing or virtualization management is offloaded to hardware. This hardware management provides a Physical Function (PF) (management interface) and several Virtual Functions (VFs) interfaces (application interfaces) [7]. A memory-mapped I/O like PCI Express (PCIe) serves as basic I/O technology. This allows to map the PF to a control partition or hypervisor. The VFs are mapped to the corresponding application partitions. Already available means for memory management and mapping like Memory Management Unit (MMU) and IOMMU ensure the spatial separation between the application partitions and I/O interfaces.

Non-transparent bridging in context of PCIe is the non-transparent connection of two dedicated tree-like (single-root) PCIe hierarchies or address spaces together to enable multiple processors to communicate and exchange data [8]. A (single-root) PCIe hierarchy or address space is a tree-like topology with maximally one Central Processing Unit (CPU), master or root. Therefore, a communication between two root or CPUs is originally not possible. To solve this issue, an NTB connects two PCIe hierarchies by presenting itself as an end-point to both PCIe hierarchies. An NTB is constructed by two end-points back to back with an address translation functionality. Each side of an NTB opens an address window (aperture) from one PCIe single root hierarchy to the other PCIe single root hierarchy. The behavior of an NTB is considered as non-transparent, since the NTB and its address translation feature has to be setup before it allows to exchange data. It is not checked if a device or function is allowed to transfer data to a distinct destination. Interrupts are transferred over an NTB by the so-called doorbell mechanism. This mechanism consumes the interrupt on the first side of the NTB and newly generates the interrupt on the second side and transmits it to the processing unit. It is not checked if a device or function is allowed to trigger an interrupt. The current concept uses NTB technology in a different way than formerly intended to enable multi-processor communication. It extends NTBs to enable spatial separation for interrupts of shared PCIe devices in a single (multi-core) processor or multi (multi-core) processor system.

[9] uses PCIe interconnect, NTB and Intel VT-d to share a PCIe Single Root I/O Virtualization (SR-IOV) network card among multiple Intel Xeon hosts in the IT-server domain. It is suggested to use a dedicated address window in the NTB to transfer interrupts from one NTB side to the other instead of using the doorbell mechanism to improve performance. The interrupt remapping feature of Intel VT-d – the Intel implementation of an IOMMU – is able to check if a device or function is allowed to trigger an interrupt [4] [10]. AMD provides a similar technology as part of AMD-Vi or AMD IOMMU [5] [11] [12]. In contrast to this, the current paper uses PCIe interconnect, NTB technology without an IOMMU – like Intel VT-d – to share a PCIe SR-IOV or PCIe multifunction device while still providing spatial separation for data transactions and interrupts in a mixed-criticality real-time embedded system. The current concept presents a more general interrupt separation solution, which does not rely on special interrupt separating features of Intel VT-d or AMD IOMMU.

[6] uses NTB technology to emulate an external IOMMU to provide spatial separation for data transactions of I/O devices like the separation feature of an IOMMU for a single (multi-core) computing host lacking an IOMMU. It is enforced that transactions (for example a DMA write) initiated by I/O device(s) flow over the NTBs. The control engine in the NTB checks the target address and source / origin ID (e.g. PCIe ID) of these transactions. A rule set in the control engine (e.g. white list) decides whether to block the transaction or pass the transaction and translate the target address to the defined target address in the (bus) address space on the other side of the NTB. [13] extends this idea to provide spatial separation for sharing I/O devices among multi (multi-core) processor systems which usually do not have means for separation like an IOMMU. The current paper extends this approach to increase the separation granularity further to provide spatial separation also for interrupts of I/O devices in a single (multi-core) processor system as well as a multi (multi-core) processor system, whose processors lack means to separate interrupts. In addition to the origin / source ID check in the NTB, the SgInt concept uses an exclusive address range (page) within the NTB aperture for the interrupts of each I/O device. Mapping target for this interrupt page is a dedicated page (alias page) in the processor that only contains the interrupt triggering register.

3   SgInt (Safeguarding Interrupts)

A fundamental assumption is a static system configuration proving low complexity. This is prioritized over dynamic flexibility to obtain a predictable and deterministic system behavior. Determinism and predictability is an essential pre-requisite to moderate the effort for the required assurance or certification process of a safety-oriented and security-oriented development project like in avionics [14]. Another assumption is the use of COTS components. This is essential to keep costs low for products with low piece numbers / volume and long life cycles like aircraft.

The SgInt concept enables the safeguarding of interrupts for hardware-based I/O virtualization for mixed-criticality embedded real-time systems using non-transparent bridges in single (multi-core) processor systems as well as in multi (multi-core) processor systems.

The already described separation mechanism (cf. [6] and [13]) using NTBs with additional checking of the target address and source / origin ID can also be extended to safeguard interrupts (cf. Figure 1). Message-signaled interrupts are the omnipresent type of interrupts in modern serial high-speed memory-mapped I/O standards, since dedicated interrupt wires are no longer available. Message-signaled interrupts can be considered as small DMA write transactions (e.g. 4 Byte). The SgInt concept uses an exclusive entry in the rule set in the NTB per I/O device (or PCIe function or application interface) for its associated interrupts (cf. Figure 1). An entry represents an address window or memory page of a typical size of 4kB. The mapping target of this entry or page is a memory-mapped page containing the interrupt trigger register of the interrupt controller. The interrupt trigger register converts the message-signaled interrupt to an actual interrupt. The access to this NTB entry is controlled by the control engine in the NTB performing the origin/source ID check (cf. Figure 1). This means that only the message-signaled interrupt sent by a distinct I/O device (or PCIe function or application interface) can pass this special interrupt window over the NTB. However, the protection granularity at page level is still not sufficient for a safe and secure handling of interrupts. The mapping target of this interrupt entry or page is a page containing this interrupt trigger register and a variety of additional control registers. Since a message-signaled interrupt is a DMA write packet, it is able to manipulate any memory-mapped control register within the target page. For example, an interrupt can trigger interrupts associated with other devices or other system-on-chip interrupts or processor interrupts by targeting another interrupt trigger register (cf. Figure 1). In addition, an interrupt can manipulate any memory-mapped control register of the target page like triggering the reset of all processing cores (cf. Figure 1). This could lead to a complete system failure. To prevent this, the granularity or precision of the origin/source ID check needs to be increased. A possibility is to isolate the interrupt trigger register within a page. This means, a page only contains this single interrupt trigger register or an alias register to this interrupt trigger register. An I/O device (or PCIe function or application interface) that is allowed to access this page can only change this register and nothing else since the page does not contain more control registers. Such a page is called alias page or page with an alias to the interrupt trigger register (cf. Figure 1).

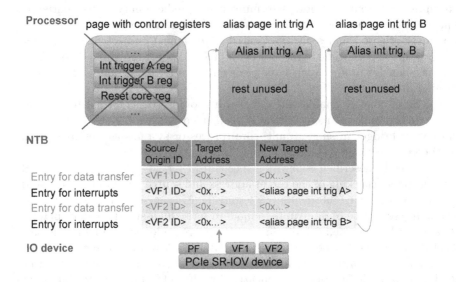

Fig. 1. SgInt (Safeguarding Interrupts): Origin/source ID check in combination with alias pages

To demonstrate an application, we have implemented the SgInt concept in the context of sharing a DMA-capable multi-function PCIe I/O card in a mixed-criticality embedded processing platform. Figure 2 depicts the implemented system setup. A Xilinx VC709 FPGA evaluation board is used as PCIe I/O card. A PLX 8749 chip serves as PCIe switch containing the two non-transparent bridges. The two system hosts are built up by two Freescale QorIQ P4080 Development Systems (P4080DS). The P4080 platform is a PowerPC-based embedded multi-core processing platform and a reference model of the Freescale QorIQ series. Freescale's Software Development Kit (SDK) Version 1.2 is used as software foundation. The avionics industry considers the PowerPC architecture-based P4080 platform as a platform candidate for embedded avionics systems [1,2,6,14,15].

For simplicity reasons, the demonstration system considers only two multi-core processors and one DMA-capable and bus-mastering capable PCIe card with two physical PCIe functions. Physical function (PF) 0 is used as management interface and application interface 1 and PF 1 servers as application interface 2. However, the SgInt concept is scalable from one application interface per processing host to multiple application interfaces per processing host with one NTB with multiple windows or multiple NTBs. An additional reason for using only two physical functions is that the SR-IOV capability of the Xilinx VC709 FPGA evaluation board is not compatible to the P4080DS. The Xilinx SR-IOV IP-core requires the optional PCIe Alternative Routing-ID Interpretation (ARI) extension to address VFs. The P4080DS does not support PCIe ARI [1]. Xilinx has

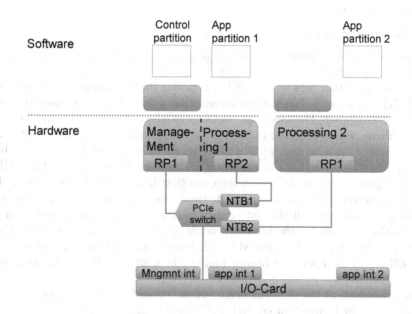

Fig. 2. Implementation of the Concept

confirmed this and we are in dialog with Xilinx to eliminate this limitation in the succeeding generation of Xilinx FPGAs.

The demonstration system encompasses two multi-core processors. If desired, the management part can be outsourced to a third management processor. The left multi-core processor runs the management section and one application section. One core and one dedicated (bus) address space or PCIe hierarchy or root port (RP) takes over the tasks of the management section. A second core and a second dedicated address space or PCIe hierarchy or root port runs one application section. This part of the demonstration system is representative to apply the concept in a single (multi-core) processing system. To be able to evaluate the concept also in multi (multi-core) processor systems, the additional second multi-processor takes over the task of another application section. This management control partition sets up the system, controls the main address space and controls the NTBs and the management interface of the I/O card. Each of the dedicated address spaces of a application section is connected to the main address spaces by an NTB. Application partition 1 running on the first multi-core processor is directly mapped to application interface 1 of the I/O card whereas application partition 2 running on the second multi-core processor is mapped to application interface 2 of the I/O card. The IOMMU of the P4080 platform has no means to safeguard interrupts of multiple PCIe devices or PCIe devices with multiple functions [2] [16]. Therefore, the spatial separation of interrupts of the two application interfaces are performed by the SgInt concept.

4 Evaluation

4.1 Evaluation Setup

The evaluation of the enforcement of the source / origin ID check for interrupts is analyzed with the following procedure:

The control partition sets up the NTB and the PCIe advanced error reporting (AER) registers. A DMA write transaction followed by a synchronization interrupt is triggered. The interrupt contains an allowed origin / source ID and target address, which complies to the rule set. Application partition 1 waits for the receiving of the interrupt while a time out timer is started. In this case, the receiving of the interrupt is expected and no time out should occur. The AER registers report no error. As a next step, another DMA write transaction with a synchronization interrupt is triggered. Here, the interrupt contains a target address associated to a disallowed origin / source ID. Application partition 1 waits for the receiving of the interrupt while a time out timer is started. The receiving of the interrupt is expected but does not occur and the time out occurs. The AER registers report the header and the first 32 data bits of the blocked packet.

The evaluation of the performance overhead (transfer time, transfer rate) of the SgInt concept is investigated with the following procedure:

The control partition configures the NTB and the I/O card. It is defined by the management interface that application interface 1 is assigned 50% of the available transfer rate and application interface 2 is assigned 50% of the available transfer rate. DMA read and write transactions hit the two application partitions. The transfer time and transfer rate of transactions are measured including the low-level software overhead and synchronization interrupts. The DMA transactions are composed of a number of 128 Byte-sized packets sent back to back. The number of packets is increased from 1 to 255. For each packet count, the measurements are run 100 times. The described measurement procedure is executed twice. One time it is conducted using the presented SgInt concept with interrupt separation. The other time it is performed using the state-of-the-art doorbell interrupt mechanism without separation (cf. Section 2 and [8]). Then both results are compared.

4.2 Evaluation Results

The evaluation result of the enforcement of the source / origin ID check for interrupts is given by the following output:

```
Test case 1: ID ok -> pass
//setup NTB
   (application interface 1 (source ID=0C00)
   is allowed to trigger sync interrupt
   (address 0xE070A140, data 0x13)
//trigger DMA write with end interrupt
//printout of application partition 1
```

```
  <no error>
//printout of PCIe Advanced Error Reporting (AER) registers
  PLX_AER_HEADER0 +0x3EFD0: 0x00000000
  PLX_AER_HEADER1 +0x3EFD4: 0x00000000
  PLX_AER_HEADER2 +0x3EFD8: 0x00000000
  PLX_AER_HEADER3 +0x3EFDC: 0x00000000

Test case 2: ID violation -> block
//setup NTB
  (source ID=0C03 is allowed
   to trigger sync interrupt
   (address 0xE070A140, data 0x13);
   application interface 1 (source ID=0C00)
   is NOT allowed to trigger the interrupt)
//trigger DMA write with end interrupt
//printout of application partition 1
  // indicating time out occurred
  ntbxpcieappdrv wait for interrupt:
  Operation not permitted
//printout of PCIe Advanced Error Reporting (AER) registers
  PLX_AER_HEADER0 +0x3EFD0: 0x40000001
  PLX_AER_HEADER1 +0x3EFD4: 0x0C00000F  //ID=0C00
  PLX_AER_HEADER2 +0x3EFD8: 0xE070A140
  PLX_AER_HEADER3 +0x3EFDC: 0x13000000
```

Figure 3 shows the relative difference of the transfer time between the SgInt concept and no interrupt separation, whereas Figure 4 depicts the relative difference of the transfer rate between the SgInt concept and no interrupt separation.

For the transfer time, the values of the SgInt concept are about 0.04% (for writes) to 0.08% (for reads) lower than the values of no interrupt separation. In case of transfer rate transactions, the data of the SgInt concept are about 0.04% (for writes) to (0.09%) for reads higher than the data of no interrupt separation.

5 Discussion and Impact

In test case 1 of the interrupt source / origin ID check, the interrupt is allowed to pass and to trigger the interrupt in the processing system. In test case 2, the origin ID of the actual sent interrupt does not comply to the origin ID of the corresponding target address in the rule set in the NTB. Therefore, the interrupt is blocked. Concluding, the origin ID check of the SgInt concept shows that the spacial separation in dependency of the origin ID can be enforced for interrupts.

The transfer time figure (cf. Figure 3 and Section 4.2) shows that the SgInt concept with separation has a 0.04% better transfer time than the state-of-the-art NTB configuration without interrupt separation. The reason for this can be explained by the nature of the state-of-the-art doorbell interrupt mechanism [8]. This mechanism consumes the interrupt on the first side of the NTB and generates a new interrupt on the second side and transmits it to the processing

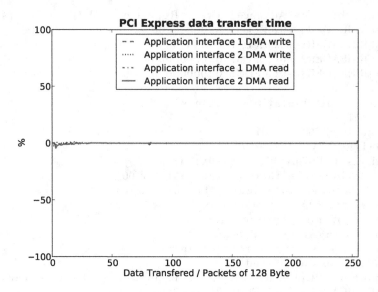

Fig. 3. Relative difference between the transfer time results using the SgInt concept and no interrupt separation

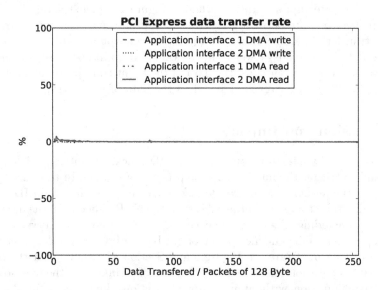

Fig. 4. Relative difference between the transfer rate results using the SgInt concept and no interrupt separation

unit. In contrast to this, the presented SgInt concept handles the interrupt like any other data packet passing the NTB. After the source / origin ID check decided to pass the packet through the NTB window, the packet is forwarded and its target address is translated. This forwarding process inclusive source / origin ID check is marginally more efficient than the traditional way of consuming and recreating without source / origin ID check of the interrupt. The figure for the transfer rate (cf. Figure 4) confirms the statements of the transfer time.

The the demonstration system considers two multi-core processors sharing one I/O card with two application interfaces. However, the scalability of the SgInt concept ranges from one application interface per processing host to multiple application interfaces per processing host with one NTB with multiple windows or multiple NTBs.

A really relevant item is that the SgInt concept can provide spatial separation for interrupts in systems, which do not have an IOMMU or have an IOMMU that is not able to safeguard interrupts. In contrast to Intel server systems using Intel VT-d [4], embedded real-time systems do not have means to protect interrupts. For these systems, the presented SgInt concept is a real benefit. The SgInt concept requires that the processor platform provides special alias pages encapsulating an interrupt trigger register (cf. Figure 1 and Section 3). The most of Freescale's PowerPC-based processors (e.g. the Freescale QorIQ families) provide three to four of such special alias pages for interrupt trigger registers. This allows to provide spatial separation for three to four application interfaces using safeguarded interrupts per processor. The SgInt concept fulfills the required separation and offers a growth of 300-400% in protected interrupts. Since the avionics industry currently has most certification-related experience for critical avionic components for the PowerPC architecture, future developments based on this architecture are focused. The aircraft certification authorities EASA and FAA lately recommended to restrict the usage of multi-core processors for safety-critical systems due to safety concerns to dual-core processor systems at the moment [17]. For future (multi-)processor systems making use of (multiple) dual-core processors (like Freescale's P5020), the presented SgInt concept is practically applicable and has still spare resources for extensions.

6   Summary and Conclusion

The presented SgInt concept enables the safeguarding of interrupts in single (multi-core) processor systems and multiple (multi-core) processor systems.

The SgInt concept uses an exclusive page within the NTB aperture for interrupts of one distinct application interface and a dedicated page in the processor only containing the interrupt triggering register as mapping target in addition to the source/ origin ID check in the NTB. The evaluation results of the SgInt concept reveals that SgInt concept slightly outperforms state-of-the-art doorbell interrupt handling in transfer time and transfer rate (by about 0.04%). The SgInt concept can provide spatial separation for interrupts in systems, which do not have an IOMMU or have an IOMMU that is not able to safeguard interrupts. This is especially important for safety-critical embedded real-time systems since these systems usually do not have means to protect interrupts. This SgInt concept is not limited to safeguard device interrupts. It can also be applied to provide spatial separation for inter-processor communication interrupts.

While this paper focuses on avionics, the results are applicable to adjacent markets which have similar stringent security and safety requirements such as automotive, railway and industrial control.

Acknowledgments. This work was supported by the projects ARAMiS and SIBASE funded by the German Federal Ministry of Education and Research (BMBF) under the funding ID 01IS11035R and 01IS13020B. We also thank Xilinx and PLX Technologies for their support. Special thanks also to our colleagues from Airbus Defence and Space, especially Peter Ganal.

References

1. Muench, D., Paulitsch, M., Herkersdorf, A.: Temporal separation for hardware-based I/O virtualization for mixed-criticality embedded real-time systems using PCIe SR-IOV. In: International Conference on Architecture of Computing Systems (ARCS) (2014)
2. Muench, D., Isfort, O., Mueller, K., Paulitsch, M., Herkersdorf, A.: Hardware-based I/O virtualization for mixed criticality real-time systems using PCIe SR-IOV. In: International Conference on Embedded Software and Systems (ICESS) (2013)
3. Pek, G., Lanzi, A., Srivastava, A., Balzarotti, D., Francillon, A., Neumann, C.: On the feasibility of software attacks on commodity virtual machine monitors via direct device assignment. In: ACM Symposium on Information, Computer and Communications Security (ASIA CCS) (2014)
4. Intel: Intel Virtualization Technology for Directed I/O (VT-d spec) (2011)
5. AMD: AMD I/O Virtualization Technology (IOMMU) Specification Rev2.0 (2011)
6. Muench, D.: IOMPU: Spatial Separation for Hardware-Based I/O Virtualization for Mixed-Criticality Embedded Real-Time Systems Using Non Transparent Bridges (TR-TX4-399). Technical report, Airbus Group (2014)
7. PCI-SIG: Single Root I/O Virtualization and Sharing Specification 1.1 (2010)
8. Regula, J.: Using Non-transparent Bridging in PCI Express Systems. Technical report, PLX (2004)
9. Tu, C.C., Lee, C.T., Chiueh, T.C.: Secure I/O device sharing among virtual machines on multiple hosts. In: International Symposium on Computer Architecture (ISCA) (2013)
10. Nguyen, T.L., Carbonari, S.R.: Message Signaled Interrupt Redirection Table (2004)
11. Hummel, M.D., Strongin, G.S., Alsup, M., Haertel, M., Lueck, A.W.: Address Translation for Input/Output (I/O) Devices and Interrupt Remapping for I/O devices in an I/O Memory Management Unit (IOMMU) (2006)
12. Serebrin, B.C., Wiederhirn, J.F., Cooper, E.M., Hummel, M.D.: Guest Interrupt Manager that Records Interrupts for Guests and Delivers Interrupts to Executing Guests (2009)

13. Muench, D., Paulitsch, M., Hanka, O., Herkersdorf, A.: MPIOV: scaling hardware-based I/O virtualization for mixed-criticality embedded real-time systems using non transparent bridges to (multi-core) multi-processor systems. In: Conference on Design, Automation and Test in Europe (DATE) (2015)
14. Muench, D., Paulitsch, M., Honold, M., Schlecker, W., Herkersdorf, A.: Iterative FPGA implementation easing safety certification for mixed-criticality embedded real-time systems. In: Euromicro Conference on Digital System Design (DSD) (2014)
15. Jean, X., Gatti, M., Berthon, G., Fumey, M.: MULCORS - Use of Multicore Processors in airborne systems. Technical report, EASA (2012)
16. Freescale: P4080 QorIQ Integrated Multicore Communication Processor Family Reference Manual (2011)
17. FAA: Position Paper Certification Authorities Software Team (CAST) CAST-32 Multi-core Processors (2014)

Design

Exploiting Outer Loops Vectorization in High Level Synthesis

Marco Lattuada[✉] and Fabrizio Ferrandi

Dipartimento di Elettronica, Informazione e Bioingegneria,
Politecnico di Milano, Milan, Italy
{marco.lattuada,fabrizio.ferrandi}@polimi.it

Abstract. Synthesis of DoAll loops is a key aspect of High Level Synthesis since they allow to easily exploit the potential parallelism provided by programmable devices. This type of parallelism can be implemented in several ways: by duplicating the implementation of body loop, by exploiting loop pipelining or by applying vectorization.

In this paper a methodology for the synthesis of complex DoAll loops based on outer vectorization is proposed. Vectorization is not limited to the innermost loops: complex constructs such as nested loops, conditional constructs and function calls are supported. Experimental results on parallel benchmarks show up to 7.35x speed-up and up to 40 % reduction of area-delay product.

1 Introduction

Heterogeneous multiprocessor systems are becoming very common in a large group of embedded system application fields because of their computational power and their power efficiency. This type of architecture requires that the different tasks in which an application is decomposed are assigned to the most suitable processing element. The parts of the application which are characterized by high degree of parallelism are good candidates to be mapped on programmable hardware devices since their hardware implementation can potentially have very significant speed-up with respect to software implementation. Design by hand efficient hardware implementations can be a hard task since requires the knowledge of hardware description languages which is typically a rare expertise. To overcome or at least to mitigate this issue, High Level Synthesis [4] has been introduced: it consists of a (semi)-automatic design flow, potentially composed of several methodologies, that starting from a high level representation of a specification (e.g., a C/C++ source code implementation) produces its hardware implementation.

Loop parallelization is one of the most used techniques exploited by High Level Synthesis to take advantage of the parallelism provided by hardware platforms. An important class of loops which are good candidates to be parallelized are DoAll loops [19]. These loops are characterized by the absence of inter-iteration dependences which allows completely independent execution of different iterations. A parallel hardware implementation of this type of loop can be

© Springer International Publishing Switzerland 2015
L.M. Pinho et al. (Eds): ARCS 2015, LNCS 9017, pp. 31–42, 2015.
DOI: 10.1007/978-3-319-16086-3_3

obtained by replicating multiple times the module implementing its body. This type of approach potentially provides good results in terms of performance, but it can significantly increase the resources usage. Moreover, the obtained speed-up can be partially reduced by the concurrent accesses to shared resources (e.g., shared memory) performed by the different module replicas. The contention resolutions can indeed introduce overhead both in terms of delay in critical path (e.g., for the presence of the arbiter) and of cycles (e.g., because of the stalls introduced during resources acquisition).

This paper proposes a methodology for High Level Synthesis of DoAll loops based on vectorization [13] (i.e., introduction of functional units processing vectors of data) to mitigate these problems. The methodology does not introduce any significant change to the structure of the Finite State Machine nor to the hardware accelerator interface, so it can be easily integrated in existing High Level Synthesis design flows provided that they already support synthesis of vector operations. Its main contributions are the following:

- It extends the applicability of vectorization in High Level Synthesis by allowing vectorization of complex loops (i.e., loops that contain nested loops, conditional constructs and function calls).
- It allows to selectively combine vectorization with local pipelined computation potentially exploiting benefits of both the approaches.

The rest of the paper is organized as follows. Section 2 presents related work while Section 3 presents a motivational example. Section 4 describes the proposed methodology whose experimental results are presented in Section 5. Finally Section 6 presents the conclusions of the paper.

2   Related Work

Synthesis of DoAll loops is a very well studied topic of High Level Synthesis so that many approaches have been proposed to address this problem. Identification of this type of loops can be performed by means of Polyhedral methodologies, which allow to analyze and transform source code specifications exposing the different possibilities of parallelizing a loop. An example of framework aiming at performing such type of transformations is presented in [19]: this framework is able to systematically identify effective access patterns and to apply both inter- and intra- block optimizations, exposing several types of possible parallelization. The framework then evaluates each of them, and when estimated it as profitable, applies it to the specification source code. Despite completeness of existing frameworks and methodologies for polyhedral analysis, this type of techniques is still limited to loops with limited irregularity in their structure. For this reason, most of the recent synthesis techniques for DoAll loops start from applications where parallelism has already been identified. Papakonstantinou et al. [15] proposed the automatic synthesis of applications written with CUDA programming model. The proposed approach adopts *FCUDA*, a design flow which translates the CUDA code into task-level parallel C code. This code is then provided as input to AutoPilot which performs the actual synthesis producing a multi accelerators system. In a similar way, Choi et al. [2] proposed the automatic synthesis of applications already parallelized, but they start from applications exploiting pthreads and OpenMP API. In this case, the methodology directly produces parallel hardware implementations of the loops which have been annotated with `#pragma omp for` (they are DoAll loops with compile time known number of iterations). The parallel architecture is obtained by replicating multiple times the hardware accelerator which implements the body loop. This approach does not have any applicability limitation, but implies to replicate multiple times the whole implementation of the loop and requires a processor to synchronize the execution of the accelerators, with a significant increase of resources usage. A similar approach (i.e., the automatic synthesis of OpenMP annotated applications) was proposed in [3] but targeting heterogeneous systems implemented onto FPGAs. All these approaches, since the different accelerator replicas potentially access at the same time to external data, require to add logic to control resources contention, potentially delaying requests performed by the single accelerators.

Parallelization of complex DoAll loops (i.e., outer loops) by means of vectorization was proposed for SIMD processors [13]: loops are vectorized during compilation for SIMD architectures, even if they contain other loops or conditional constructs, provided that some conditions are met. In particular the outer and the inner loops must be countable and all the conditional constructs must be removable by means of if-conversion. Moreover, ad-hoc analyses and transformations are applied trying to maximize the number of aligned accesses. A similar approach is proposed in this paper, but it is adopted during the synthesis of hardware accelerators. Finally, the effects of using vector functional units in High Level Synthesis have already been evaluated in [17]. The authors proposed the adoption of configurable vector functional units which can implement at the same time both scalar operations and vector operations. This approach produces better solutions both in terms of performances and power consumption, showing the effectiveness of using parallel functional units, but it is limited to the parallelization of some operations of the specification.

3   Motivational Example

In this section a small motivational example is presented showing the potential advantages of the outer loop vectorization with respect to other loop optimization techniques when applied in High Level Synthesis. The example, presented in the left part of Fig. 1, consists of a brief fragment of code containing two nested loops. The outer loop is characterized by a fixed number of iterations (16) while the number (k) of iterations of inner loop cannot be computed at compile time. Moreover, the iterations of the outer loop can be parallelized while the iterations of the inner loop have to be executed in sequence. To allow the application of the most common types of loop parallelization techniques, the source code in the left part of Fig. 1 has been transformed by means of if-conversion removing

	Initial Code	Pre-Processed Code	Transformed Code
A	`for(i=0; i<16; i++) {`	`for(i=0; i<16; i++) {`	`for(ī={0,1}; i[0]<16; ī = ī+{2,2}) {`
B	`sum = 0;`	`sum = 0;`	`s̄ūm̄ = {0,0};`
C	`for(j=0; j<k; j++) {`	`for(j=0; j<k; j++) {`	`for(j=0; j<k; j++) {`
D	`if(sum < 10) {`	`c = sum < 10;`	`c̄ = s̄ūm̄ < 10`
E		`temp = in[i][j];`	`temp[0] = in[i[0]][j];` `temp[1] = in[i[1]][j];`
F	`sum = sum + in[i][j];`	`sumS = sum + temp;`	`sumS = s̄ūm̄ + temp;`
G	`}`	`sum = c ? sumS : sum;`	`sum[0] = c[0] ? sumS[0] : sum[0];` `sum[1] = c[1] ? sumS[1] : sum[1];`
	`}`	`}`	`}`
H	`res[i] = sum/k;`	`res[i] = sum/k;`	`res[i[0]] = sum[0]/k;` `res[i[1]] = sum[1]/k;`
	`}`	`}`	`}`

Fig. 1. Example of application of the proposed methodology

1	A(0,-) A(1,-)	`ī={0,1};`

2	B(0,-)
	B(1,-)
	C(0,0)
	C(1,0)
		`s̄ūm̄={0,0};`
		
		`j=0;`

3	D(0,0)
	D(1,0)
	E(0,0)
	E(1,0)
		`c̄=s̄ūm̄<10;`
		
		`temp[0]=in[i[0]][j];`
		`temp[1]=in[i[1]][j];`

4	F(0,0)
	F(1,0)
	C(0,1)
	C(1,1)
		`sumS=s̄ūm̄+temp;`
		
		`j++;`

5	G(0,0) G(1,0)	`sum[0] = c[0] ? sumS[0] : sum[0];` `sum[1] = c[1] ? sumS[1] : sum[1];`

6	D(0,1)
	D(1,1)
	E(0,1)
	E(1,1)
		`c̄=s̄ūm̄<10;`
		
		`temp[0]=in[i[0]][j];`
		`temp[1]=in[i[1]][j];`

7	F(0,1)
	F(1,1)
	C(0,2)
	C(1,2)
		`sumS=s̄ūm̄+temp;`
		
		`j++;`

5	G(0,1) G(1,1)	`sum[0] = c[0] ? sumS[0] : sum[0];` `sum[1] = c[1] ? sumS[1] : sum[1];`
9	H(0,-) H(1,-)	`res[i[0]]=sum[0]/k;` `res[i[1]]=sum[1]/k;`

Fig. 2. Execution trace of the first two iterations of outer loop when outer loop vectorization is applied

the conditional construct instruction D. Moreover, the complex instruction F has been decomposed into two simpler instructions (the reading from the matrix and the sum). The result of these transformations is shown in the central part of Fig. 1 where instructions E and G have been added. Nevertheless, the presence of a nested and non parallelizable loop with an unknown number of iterations prevents the application of some loop optimization techniques, but not of the proposed.

The only other loop parallelization technique which can be applied to the loops of Fig. 1 without any further change is the *Unrolling of inner loop* [6]. However, the instructions belonging to consecutive iterations of the loop cannot be executed in parallel because of data dependence between G and D, limiting the benefit of adopting this optimization. The *Unrolling of outer loop* [6], the *Pipelining of inner loop* [6], the *Pipelining of outer loop* [11] and the *Vectorization of inner loop* [12] cannot be applied to the example because of the variable number of iterations of inner loop and because of inter-iterations data dependence.

On the contrary, outer loop vectorization can be applied to the considered example: the right part of Fig. 1 shows the results of the optimization, while Fig. 2 reports which are the operations executed by an accelerator synthesized with the proposed methodology in each control step during first iteration of outer loop. For the sake of brevity and simplicity, it is assumed that the execution time of each synthesized instruction is one clock cycle, that chaining is not exploited and that k=2. A pair of indices has been associated to each instruction: the first index is the relative iteration number of the outer loop to which the instruction belongs while the second index is the relative iteration number of the inner loop. The effects of the outer vectorization are that the first iteration of nested loop executed during first iteration of DoAll loop is executed in parallel with first iteration of nested loop executed during second iteration of DoAll loop and so on. The details about the proposed solution and about how this can been obtained will be presented in the following section.

4   Proposed Methodology Flow

The proposed methodology is integrated in a High Level Synthesis flow and aims at synthesizing a parallel hardware accelerator by means of outer loop vectorization. A fixed number P of iterations of the loop is coupled and merged so that the execution of an iteration of the transformed loop corresponds to the execution of P iterations of the original loop. P identifies the degree of introduced parallelism: different loops can be parallelized with different degrees of parallelism and different implementations of the same loop can be obtained by varying its degree of parallelism.

The significant part of the proposed methodology flow consists of the transformations applied to the loop to be synthesized. These transformations can be applied with similar results to the source code or to the high level intermediate representations adopted in the first phases of a High Level Synthesis design flow. The direct manipulation of high level representations allows to easily integrate the proposed methodology in existing High Level Synthesis flows, provided that they support vector functional units. The methodology assumes that vector variables are synthesized as registers: if vector variables were mapped on BRAM, the methodology is still applicable, but the memory accesses overhead would completely nullify the benefits of the vectorization.

A loop can be synthesized with the proposed methodology if:

1. it is a DoAll loop, i.e., all iterations can be executed in parallel;
2. the number n of its iterations is multiple of the degree of parallelism P: $n\%P = 0$;
3. nested loops are not controlled by conditional constructs (i.e., nested loops are not contained in a *then* or in a *else* block; polyhedral transformations can help to remove violations to this constraint;
4. the number of iterations of nested loops does not depend on a value computed in the outer loop.

Note that the loop to be parallelized and the nested loops can contain conditional constructs which will be removed by if-conversion. Moreover, it is not required that nested loops are DoAll loops nor countable loops, but only that their iterations number does not depend on a value computed in the outer loop since they will be not internally parallelized nor unrolled. Indeed, the vectorization of the outer loop implicitly creates multiple copies of the inner loops. Each copy will be executed sequentially, but the different copies will be executed in parallel and in a completely synchronized way. The synchronization is implicit and it is guaranteed by the fourth precondition. Second constraint can potentially be removed by adding the possibility to execute in an ad-hoc way the last $n\%P$ iterations of the loop. In a similar way, also the constraint on the number of iterations of nested loops can be removed.

The proposed methodology flow is composed of several steps:

1. *Loops Analysis*: the specification is analyzed to identify DoAll loops.
2. *PreProcessing transformation*: conditional constructs in the loops are removed by transforming instructions controlled by them in speculated or predicated instructions; complex instructions are decomposed in simpler instructions.
3. *Instructions classification*: each instruction of the loops is analyzed to identify if it controls the execution of a loop and, if not, if it has to be transformed in a vector instruction or in a set of scalar instructions.
4. *Instructions transformation*: instructions which control execution of loops are transformed to support parallel execution of iterations; other instructions are transformed in vector instructions or in sets of scalar instructions according to how they have been classified.
5. *Synthesis*: the transformed loops are synthesized by means of High Level Synthesis flow.

In the following each of these steps will be detailed and its application to the example of Fig. 1 will be shown.

Loops Analysis. The source code or its high level intermediate representation is analyzed to identify DoAll loops. How this analysis is performed is out of the scope of this paper: all state of the art techniques such as polyhedral analyses can be exploited. However, since not all the DoAll loops can be actually identified by static analyses, loops which have to be parallelized by means of vectorization can be directly annotated by the designer with annotations like OpenMP pragma simd [14].

The outmost loop of Fig. 1 has been annotated with OpenMP pragma simd to be synthesized with the proposed methodology.

Preprocessing Transformation. In this step the original specification is modified to remove complex instructions and conditional constructs (i.e., if). First objective is achieved by replacing complex operations (i.e., operations which require more than one functional unit to be synthesized) with simpler operations. Second objective is obtained by applying if-conversion by means of speculation [7] and predication [10]. The recursive application of these transformations to the body of the DoAll loop and to its nested loops removes all the conditional constructs allowing to apply the following steps of the methodology. Note that, since this transformation is required to apply the loop vectorization, it always has to be performed, even when it is not profitable because of possible mispeculations.

The result of applying these transformations to the example is shown in the centre part of Fig. 1. Instruction F has been decomposed into two operations E and F (a read from a matrix and a sum), then instruction D has been transformed in a boolean assignment, while instruction E and instruction F have been speculated.

Instructions Classification. During this phase of the methodology each instruction which is part of the analyzed loop or of a nested loop is classified into four different classes:

- *Vector instructions*: they will be transformed into vector instructions; in the presented example they are B, D, and F.
- *MultiScalar instructions*: they will be transformed into P scalar instructions; in the presented example they are E, G and H.
- *DoAll loop instructions*: they are the instructions controlling the execution of the DoAll loop; in the presented example A is the only one;
- *Nested loop instructions*: they are the instructions controlling the execution of nested loops; in the presented example C is the only one.

The reason for which the second class has been introduced depends on how a vector instruction can be implemented:

① *Single scalar unit*, i.e., a single scalar functional unit which executes P scalar operations in sequence; this is the worst solution in terms of clock cycles, but the best in terms of area.

② *Single pipeline unit*, i.e., a single pipeline functional unit which executes P scalar operations in pipelined way; for complex operations (i.e., operations which require more than one cycle) it provides good performances (better than ①) with a slight area increment.

③ *Multiple scalar units*, i.e., P scalar functional units which execute P scalar operations in parallel; this is the best solution in terms of clock cycles, but the worst in terms of area.

④ *Vector parallel unit*, i.e., a single vector functional unit; it provides the same performances of ③ but better area savings because of better resource sharing [8] [5] and smaller controller complexity [9].

If the second class of instructions was not introduced, all operations would be synthesized as ④, producing the best solution in terms of performance, but the increment of area with respect to the non parallelized solution would be too large. Moreover some operations cannot be implemented in this way (e.g., non aligned memory accesses).

On the contrary, the introduction of the second class of instructions provides more flexibility to the High Level Synthesis design flow because allows to perform outer loop vectorization of loops containing instructions which cannot be vectorized. Moreover the choice between ①, ② and ③ allows to explore different possible trade-offs between area and performance in the produced solutions.

Note that classifying an instruction as *Vector* or *MultiScalar* determines only if an instruction will be synthesized as ④ or not. Since the choice between ①,

② and ③ does not concern vector functional units, this can be demanded to the rest of the High Level Synthesis design flow. The proposed methodology classifies as *MultiScalar* all the instructions which cannot be implemented by vector functional units (e.g., non-contiguous memory accesses) and all the instructions that require more than one clock cycle to be executed.

In the analyzed example, instructions E and G have been classified as *MultiScalar instructions* since vector functional units which implement these types of operations (non-contiguous load and conditional assignment) are not available. Finally, since the division requires more than one cycle, instruction H has been classified as *MultiScalar instruction*. In this way the 2 divisions can be synthesized as ① (1 divisor), ② (1 divisor which executes the two divisions in pipeline) or ③ (2 different divisors) according to the choices taken by the rest of the High Level Synthesis design flow.

Instructions Transformation. Different types of transformations are applied in this step. For the sake of brevity, it will be presented only how to transform simple `for` loops, but the proposed methodology can be applied even with different patterns (e.g., `while` loops). All the scalar variables defined inside the DoAll loop (with the exception of the induction variables of the nested loops) are transformed in vector variables, while the variables defined outside the DoAll loop are not modified. In the considered example i, `res`, `sum`, `sumS`, and `temp` are vectorized while j, and k are not.

DoAll loop instructions are transformed to support simultaneous execution of multiple iterations of the parallelized loop. The transformations to be applied are the following:

- primary induction variable is initialized with the values it would assume during first P iterations of the loop; in the presented example it is initialized to {0,1}.
- increment instruction is transformed in a vector instruction; the added constant is the increment of the sequential loop multiplied by P; in the presented example i++ is transformed in i = i + {2,2} since $P = 2$.
- guard instruction is not transformed in a vector instruction; changes to operands can be necessary to extract the scalar variables from the vector variables and to fix the loop termination; in the presented example i<16 is transformed in i[0]<16.

If secondary induction variables are present, further changes can be necessary.

Nested loop instructions have to be transformed to support simultaneous execution of implicit multiple copies of the nested loops. The transformations to be applied in case of `for` instructions are limited to their operands. In the presented example, operands of `for(j=0; j<k; j++)` have not to be changed since j is defined in this instruction and k is not defined inside the DoAll loop.

Each *Vector instruction* is transformed in a single vector instruction which directly writes a whole vector variable. Finally, each *MultiScalar instruction* is transformed in P scalar instructions, each of which writes a different element of a vector variable. The input variables of each instruction are opportunely modified to correctly manage scalar/vector data. The instructions to extract scalar values from vector variables (e.g., `var_0 = var[0]`) and to compose vector variables starting from scalar variables (e.g., `var = {var_0, var_1}`) may need to be added.

Synthesis. After that the previous steps of the proposed methodology flow have been applied, state-of-the-art High Level Synthesis flows can be applied. Since the transformed intermediate representation contains vector instructions, the design flows have to support synthesis of vector functional units.

5   Experimental Results

To evaluate the proposed methodology, this has been implemented in Bambu [16], a modular framework for High Level Synthesis developed at Politecnico di Milano. Since the identification of the DoAll loops is out of the scope of this paper, this type of analysis has not been implemented: benchmarks have to be annotated by hand with a `#pragma omp simd` [14] to be vectorized. The degree of parallelism of each loop can be specified by the designer by means of the `safelen` clause associated with each `#pragma omp simd`.

The proposed methodology has been verified on a set of parallel benchmarks distributed with Legup [2]. In OpenMP benchmarks each `#pragma omp for` has been replaced with `#pragma omp simd`, while pthread benchmarks have to be refactorized to replace pthread parallelism with `#pragma omp simd`. The proposed methodology cannot be applied to all the distributed benchmarks: some of them do not contain DoAll loops or contain DoAll loops which do not satisfy the constraints listed in Section 4.

Different degrees of parallelism have been considered: 1 (absence of parallelism), 2, 4 and 8. For each degree and for each benchmark a different hardware accelerator is produced by *Bambu*. The tool has been configured with maximum level optimization (-O3), to store input and output data on a dual port pipelined memory external to the hardware accelerator and to target 100MHz frequency. Two target platforms have been considered: the Xilinx Zynq-7000 xc7z020 and the Altera Cyclone II EP2C70F896C6. The solutions produced by High Level Synthesis have been finally synthesized with Xilinx Vivado [18] and Altera Quartus II [1]. The synthesis results obtained after place and route on different benchmarks with different degrees of parallelism are presented in Table 1. The area results refer only to the synthesized accelerator since the produced parallel hardware architectures, differently from the ones presented in [2], do not require any external processor nor external controller to be integrated in the system. Memory utilization has not been reported since all the benchmarks have been synthesized assuming that input and output data are stored in external memories. The results obtained on the different platforms are similar, so that the proposed methodology can actually be considered as appliable to different families of FPGAs. Moreover the results show how it is effectively able to save resources with respect to the complete duplication of loop implementation: the area of the produced solutions indeed growths less that the parallel degree.

Table 1. Experimental Results of applying the proposed methodology

Benchmark	Par. Degree	Xilinx Zynq-7000 xc7z020				
		Area(Ratio) LUT FF Pairs	DSPs	Cycles(Speedup)	FMax (Ratio)	Product Ratio
Add	1	344 (1)	0	20018 (1)	165.21 (1)	1
	2	573 (1.67)	0	10014 (2.00)	171.73 (1.03)	0.80
	4	1245 (3.61)	0	7512 (2.66)	157.98 (0.95)	1.42
	8	2571 (7.47)	0	6261 (3.19)	135.34 (0.81)	2.85
Boxfilter	1	3880 (1)	0	492910 (1)	95.43 (1)	1
	2	7100 (1.83)	0	176024 (2.80)	102.57 (1.07)	0.60
	4	14803 (3.81)	0	104022 (4.73)	103.19 (1.08)	0.74
	8	27966 (7.20)	0	70021 (7.03)	100.35 (1.05)	0.97
Dotproduct	1	567 (1)	3(1)	30024 (1)	131.03 (1)	1
	2	917 (1.61)	6 (2)	18020 (1.66)	107.50 (0.82)	1.18
	4	1700 (3.00)	12(4)	12018 (2.49)	116.69 (0.89)	1.34
	8	3332 (5.87)	24 (8)	9017 (3.32)	110.75 (0.84)	2.08
Hash	1	722 (1)	0	192041 (1)	121.64 (1)	1
	2	1442 (1.99)	0	108029 (1.77)	118.19 (0.97)	1.08
	4	2318 (3.21)	0	78025 (2.46)	109.69 (0.90)	1.35
	8	4570 (6.32)	0	63023 (3.08)	101.38 (0.83)	2.33
Histogram	1	2655 (1)	0	202101 (1)	129.99 (1)	1
	2	3751 (1.41)	6 (-)	72100 (2.80)	102.79 (0.79)	0.63
	4	6620 (2.49)	12 (-)	45094 (4.48)	116.65 (0.89)	0.62
	8	12158 (4.57)	24 (-)	31591 (5.74)	107.34 (0.82)	0.86

Benchmark	Par. Degree	Altera Cyclone II EP2C70F896C6				
		Area(Ratio) Logic Elements	DSPs	Cycles(Speedup)	FMax	Product Ratio
Add	1	360 (1)	0	40018 (1)	166.39 (1)	1
	2	649 (1.80)	0	20014 (2)	161.32 (0.96)	0.92
	4	1495 (4.15)	0	12512 (3.19)	147.23 (0.88)	1.46
	8	2599 (7.21)	0	8671 (4.61)	139.02 (0.83)	1.87
Boxfilter	1	4643 (1)		529905 (1)	117.03	1
	2	8291 (1.78)		184028 (2.87)	102.87 (0.87)	0.70
	4	17924 (3.86)		108024 (4.90)	89.93 (0.76)	1.02
	8	Not Available				
Dotproduct	1	668 (1)	6 (1)	36025(1)	141.58 (1)	1
	2	1238 (1.85)	12 (2)	21021 (1.71)	123.43 (0.87)	1.24
	4	2101 (3.14)	24 (4)	13519 (2.66)	124.08 (0.87)	1.34
	8	3604 (5.39)	48 (8)	9768 (3.68)	128.25 (0.90)	1.61
Hash	1	850 (1)	0	288050 (1)	121.15 (1)	1
	2	1413 (1.66)	0	144034 (1.99)	103.91 (0.85)	0.97
	4	3000 (3.52)	0	96028 (2.99)	91.16 (0.75)	1.56
	8	4885 (5.74)	0	72025 (3.99)	95.50 (0.78)	1.82
Histogram	1	3161 (1)	0	238011 (1)	132.14 (1)	1
	2	4965 (1.57)	8 (-)	90114 (2.64)	112.57 (0.85)	0.69
	4	8191 (2.59)	16 (-)	54108 (4.39)	105.45 (0.79)	0.73
	8	15421 (4.87)	32 (-)	36103 (6.59)	107.35 (0.81)	0.91

The maximum resource saving has been obtained for *Histogram* benchmark when targeting both platforms with parallel degree of 8: more than 40%. The resource saving however is not effective on the usage of DSPs: their number growths linearly in *Dotproduct* benchmark while in case of *Histogram* benchmark they have been introduced only in vectorized implementation. On *Boxfilter* (when P=2 and P=4) and on *Histogram* (when P=2) the obtained speed-up is more than linear (i.e., it is larger than parallel degree). Further gain with respect to the linear speed-up is due to the if-conversion preprocessing phase which allows to improve the performances of the circuit implementation even when vectorization is not applied. However, for all the benchmarks the real speed-up grows less than parallel degree. The main cause of this reduction in speed-up growing is the considered memory architecture which has only two ports. The number of ports limits the exploitation of parallelism since limits to two the number of simultaneous memory accesses. Even if memory accesses are pipelined, solutions where degree of parallelism is larger than 2 are slowed and cannot achieve maximum performances. Memory partitioning, by increasing the number of possible concurrent accesses, can solve this problem, but it is not supported by *Bambu*.

The introduction of vector functional units does not decrease very much the maximum frequency of the circuits. In the worst case (*Hash* benchmark implemented on Altera board with $P = 4$) the maximum frequency is reduced of 25%. Note that the increasing of the parallel degree does not always imply a decreasing in the maximum frequency. There are specifications (e.g., *Boxfilter* when implemented on Zynq) for which the introduction of vectorization increases the maximum frequency. The gain in terms of area-delay product for most complex benchmarks (e.g., *Boxfilter* and *Histogram*) is quite significant (up to 40% obtained on *Boxfilter* on Zynq with P=2) since the performances grow faster than resource utilization thanks to the if-conversion and to the local pipelined computation. However, there is a general gain in terms of area-delay product also for most of the other benchmarks when the considered parallel degree is 2. On the contrary, because of the performances limitations due to memory accesses, the solutions with higher parallel degree present worse results.

Finally, it has to be highlighted that direct comparison of the results of the proposed methodology and the results presented in [2] is not possible, not only for the different analyzed benchmarks but also for the different types of built architectures. Differently from [2] indeed, the parallel accelerators built with the proposed methodology do not require to be coupled with a controller processor. For this reason, this has not been included in the resource utilization statistics in non-vectorized architecture nor in the vectorized, resulting in smaller area occupations and in smaller area-delay savings.

6 Conclusions

In this paper a methodology for the synthesis of parallel accelerators based on vectorization has been presented. This methodology is able to synthesize by means of outer loop vectorization also irregular loops: nested loops, conditional constructs and operations which cannot be vectorized are supported. Since it transforms high level specifications, it can be easily integrated in existing design flows if they support synthesis of vector functional units. Experimental results show the effectiveness of the proposed methodology: the parallel produced solutions present a significant speed-up with a limited resource usage growth with respect to non vectorized solutions.

References

1. Altera: Quartus II (2013). http://www.altera.com
2. Choi, J., Brown, S., Anderson, J.: From software threads to parallel hardware in high-level synthesis for fpgas. In: FPT '13, pp. 270–277, December 2013
3. Cilardo, A., Gallo, L., Mazzocca, N.: Design space exploration for high-level synthesis of multi-threaded applications. Journal of Systems Architecture **59**(10, Part D), 1171–1183 (2013)
4. Cong, J., Liu, B., Neuendorffer, S., Noguera, J., Vissers, K., Zhang, Z.: High-level synthesis for fpgas: From prototyping to deployment. IEEE TCAD **30**(4), 473–491 (2011)
5. Cong, J., Jiang, W.: Pattern-based behavior synthesis for fpga resource reduction. In: FPGA 2008, pp. 107–116. ACM, New York (2008)
6. Fingeroff, M.: High-Level Synthesis Blue Book. Xlibris Corporation (2010)
7. Gupta, S., Savoiu, N., Kim, S., Dutt, N., Gupta, R., Nicolau, A.: Speculation techniques for high level synthesis of control intensive designs. In: DAC 2001, pp. 269–272. ACM, New York (2001)
8. Hadjis, S., Canis, A., Anderson, J.H., Choi, J., Nam, K., Brown, S., Czajkowski, T.: Impact of fpga architecture on resource sharing in high-level synthesis. In: FPGA 2012, pp. 111–114. ACM, New York (2012)
9. Kurra, S., Singh, N.K., Panda, P.R.: The impact of loop unrolling on controller delay in high level synthesis. In: DATE '07, pp. 391–396 (2007)
10. Mahlke, S.A., Lin, D.C., Chen, W.Y., Hank, R.E., Bringmann, R.A.: Effective compiler support for predicated execution using the hyperblock. SIGMICRO Newsl. **23**(1–2), 45–54 (1992)
11. Morvan, A., Derrien, S., Quinton, P.: Polyhedral bubble insertion: A method to improve nested loop pipelining for high-level synthesis. IEEE TCAD **32**(3), 339–352 (2013)
12. Naishlos, D.: Autovectorization in GCC. In: GCC Developers Summit, pp. 105–118 (2004)
13. Nuzman, D., Zaks, A.: Outer-loop vectorization: revisited for short simd architectures. In: PACT 2008, pp. 2–11. ACM, New York (2008). http://doi.acm.org/10.1145/1454115.1454119
14. OpenMP: Application Program Interface, version 4.0, July 2013
15. Papakonstantinou, A., Gururaj, K., Stratton, J.A., Chen, D., Cong, J., Hwu, W.M.W.: Efficient compilation of cuda kernels for high-performance computing on fpgas. ACM TECS **13**(2), 1–26 (2013)
16. Pilato, C., Ferrandi, F.: Bambu: A modular framework for the high level synthesis of memory-intensive applications. In: FPL 2013, pp. 1–4, September 2013
17. Raghunathan, V., Raghunathan, A., Srivastava, M., Ercegovac, M.: High-level synthesis with simd units. In: ASP-DAC 2002, pp. 407–413 (2002)
18. Xilinx: Vivado Design Suite (2013). http://www.xilinx.com
19. Zuo, W., Liang, Y., Li, P., Rupnow, K., Chen, D., Cong, J.: Improving high level synthesis optimization opportunity through polyhedral transformations. In: FPGA 2013, pp. 9–18. ACM, New York (2013)

Processing-in-Memory: Exploring the Design Space

Marko Scrbak[1], Mahzabeen Islam[1], Krishna M. Kavi[1(✉)],
Mike Ignatowski[2], and Nuwan Jayasena[2]

[1] University of North Texas, Denton, USA
{markoscrbak,mahzabeenislam}@my.unt.edu, krishna.kavi@unt.edu
[2] AMD Research - Advanced Micro Devices, Inc., Sunnyvale, USA
{mike.ignatowski,nuwan.jayasena}@amd.com

Abstract. With the emergence of 3D-DRAM, Processing-in-Memory has once more become of great interest to the research community and industry. In this paper, we present our observations on a subset of the PIM design space. We show how the architectural choices for PIM core frequency and cache sizes will affect the overall power consumption and energy efficiency. Our findings include detailed power consumption modeling for an ARM-like core as a PIM core. We show the maximum number of PIM cores we can place in the logic layer with respect to a power budget. In addition, we explore the optimal design choices for the number of cores as a function of frequency, utilization, and energy efficiency.

Keywords: Processing-in-memory · 3D-DRAM · Big data · MapReduce

1 Introduction

Over the last decade, we have witnessed the Big Data processing evolution. Existing commodity systems, which are widely used in the Big Data processing community, are becoming less energy efficient and fail to scale in terms of power consumption and area. [20] clearly shows that this is also true for any Scale-Out workloads in general. With the evolution of new emerging DRAM technologies, in particular 3D-DRAM, Processing-in-Memory (PIM) has again become of great interest to the research community as well as the industry [2,15]. When it comes to Big Data processing, systems with 3D-DRAM including PIM could prove to be more energy efficient and powerful than traditional commodity systems. Recent studies [8,14,18] have shown the potential use of PIM in 3D-DRAM chips. However, in order to prove the efficiency and usability of PIM, a much larger design space needs to be explored. This includes both software and hardware related design choices as well as tackling the challenges which arise from such a complex heterogeneous system. From a software perspective, challenges such as programmability, scalability, programming interfaces, and usability need to be explored. Major hardware challenges include PIM core micro-architecture, interconnection networks, and interfaces. In this paper, we present our observations

© Springer International Publishing Switzerland 2015
L.M. Pinho et al. (Eds): ARCS 2015, LNCS 9017, pp. 43–54, 2015.
DOI: 10.1007/978-3-319-16086-3_4

for a subset of architectural choices for the PIM cores, e.g. core architecture, frequency, and cache sizes to maximize energy efficiency. Our goal is to explore a part of the large design space and investigate the trade-offs between certain design choices. We believe that our observations can be useful for narrowing down some architectural choices. We focus on an ARM-like energy-efficient core as a PIM core and evaluate design choices for caches, core frequency, and number of cores for a set of Big Data analyses benchmarks based on MapReduce. Our findings and observation include:

- How cache size and core frequency affect the performance of a single PIM core and total power consumption
- How these parameters and metrics translate to overall energy efficiency
- Power decomposition for different system components
- Potential number of cores we can place in the logic layer within a power budget
- Possible design choices for number of cores as a function of frequency, utilization, and energy efficiency

The rest of the paper is organized as follows. Section 2 covers the background and related studies, and Sect. 3 describes benefits and challenges of PIM in 3D-DRAM. Section 4 shows our contribution to the design space exploration. In Sect. 5 we describe the methodology and in Sect. 6 we present our results followed by a discussion. We conclude with Sect. 7 and discuss the future work.

2   Background and Related Work

2.1   3D-DRAM Memory

3D-DRAM memory provides memory access with lower latency, higher bandwidth and lower power consumption. A prototype of such 3D-DRAM is already available from Micron [21]. A group of different vendors, Hybrid Memory Cube Consortium (HMCC) [10], are working on expanding 3D-DRAM capabilities. Current prototype 3D-DRAM, known as Hybrid Memory Cube (HMC) has a capacity of 4GB and can provide maximum memory bandwidth of 320GB/s [10]. 3D-DRAM memory is typically going to consist of several layers of DRAM (nMOS) dies stacked on top of each other with a logic layer (CMOS) sitting on the bottom of the stack. Communication between different layers is done through high speed TSVs (Through Silicon Vias) [9,10]. The logic die contains necessary interfacing circuits for the DRAM dies, and it still has enough area to accommodate additional logic [14,18]. The proposed TDP budget of the logic layer is conservatively set at 10W [18].

2.2   An Overview on PIM

Processing-in-Memory (PIM) is the concept of putting computation as close as possible to memory to get faster access to memory and achieve higher bandwidth. Processing logic can be integrated in different levels of the storage hierarchy, e.g.

cache, memory (DRAM), permanent storage (Solid State Drive-SSD). In this study, we focus only on processing in DRAM memory.

Research in the area of PIM can be categorized into two eras from the implementation point of view. In the first era, researchers relied on a processing technology that tried to combine both logic and DRAM cells on a single die. However the incompatibilities in the manufacturing process of these different types of devices made it difficult to integrate DRAM with logic [15,22]. The invention of 3D-die stacking technology breathed a new life for PIM research. 3D-Die stacking enables two disparate technologies to be integrated in the same die. It provides a very useful way of constructing a single die that can offer both dense memory and fast logic. Also, some other common challenges anticipated by the researchers of the past PIM studies seem to be easily solved with 3D-DRAM technology.

PIM, Previous Studies. From the 1990s to 2005, a number of studies proposed appropriate architectures employing PIM to achieve lower memory latency, higher memory bandwidth and high throughput. Some interesting studies from that era include EXECUBE [23], IRAM [13], FlexRAM [15], Smart Memories [24], DIVA [11], and Intelligent Memory Manager [4]. In most of the work, the researchers advocated architectures with vector [13] or SIMD type [11,15,23] processing units sitting close to the memory arrays.

PIM, Related Studies. Recently proposed Near Data Computing (NDC) architecture [14] and PIM for MapReduce applications [8] propose to integrate simple ARM cores as PIM cores in 3D-DRAM memory and have shown performance and energy gains. In our study, we closely resemble the architecture but the goal of our study differs. In this paper, we explore the design space of PIM cores utilizing MapReduce applications as a use case. In TOP-PIM [18] the researchers presented a 3D-DRAM PIM model with GPUs as PIM cores. For different process technologies, they have shown significant energy efficiency with little or no performance degradation for different HPC and graph applications. Other studies [2,3,15] have provided useful insights on research directions for PIM-augmented 3D-DRAM systems.

3   PIM Integrated 3D-DRAM: Looking into the Future

In data center systems we need to process large amounts of data as fast as possible. The main bottleneck in achieving higher speed processing is the gap between processor and memory speed. Here we discuss the two most important issues which create this problem, namely latency and bandwidth. Energy efficiency is another crucial requirement for today's data centers. 3D-DRAM memory cubes provide memory accesses with lower latency, higher bandwidth and lower power consumption. PIM cores integrated in the logic layer of 3D-DRAM are expected to capitalize these benefits.

Latency. Memory access latency for a commodity processor can be divided in two parts [13]. The first part is the time to send the address bits to the DRAM. This includes lookups in the cache hierarchy, memory controller overhead, multiplexing the address over the system memory bus, and reaching the DRAM pins, etc. The second part is the core DRAM access latency, which may include row precharge time (tRP), row address to column address delay time (tRCD) and column access delay time (tCAS). DRAM core latency is approximately 40-50ns [5,14]. PIM core's DRAM access latency will be reduced by the lookup time for L2 and L3 caches as it only has L1 caches. In addition, the off-chip memory bus delay can be avoided as the PIM cores reside in the same stack as the DRAM dies and are connected with high speed TSVs. The reduction in DRAM access latency is expected to be at least 30% [2].

Bandwidth. Today's processors, which typically have superscalar pipelines, support Out-Of-Order execution, and support speculation need an excessive amount of data per second. A good part of data can be supplied by large caches. However, present data intensive applications, e.g. Scale-Out applications [20], do not benefit from deep cache hierarchies and demand more memory accesses resulting in a high bandwidth requirement. Additionally, non-blocking and prefetch-enabled caches increase this requirement. The invention of 3D-DRAM memory can provide a viable solution to the high bandwidth requirement. Current prototypes [10] offer as much as 320GB/s off-chip memory bandwidth. Ser-Des links are used to support this high memory bandwidth. Each Ser-Des link can support 40GB/s while consuming high power, and in order to provide 320GB/s, 8 such links are required. This bandwidth (320GB/s) is also available to the logic die sitting at the bottom of the stacked DRAM dies through TSV buses. If we integrate PIM cores into the logic layer they will be able to utilize the high bandwidth without requiring Ser-Des links.

Power. The memory subsystem (memory chip, I/O interface and link) is power hungry, and in modern Petascale systems, it consumes approximately 35% of the total system power budget and is anticipated to consume more than 60% in future Exascale systems [6]. 3D-DRAM will be able to provide 72% less energy per bit as compared to current DDR4 DRAM systems [17]. Nonetheless accessing off-chip memory has high overhead in terms of energy. Studies have shown that around 50%-70% of the DRAM access energy is consumed by the interfaces [6,7]. Other studies show that approximately 20-30 pJ/b are spent when transferring data over DRAM buses [7], 5-10 pJ/b for Ser-Des links, and it is expected to be only 30-110 fJ/b when traversed along 3D TSV [18]. Thus, PIM integrated systems would be more energy efficient when running data-intensive workloads.

Challenges. There exist a number of issues which need to be solved for PIMs to be effective. The crucial challenge is designing an appropriate system architecture. This involves many design parameters, such as, the host processor, PIM processors, the memory hierarchy, communication channels, interfaces, etc.

Also a number of changes must be made to the operating system (e.g. memory management), programming framework (e.g. libraries), and programming models (e.g. synchronization, coherence, data layout).

4 PIM Design Space Exploration

A general model of a PIM augmented architecture using 3D-DRAM has been proposed by Zhang et al. [2] and a similar model has been used in recent studies [8,14] as well. We use the same model for our studies. The model consists of a host processor connected to one or many 3D-DRAM modules where each 3D-DRAM module has several PIM cores residing in the logic layer (Fig. 1). The host processor views all the 3D-DRAM modules as one physical address space shared between the host processor and the PIM cores.

Previous studies have shown high performance gains and energy reductions for PIM-augmented architectures running MapReduce workloads [8,14]. However, the power analyses performed in these studies, for ARM-like PIM cores, are not accurate. The overall power consumption of the PIM core is underestimated, and not all power components are considered, e.g. cache power. Furthermore, the studies are limited for a fixed cache size and core frequency.

In this paper, our goal is to explore the design space of the PIM cores in terms of cache sizes, operating frequency, the number of cores for a specific microarchitecture, and perform more realistic power estimations. We take an in-order, single issue, ARM-like core and perform simulations for different MapReduce workloads. Our focus is on the map() phase of MapReduce workloads because they are data intensive and highly parallelizable. We have used gem5 [19] to capture the performance statistics of the core and McPAT [25] and CACTI-3DD [26] for the power analyses.

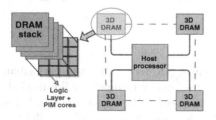

Fig. 1. A PIM augmented system comprising of 4 3D-DRAM cubes with several PIM cores embedded in the logic layer.

The architectural choices for cache size and frequency for the PIM cores will depend on two metrics, i.e. power consumption and energy efficiency. Total power consumption of a PIM core is an important factor because it limits the number of cores we can place in the logic layer within a power budget of 10W. We define the energy efficiency as useful work done per unit of energy (Work/Joule). We do not focus solely on total execution time, because it would imply the largest cache size and highest frequency as optimal choices. This is not a good approach because we want to minimize the power consumption while maximizing the performance. We performed experiments with varying L1 cache sizes with and without enabled prefetching. We have observed a moderate cache size with prefetch offers the best energy efficiency. The reason behind this is the low temporal locality and streaming-like behavior of map() phases in MapReduce workloads. Note that including another level of cache would consume a significant amount of power without providing a significant performance improvement. We also vary the PIM core frequency and adjust the supply voltage accordingly [27] to ensure a minimal supply voltage. There will be an optimal frequency for which we get the best energy efficiency. Because the power increases exponentially and execution time reduces linearly, higher frequencies than optimal will result in low energy efficiency due to high power. Lower frequencies will result in lower energy efficiency due to high execution times.

We also calculate the maximum number of cores we can place in the logic layer within the power budget of 10W. Note that the maximum number of cores may not be the optimal choice since the utilization of the cores will depend on the application which will run on the PIM cores. We therefore evaluate the optimal number of cores we want to place in the logic layer with respect to minimal execution time and minimal energy spent. We calculate the execution times using Amdahl's law for different possibilities of serial fractions. We reason that, although the computation done on PIM cores is typically going to be parallel, there may be some overhead due to communication, synchronization, or load imbalance. We observe that the more overhead we have, the fewer cores we want in the logic layer. We do not get significant performance gains with increasing the number of cores but add unnecessary power consumption. If we do not place the maximum number of cores, we hardly utilize the available bandwidth within a 3D stack. This leads to a conclusion that a SIMD/VLIW/vector processor architecture, which can consume much more bandwidth, should be considered as a PIM core. We plan to investigate such designs in the future.

5   Methodology

We used the gem5 simulator [19] to capture the performance statistics needed for our power and energy efficiency evaluation. We used the "minor" CPU, an in-order, single-issue CPU model with support for ARM ISA. We are aware that this model is not as detailed, but it is the only available in-order model with ARM ISA support. We used a simple DRAM model with a fixed latency of 40ns [14] to match the latency of the 3D-DRAM. We ran four different microbenchmarks, written in the C programming language, which capture the map() function behavior of common MapReduce applications. After input reading, we take a snapshot of the execution and simulate the run only for the map() function, which is approximately 500 million instructions. We perform the simulations for four micro-benchmarks, wordcount, histogram, linear regression, and string match. We vary the L1 cache sizes and core frequencies. L1 cache means split instruction and data caches of the same size, e.g. 16KB L1 cache means a 16KB L1 instruction and 16KB L1 data cache. We use a 64B block size for cache.

For the power consumption modeling we used McPAT [25], a power modeling tool with support for power, area and timing optimization. The tool uses a CPU model description and the corresponding performance statistics for an application run. We take the needed input parameters from gem5 statistics outputs and feed them into McPAT. We do so for each benchmark we run with different cache sizes and frequencies. We adjust the supply voltage for each frequency accordingly. This also allows us to capture the correct increase in power while varying the frequency. The chosen voltage-frequency pairs mimic those in [27]. To keep the static power consumption low, we allow power-gating. All the power estimations were conducted with respect to the 40nm process, and technology parameters follow the ITRS roadmap. We have modeled a 3D-DRAM with respect to JEDEC-HBM [12] standard using CACTI-3DD [26]. We obtained the 3D-DRAM access energy of 3.98pJ/bit which is close to 3.7pJ/bit as presented in [14]. The next section describes the experiments and results in more detail followed by a discussion.

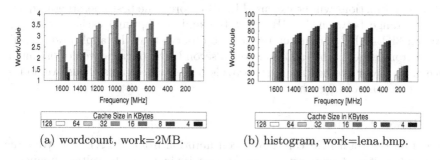

(a) wordcount, work=2MB.   (b) histogram, work=lena.bmp.

Fig. 2. Energy efficiency for two MapReduce workloads. (a) A configuration with 16KB L1 cache and a frequency of 800MHz results in the best energy efficiency. A frequency of 1GHz provides almost the same energy efficiency and represents a better alternative in terms of performance at the cost of higher power consumption. (b) A configuration with 4KB cache and 1GHz frequency results in the best energy efficiency.

6   Results and Discussion

6.1   PIM Core Frequency and Cache Size

We use the collected statistics from gem5 to evaluate what would be good architectural choices for cache sizes and core frequencies. In order to do that, we look at the overall energy efficiency for different cache size-frequency pairs. The goal is to find an optimal point where we get the most out of the PIM core for the lowest possible power consumption. For that, we take the total execution time obtained from gem5 and the power consumption of the core obtained from McPAT [25]. We include both static and dynamic power consumption, for the core and caches, as well as the dynamic 3D-DRAM power obtained from CACTI-3DD [26]. It is important to include the dynamic DRAM power consumption because smaller cache sizes can create more accesses to the DRAM and result in increased overall power consumption. We calculate the energy efficiency, E_{eff} as $E_{eff} = 1/Energy$ where,

$$Energy = (CPU\_Power \times Total\_Execution\_Time)$$
$$+ (Number\_of\_Memory\_Access \times DRAM\_Access\_Energy) . \quad (1)$$

Figure 2 shows the overall PIM core energy efficiency in Work/Joule for two distinct workloads: wordcount and histogram. We do not present the data for the other two workloads since they exhibited similar behavior as that of histogram. The data shows that, for applications like wordcount, a PIM core with 16KB L1 cache running at 800MHz frequency is the most energy efficient choice. For applications similar to histogram a 4KB L1 cache and a frequency of 800MHz results in the most energy efficient setup. We acknowledge that the actual values for cache sizes and operating frequencies may be benchmark dependent, and we plan to conduct further experiments with several other benchmarks. Our goal here is to present an approach for exploring these design choices. We do, however, believe that, if we are using ARM like cores, for most MapReduce applications, where map functions will be executed by PIM cores, the best operating frequencies will range between 600MHz-1000MHz and the optimal cache sizes range between 8KB-32KB. From our results, we observe that the applications don't benefit from larger caches and therefore a second level of cache would just introduce more power overhead and not provide performance gains. Thus, we do not evaluate the use of L2 caches.

6.2 Power Consumption

We obtain the total PIM core power consumption from McPAT [25]. We scale the supply voltage to support various frequencies by using the voltage-frequency pairs as in [27]. We separate the power consumption into four different components: static core power, dynamic core power, static cache power, and dynamic cache power. The power consumption will depend on both frequency and supply voltage and, therefore, will scale exponentially. Figure 3 shows the breakdown of different power components within a PIM core. For a cache size of 32KB and core frequency of 1GHz, the total PIM power consumption (including cache power) is around 500mW. The core dynamic power is roughly 50mW which supports the published data for an energy-efficient in-order ARM core [16]. Previous studies [8,14] used the power specifications for the same ARM core and took into consideration only the core dynamic power consumption. However, we notice that the core static power and the cache power are the most significant components and should be taken into account. Even after allowing for power-gating, static power consumption is high. This implies that the PIM cores should be turned off whenever they are not performing computation. We include the dynamic power of the DRAM to capture the effects of cache sizes.

6.3 Number of PIM Cores

The maximum number of PIM cores that can be placed in the logic layer of a 3D-DRAM will depend on the PIM core power consumption as well as the

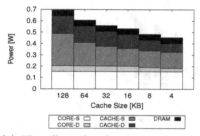 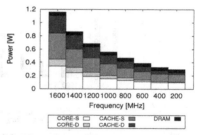

(a) The effect of cache size on the power consumption for a fixed frequency 1GHz.

(b) The effect of frequency on the total power consumption for a fixed L1 cache size of 32KB.

Fig. 3. Power decomposition for PIM core components. A significant portion of the power comes from the static power for core and cache. A configuration with a cache size of 32KB, and core frequency of 1GHz, consumes 153mW of static and 50mW of dynamic core power, and 173mW of static and 131mW of dynamic cache power. The DRAM dynamic power consumption is 51mW. The power consumption was modeled using McPAT with enabled power-gating.

power limit of the logic layer. Researchers have proposed a conservative power budget of 10W for the logic layer [18]. Figure 4 shows the maximum number of cores, within that power budget, for different setups. For 800MHz and 16KB L1 cache, we can put up to 26 cores in the logic layer. Due to various parallel overheads, the code which will run on the PIM cores may result in lower utilization of the PIM cores. Therefore, we reason about a good number of PIM cores with respect to Amdahl's law. The rate at which the power increases with the number of cores will be higher than the obtained speedup. We are trying to find the trade-off between energy consumption and execution time. We do that by calculating the execution times for different numbers of cores using Amdahl's law for different parallel overheads (serial fractions). For specific core parameters (cache, frequency), we obtain the execution time from a gem5 simulation when using a single core. We then vary the number of cores, for different parallel overheads, and calculate the execution times by using Amdahl's law. The obtained execution time for n cores, Total_Execution_Time(n), is used to calculate the energy consumed by n cores, E(n).

$$E(n) = n \times CPU\_Power \times Total\_Execution\_Time(n) \ . \tag{2}$$

We compute E(n) for different frequencies so we can observe different design alternatives. We plot the time-energy pairs in a 2D plane. The points closest to the optimum point (0,0) will be the configurations which are optimized for both performance and energy. Figure 5 shows how the desired number of cores changes because of Amdahl's law. The general observation is the more overhead we have, the fewer cores we want in the logic layer. For a parallel overhead of 1% we want as many as 16-24 cores, for 10% overhead 8-12 and for 30% 4-6 cores.

The desired number of cores depends on the parallel overhead and is subject to Amdahl's law. Therefore, it would be wise to choose highly parallelizable

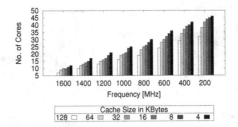

Fig. 4. Maximum number of PIM cores we can place in the logic layer within a power budget of 10W. We can place as many as 26 ARM-like PIM cores, with a 16KB L1 cache running on 800MHz, and not exceed the 10W power budget.

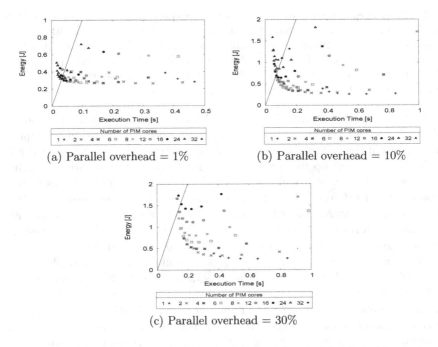

Fig. 5. Time-Energy pairs for 3 different parallel overheads. The desirable number of PIM cores are those closer to the (0,0) coordinate. As the parallel overhead increases, the configurations with more cores "drift away" because more cores do not provide additional performance and increase the power consumption. The black line represents the 10W power budget. All the configurations which are on the left-hand side of the slope are not possible, since they exceed the power limit. For a parallel overhead of 1% we want as many as 16-24 cores, for 10% overhead 8-12 and for 30% 4-6 cores. For each number of cores, we plot the points for different frequencies starting with the largest frequency (1600MHz) on the left most side and ending with the lowest frequency (200MHz) on the right most side. Note that the 800MHz frequency still gives the best results in terms of energy and time.

applications with no parallel overhead to run on PIM. If we assume that more general applications are going to run on PIM we might consider putting less cores and not waste additional energy.

7 Conclusion and Future Work

In this paper, we presented our observations on a subset of architectural choices for PIM cores. As a use case, we have used map() phases of several MapReduce workloads. Our study shows that a PIM core running at 800MHz clock frequency, with 16KB instruction cache and 16KB data cache, provides the best energy efficiency. In addition, we have shown the power consumption components and calculated the maximum number of cores we can place in the logic layer. Also, we have shown how the parallel overhead of a program can limit the advantage of having a larger number of cores in the logic layer.

In the future we want to explore other possible micro-architectures for PIM cores such as simple RISC cores, VLIW processors, vector processors and Dataflow. Also, we would like to characterize which applications benefit from a PIM architecture and how to exploit the possible benefits.

Acknowledgments. This work is conducted in part with support from the NSF Net-centric IUCRC and AMD. We acknowledge Jim Buchanan's help in making this paper more readable.

References

1. Kogge, P.M., Jay, B.B., Sterling, T., Guang, G.: Processing in memory: chips to petaflops. In: Workshop on Mixing Logic and DRAM: Chips that Compute and Remember at ISCA, vol. 97 (1997)
2. Zhang, D.P., Jayasena, N., Lyashevsky, A., et al.: A new perspective on processing-in-memory architecture design. In: Proceedings of the ACM SIGPLAN Workshop on Memory Systems Performance and Correctness, p. 7. ACM (2013)
3. Loh, G., Jayasena, N., Oskin, M., et al.: A processing in memory taxonomy and a case for studying fixed-function PIM. In: WoNDP: 1st Workshop on Near-Data Processing (2013)
4. Rezaei, M., Kavi, K.M.: Intelligent memory manager: Reducing cache pollution due to memory management functions. Journal of Systems Architecture **52**(1), 41–55 (2006)
5. Chang, D.W., Byun, G., Kim, H., et al.: Reevaluating the latency claims of 3D stacked memories. In: Design Automation Conference (ASP-DAC), 2013 18th Asia and South Pacific, pp. 657–662. IEEE (2013)
6. Gara, A.: Energy efficiency challenges for exascale computing. In: ACM/IEEE Conference on Supercomputing: Workshop on Power Efficiency and the Path to Exascale Computing (2008)
7. Keckler, S.W., Dally, W.J., Khailany, B.: GPUs and the future of parallel computing. IEEE Micro **31**(5), 7–17 (2011)

8. Islam, M., Scrbak, M., Kavi, K.M., Ignatowski, M., Jayasena, N.: Improving node-level MapReduce performance using processing-in-memory technologies. In: Lopes, L., et al. (eds.) Euro-Par 2014, Part II. LNCS, vol. 8806, pp. 425–437. Springer, Heidelberg (2014)

9. Black, B., Annavaram, M., Brekelbaum, N., DeVale, J., et al.: Die stacking (3D) microarchitecture. In: Micro, pp. 469–479. IEEE (2006)

10. Hybrid Memory Cube Consortium. http://hybridmemorycube.org/

11. Draper, J., Chame, J., Hall, M., et al.: The architecture of the DIVA processing-in-memory chip. In: Proceedings of the Supercomputing, pp. 14–25. ACM (2002)

12. JEDEC.http://www.jedec.org/category/technology-focus-area/3d-ics-0

13. Patterson, D., Anderson, T., Cardwell, N., et al.: A case for intelligent RAM. Micro **17**(2), 34–44 (1997)

14. Pugsley, S.H., Jestes, J., Zhang, H.: NDC: analyzing the impact of 3D-stacked memory+logic devices on mapreduce workloads. In: International Symposium on Performance Analysis of Systems and Software (2014)

15. Torrellas, J.: FlexRAM: toward an advanced intelligent memory system: a retrospective paper. In: Intlernational Conference on Computer Design, pp. 3–4. IEEE (2012)

16. ARM. http://www.arm.com/products/processors/cortex-a/cortex-a5.php

17. Graham, S.: HMC overview. In: memcon Proceedings (2012)

18. Zhang, D., Jayasena, N., Lyashevsky, A., et al.: TOP-PIM: throughput-oriented programmable processing in memory. In: Proceedings of international symposium on High-performance parallel and distributed computing, pp. 85–98. ACM (2014)

19. gem5 Simulator System. http://www.m5sim.org

20. Ferdman, M., Adileh, A., Kocberber, O., et al.: A case for specialized processors for scale-out workloads. In: Micro, pp. 31–42. IEEE (2014)

21. Hybrid Memory Cube, Micron. http://www.micron.com/products/hybrid-memory-cube

22. Brockman, J.B., Kogge, P.M.: The Case for Processing-in-Memory. In: Reports in University of Notre Dame (1997)

23. Kogge, P.M.: EXECUBE-A new architecture for scaleable MPPs. In: International Conference on Parallel Processing, vol. 1, pp. 77–84. IEEE (1994)

24. Mai, K., Paaske, T., Jayasena, N., et al.: Smart memories: a modular reconfigurable architecture, vol. 28, no. 2. ACM (2000)

25. McPAT, HP Labs. http://www.hpl.hp.com/research/mcpat/

26. Chen, K., Li, S., Muralimanohar, N., et al.: CACTI-3DD: architecture-level modeling for 3D die-stacked DRAM main memory. In: Proceedings of the Conference on Design, Automation and Test in Europe, pp. 33–38. EDA Consortium (2012)

27. Spiliopoulos, V., Bagdia, A., Hansson, A., et al.: Introducing DVFS-management in a full-system simulator. In: Modeling, Analysis & Simulation of Computer and Telecommunication Systems (MASCOTS), pp. 535–545. IEEE (2013)

Cache- and Communication-aware Application Mapping for Shared-cache Multicore Processors

Thomas Canhao Xu[✉] and Ville Leppänen

Department of Information Technology, University of Turku,
20014 Turku, Finland
canxu@utu.fi

Abstract. We propose and study a mapping algorithm optimized for shared-cache multicore processors. Performance requirement of modern applications is constantly growing. Processing huge amount of data in real-time is a trend even for mobile devices. It is common to find a octa-core processor in mobile phones or tablets. We will be able to see embedded devices with tens of cores in the next few years, if the trend continues. Conventional mapping algorithms are not well designed for shared-cache multicore processors. We discuss the importance of application mapping in terms of inter-application communication and shared-cache access delay. An algorithm is proposed with optimizations of the two aspects. We introduce a method with low computation complexity. First the mapping region is calculated with the congregate degree of nodes, then the region is expanded with a strategy in which the nearest nodes with lowest average cache latency are selected. The comparison with other mapping algorithms shows up to 13.9% improvement in average inter-application communication distance, with near optimal values considering the average cache latency. The results from real applications show that, the execution time and power consumption of the proposed algorithm has improved for 8% and 16.7% respectively, compared with an incremental mapping algorithm.

1 Introduction

Performance demanding applications such as games, real-time multimedia processing, real-time remote sensing and wireless signal processing have penetrated people's daily life deeper than ever before. These applications generate and process huge amount of data. Processing the data relies on efficient hardware, smart algorithm and support from the middleware. To improve the performance of data processing, parallel algorithms and multicore systems are widely used. Employing more and more cores in a single chip is a trend for multi-threaded applications with increasing performance requirements. Recent semiconductor technology has made it possible to integrate more general-purpose processor cores into a single chip. Even smart phones and tablets are equipped with quad- or octa-core processors nowadays. It is predictable that in the near future, tens of cores on a single chip will appear on the market. However, the communication infrastructure of current multicore processors are mainly based on share bus, which can

L.M. Pinho et al. (Eds): ARCS 2015, LNCS 9017, pp. 55–67, 2015.
DOI: 10.1007/978-3-319-16086-3_5

have performance bottleneck as the number of on-chip components increases. To handle the communication requirements of future multicore systems, the Network-on-Chip (NoC) concept has been proposed as a promising alternative to the conventional bus-based communication mechanism [5].

Figure 1 presents an NoC with 16 nodes. The nodes are connected by network links and routers (R). Processing Elements (PE) are attached to the routers. On-chip data such as control messages and cache data messages are generated by the cores and L1/L2 caches and sent to the routers via network interfaces (NI). Each router includes several ports for connecting local NI and four cardinal directions, where each port consists of several Virtual Channels (VC) and input buffers. The router controls

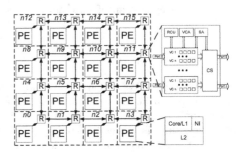

Fig. 1. NoC with 4×4 mesh

message flow, e.g. serialization and routing, with Routing Computation Unit (RCU), Virtual Channel Allocator (VCA) and Switch Allocator (SA). Components are connected by a Crossbar Switch (CS). NoC processors such as Intel SCC, Tilera TILE and KALRAY MPPA are manufactured both for research and commercial use [8].

Application/task mapping consists of finding a mapping region for a given application task with a set of constraints and requirements, e.g. performance, energy cost, efficiency and network congestion. These metrics can be affected drastically with different mapping decisions. The application mapping algorithm itself should be efficient in a dynamic system, since finding the best or optimal solution is an NP-hard problem in many cases [21]. First fit algorithm is widely used in modern operating systems, in which the first available processor in the processor list is selected [7]. Several mapping algorithms for traditional architectures have been explored and investigated by previous researches [15] [9]. To reduce the access latency to different memory modules, application mapping for Non-Uniform Memory Access (NUMA) and cache coherent NUMA systems are discussed in [6] and [13]. Due to the size and computation complexity, researchers studied heuristic mapping algorithms under different NoC architectures and constraints. For example, a greedy heuristic approximation algorithm for three-dimensional NoCs is studied in [21], while Chou et al. discussed an incremental mapping algorithm with efficiency optimizations [4]. Real-time mapping algorithms in NoC platforms are investigated in [10] and [2].

In shared-cache multicore processors, the shared last level cache is one of the most important aspects in determining application performance, due to the fact that cache access latency may take a significant part of total execution time for applications [25]. The impact of shared-cache is even higher for NoCs since cache slices are usually distributed to different nodes [3] [20]. Previous researches have focused on optimizing the compactness of mapping region, i.e. nodes in the mapping region should be closer to each other if possible [4] [7]. However the latency of shared-cache is not investigated. In this paper, we propose and study a novel heuristic application mapping algorithm which aims to optimize the application delay to shared cache. In addition the average compactness of the resulting mapping region is even better than that in the previous studies.

2   On-chip Communication of Applications

For shared-cache multicore processors, the on-chip communication of multi-threaded applications can be classified as two types: inter-application communication and shared-cache access. In general, the multi-threaded application is mapped to certain nodes of the processor. Inter-application communication means data exchange among multiple threads in an application, while shared-cache access means fetching/storing data from/to the shared cache. Figure 2 shows several cases for the two types of communication. We investigate the Manhattan Distance (MD) which represents the number of hop counts between two nodes. In Figure 2a, a 4-thread application is mapped to four corners of the mesh network, while in Figure 2b the application is mapped to the centre. Apparently, in terms of inter-application communication, Figure 2b shows a better mapping since the communication delay among nodes is lower. In consideration of shared-cache access, the average MD from node 0 to other nodes is 3 (Figure 2c), while the metric for node 5 in Figure 2d is reduced to 2. A thread running on node 5 has faster access to shared-cache compared with node 0.

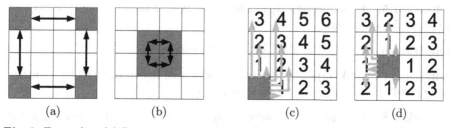

(a)   (b)   (c)   (d)

Fig. 2. Examples of different mapping strategy for a 4-thread application ((a) and (b), arrow shows communication distance between nodes), and distances to the shared cache of node 0 and 5 ((c) and (d), the routing paths are shown as arrows, while numbers indicate the distance in hop count. Notice that not all routing paths are illustrated for clarity).

Based on the aforementioned analysis, obviously the inter-application communication latency and shared-cache latency are strongly related to the mapping strategy of multi-threaded applications. The mapping algorithm should evaluate the two metrics for optimizing performance of applications. Specifically, modern applications have higher and higher demand on communication and data exchange. Conventional application mapping algorithms that have not been optimized for these aspects can lead to performance bottlenecks and reduced efficiency for multi-threaded applications.

3   The Proposed Mapping Algorithm

In this section, a model is defined for the multicore platform. We analyse the aspects that are affecting application performance. A novel application mapping algorithm aiming at optimizing these factors is proposed for shared-cache multicore processors. We also explore limitations of the proposed algorithm.

3.1   Multicore Platform Model

We present definitions of the multicore platform and the fundamentals of the mapping problem. Homogeneous NoC with mesh-based interconnect is presumed here for simplicity.

Definition 1. *A NoC $N(P(X,Y))$ consists of a mesh network $P(X,Y)$ of width X, length Y with $X \times Y$ nodes. Each node consists of a PE, an NI and a router. Each PE contains a core (single thread), a private L1 cache and a shared last level cache (L2 cache). Figure 1 illustrates a NoC of $N(P(4,4))$.*

Definition 2. *Each node n_i is denoted by a coordinate (x,y), where $0 \leq x \leq X-1$ and $0 \leq y \leq Y-1$. The coordinate can be represented as $i = y \times X + x$.*

Definition 3. *The Manhattan Distance between $n_i(x_i, y_i)$ and $n_j(x_j, y_j)$ is MD (n_i, n_j), $MD(n_i, n_j) = |x_i - x_j| + |y_i - y_j|$.*

Definition 4. *Two nodes $n_1(x_1, y_1)$ and $n_2(x_2, y_2)$ are connected by a router and related link only if they are adjacent, e.g. $|x_1 - x_2| + |y_1 - y_2| = 1$.*

Definition 5. *An application $A_i(t)$ has t threads, and therefore must be mapped to t cores for execution.*

Definition 6. *$n_{Available}$ is a list of available nodes in $P(X,Y)$.*

Definition 7. *$R_i(A_i(t))$ is the destination mapping region in $P(X,Y)$, consisting of a list of nodes n_t with t nodes for $A_i(t)$.*

Definition 8. *Average Cache Latency (ACL_{n_i}) is the average latency for a node n_i accessing the shared last level cache. The ACL_{n_i} is calculated as:*

$$ACL_{n_i} = \frac{\sum MD(n_i, n_j)}{X \times Y} \tag{1}$$

Such that: $0 \leq j \leq X \times Y - 1$.

Definition 9. *Average Inter-application Latency ($AIL_{R_i(A_i(t))}$) is the average latency between internal nodes for an application $A_i(t)$ with a mapping region $R_i(A_i(t))$. The $AIL_{R_i(A_i(t))}$ is calculated as:*

$$AIL_{R_i(A_i(t))} = \frac{\sum MD(n_i, n_j)}{t} \tag{2}$$

Such that: $\forall i, j : n_i, n_j \in R_i(A_i(t))$.

3.2   Application Mapping and Efficiency

System performance and efficiency can be affected by the two metrics ACL and AIL. For example, a node with lower ACL has lower average latency accessing the shared cache slices, resulting improved performance and efficiency. Similarly, a mapping region with lower AIL has lower average node-node access delay which is an advantage for communication-intensive applications. We explain the two metrics with Figure 3a. Application D is mapped to four nodes n_{29}, n_{30}, n_{37} and n_{38}. It can be calculated that the ACLs of n_{30} and n_{38} are 4.75 $(\frac{304}{64})$, while these values for n_{29} and n_{37} are both 4.25 $(\frac{272}{64})$. Indeed, nodes closer to the centre of the mesh network generally have lower ACL values. For AIL of D, we must calculate the average MD between one node and all other nodes in the mapping region. Take n_{30} for instance, $MD(n_{30}, n_{29}) = 1$, $MD(n_{30}, n_{38}) = 1$ and $MD(n_{30}, n_{37}) = 2$, therefore the average MD of n_{30} to other nodes in the mapping region is 1 $(\frac{4}{4})$. Similarly this metric can be calculated for n_{29}, n_{37} and n_{38}, and the AIL of D is the mean value of four. Both C and D are possible mapping regions for an application with 4 threads, however D is preferable since the two metrics are lower than that in C (ACL and AIL for C are 5.5625 and 3.25, while for D the two metrics are 4.625 and 1, respectively).

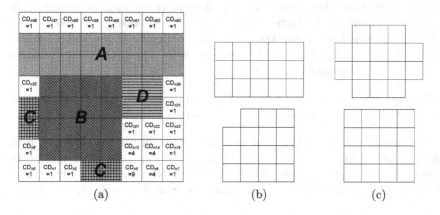

(a)   (b)   (c)

Fig. 3. Examples of different mapping schemes. (a), an example of four applications A (16 threads), B (16 threads), C (4 threads) and D (4 threads) running in an 8×8 NoC. (b), two mapping regions for a 15-thread application. (c), two mapping regions for a 16-thread application.

It is relatively easy to find a mapping region with lowest value of one metric. For example, to find a mapping region with lowest ACL, the algorithm can sort all available nodes with ACL, and output the required number of nodes with lowest ACL. We will evaluate this strategy in the experiments. The minimal ACL strategy works well for single-thread applications. However, for an application with more threads, the resulting mapping region can be fragmented, leading to poor inter-application communication and even congestion of the on-chip network [24]. For example, application C in Figure 3a can cause congestion to B, since the network resources in B are contended with the traffic of D. To decrease congestion and reduce the delay of inter-application communication, intuitively, the algorithm can enumerate all mapping possibilities and output the region with lowest AIL. Nevertheless the time spent for exhaustive enumeration increases rapidly as the size of the inputs grows: assuming all nodes in the mesh are available, a 4-thread application in a 4×4 mesh has $\binom{16}{4} = 1{,}820$ mapping possibilities, while a 10-thread application in an 8×8 mesh has $\binom{64}{10} = 151$ billion mapping possibilities. It is questionable whether the trade-off of exhaustive enumeration is worthy for generating the optimal result. Practically, heuristic and stochastic algorithms, as well as simulated annealing and linear programming are widely used to achieve relatively good results with low computational complexity. Here the proposed algorithm is based on heuristics. In general, the AIL of a mapping region is lower in case the region is more *congregate* [14] [23]. In this paper, more *congregate* means that the shape of a region is closer to a square. Figure 3a shows two applications A and B both with 16 threads. The AIL of B is lower than that in A, since B is more congregate than A ($AIL_{R_B(A_B(16))} = 2.5$, $AIL_{R_A(A_A(16))} = 3.125$, 4×4 square compared with 8×2 rectangle). Another example is shown in Figure 3b, in which the AIL of the upper mapping region is higher than that in the lower (2.49 and 2.42). Notice that it is not always true the AIL of a square region is the lowest among all regions. Figure 3c illustrates two regions with 16 nodes, in which the AIL of upper region is better than the square shaped region (2.484 and 2.5 respectively), despite the fact that the difference is only 0.64%. We define *Congregate Degree* based on the above analysis:

Definition 10. *Congregate Degree (CD_{n_i}) is the maximum number of available nodes for n_i in the $x + y+$ (right-up) direction, in a square shape.*

Apparently CD of an occupied node is 0, for other nodes the value is the square of an integer. For instance in Figure 3a, $CD_{n_5} = 9$, which means that for n_5, the maximum number of free nodes in a square shape in the right-up direction is 9. The CDs of other free nodes are indicated in the figure as well.

3.3   The Proposed Algorithm

The number of nodes requested by an application can be equal, larger or smaller than the CD of a node. Therefore the region should be shrunk or expanded accordingly. Furthermore, the search space, i.e. the number of candidate mapping regions should be limited for higher efficiency. We define a variable R_{max} to limit the maximum number of regions in the candidate list. Larger R_{max} increases the search space, spends more time for calculation and possibly generates better results. We will explore the quality of the algorithm with different cases where $R_{max} \le \sqrt{X \times Y}$. Another problems is, which node should be the first to explore. We discovered that nodes in the central part of the mesh network have lower ACL values than nodes in the border, therefore the algorithm explores from the node with minimum ACL.

The region will be added to the candidate region list, in case the number of tasks in an application equals to the CD of a node ($Case$ 1). If CD_{n_i} is larger than the number of tasks in an application, and the number of tasks can be represented by a square (e.g. applications with 1, 4, 9, 16... tasks), then the smallest CD_{n_i} that is closest to the number of requested nodes is added to the candidate list ($Case$ 2.1). Otherwise the aforementioned square region must be expanded. For instance, an application with 6 threads will be mapped to CD_{n_i} = 4 if available, then expanded with 2 nodes ($Case$ 2.2). Notice that CD_{n_i} represents the maximum number of free nodes in a square, while the smaller squares in CD_{n_i} can be evaluated if necessary. In Figure 3a, despite the fact that $CD_{n_5} = 9$, it can be estimated for an application with 4 tasks. The last case is for CD_{n_i} smaller than the number of tasks in an application: the region should be expanded and then placed to the candidate region list ($Case$ 3). To minimize AIL and improve the cohesion of the expanded region while maintaining better ACL, we propose a nearest, lowest ACL expanding strategy. The algorithm explores adjacent nodes near the current region in terms of MD, nodes with lowest average MD to the current region are added to the expanded region. A node is favourable if it has lower ACL. Finally, the candidate regions are assessed with both ACL and AIL, we define Normalized Average Latency (NAL):

Definition 11. *Normalized Average Latency ($NAL_{R_i(A_i(t))}$) is the weighted average latency of a mapping region $R_i(A_i(t))$:*

$$NAL_{R_i(A_i(t))} = \frac{\frac{\sum_{n_j \in R_i(A_i(t))} ACL_{n_j}}{t} - ACL_{min}}{ACL_{min}} + \frac{AIL_{R_i(A_i(t))} - AIL_{min}}{AIL_{min}} \quad (3)$$

where ACL_{min} and AIL_{min} represent the minimum ACL and AIL of all candidate regions.

In the destination multicore platform, given an application $A(t)$, we define the problem as finding a mapping region $R(A(t))$ with optimizations of both ACL and AIL. The pseudo code of the proposed algorithm is demonstrated in Algorithm 1. The computation complexity of the proposed algorithm is linear, determined by $n_{Available}$ and R_{max}. Higher amount of available nodes will lead to increased search space, similarly exploring more candidate regions will result more time for calculation. Overall the computation cost of the proposed algorithm is relatively low. The exact time cost will be explored in the experiments. The main problem of the proposed algorithm is that, the available maximum CD_{n_i} may reduce quickly when applications are mapped to the network, causing fragmentation. This is due to the fact that the algorithm starts to explore nodes with lowest ACL which are in the centre of the network. Limiting the maximum usable nodes is a solution for fragmentation and will be studied in the following section. In addition, the proposed algorithm assumes applications with certain amount of cache accesses and inter-application communication, while unique applications with low amount of cache accesses and/or inter-application communication may not benefit that much from the algorithm.

Algorithm 1. Pseudo code of the proposed mapping algorithm

Input: The configuration of the NoC $N(P(X,Y))$; list of current available nodes $n_{Available}$; ACL for all nodes; R_{max} as the maximum number of regions in the list of candidate regions $R_{Candidate}$; an application with t threads $A(t)$

Output: A mapping region $R(A(t))$ for the application

$\forall n_i \in n_{Available}$: {
calculate and sort all ACL_{n_i} as ACL_{sorted}
calculate all CD_{n_i}
}

$\forall ACL_{sorted}$ **if** $CD_{n_i} > t$ **then**
   Shrink the region to $\lfloor \sqrt{t} \rfloor$
   Expand the region according to the nearest, lowest ACL strategy if $t > \lfloor \sqrt{t} \rfloor^2$
   Place the region into the candidate list $R_{Candidate}$ until reaching R_{max}
   else if $CD_{n_i} = t$ **then**
     | Place the region into the candidate list $R_{Candidate}$ until reaching R_{max}
   end
   else
     Expand the region according to the nearest, lowest ACL strategy
     Place the region into the candidate list $R_{Candidate}$ until reaching R_{max}
   end
end

Calculate and return the region with lowest NAL in $R_{Candidate}$

---

4   Experimental Evaluation

In this section, we evaluate the performance of different mapping algorithms with synthetic and real application. Theoretical performance metrics such as ACL, AIL and time cost, as well as application performance metrics are investigated.

4.1   Synthetic Result Analysis

We first evaluate mapping results using synthetic traces. Here, Task Graph Generator [18] is selected to generate 10,000 tasks with 1 to 16 threads. By applying the same task input set and sequence, we investigate the proposed mapping algorithm with different number of search space ($P - SS*$), the First Fit mapping algorithm in Solaris 9 (FF), the incremental mapping algorithm in [4] (INC), the mapping algorithm that always choose nodes with minimum ACL ($MACL$) and random mapping ($RAND$). The tasks enter and leave the system with first-in-first-out sequence. We also explore networks with different utilization, since lower utilized networks generally have higher number of available nodes and therefore have higher potential to generate better results. In case the number of available nodes are not enough for the next application, the earliest application will be removed. The quality of mapping results is measured by AIL and average

ACL of all nodes in the mapping region ($AACL$). Lower values are preferable under the same condition. The results are presented in Table 1.

In terms of $AACL$, mapping algorithm $MACL$ achieved lowest value in all cases. This is due to the fact that $MACL$ always chooses next node with lowest ACL. It is noteworthy that the $AACL$ results of the proposed algorithm are basically identical with $MACL$ regardless of the search space, implying that our algorithm achieves near optimal values in terms of cache latency. Increasing the network utilization leads to higher $AACL$ for all algorithms, and the difference of $AACLs$ for these algorithms is smaller in case the network is saturated. Notice that the proposed algorithm generated best $AACL$ under full network utilization, although the improvement is relatively small ($\approx 1\%$). Overall, the $AACL$ for $P - SS1$ has improved by 5.2% and 7.4% under 70% network utilization, compared with FF and INC respectively. The number of search space plays a key role in consideration of AIL. For example, increasing the size of search space from 1 to 8 results a 16.7% AIL improvement on average. However the time consumed by searching a better region increases linearly. We note that the time spent for making mapping decision is considerably low even for $P - SS8$ (magnitude of μs). It can be neglected for most non-realtime systems, taking human reaction time and program execution time into account (magnitude of ms or higher). On average, compared with INC, the $AILs$ of $P - SS8$ has improved 10.8%, 12.6%, 13.9% and 2.1% under 70% to 100% network utilization, respectively. In conclusion, the proposed algorithm provides best AIL and $AACL$ in most cases, with reasonable computation complexity.

Table 1. Result of different mapping algorithms with different Node Utilization (NU), the unit of time μs is the average time of mapping decisions. System configuration: C/gcc 4.7.2, Linux 3.6.11, Core i7 920 3.7 GHz, 8GB Memory.

NU=0.7	P-SS1	P-SS2	P-SS4	P-SS8	FF	INC	MACL	RAND
AIL	1.923	1.815	1.714	1.663	2.753	1.866	3.256	4.204
AACL	4.851	4.844	4.848	4.846	5.116	5.239	4.812	5.267
Time	86.1	110.4	161.2	263.9	63.3	79.8	63.8	65.3
NU=0.8	P-SS1	P-SS2	P-SS4	P-SS8	FF	INC	MACL	RAND
AIL	2.063	1.922	1.777	1.718	2.842	1.967	3.516	4.212
AACL	4.983	4.980	4.981	4.981	5.114	5.217	4.949	5.257
Time	80.5	102.0	144.6	231.4	61.5	74.0	61.7	63.2
NU=0.9	P-SS1	P-SS2	P-SS4	P-SS8	FF	INC	MACL	RAND
AIL	2.299	2.080	1.910	1.829	2.909	2.126	3.742	4.295
AACL	5.089	5.088	5.089	5.091	5.153	5.226	5.080	5.254
Time	91.1	93.3	129.8	203.9	60.0	69.6	60.1	62.2
NU=1.0	P-SS1	P-SS2	P-SS4	P-SS8	FF	INC	MACL	RAND
AIL	2.837	2.652	2.478	2.369	2.958	2.422	4.018	4.177
AACL	5.238	5.241	5.237	5.229	5.254	5.280	5.269	5.253
Time	70.6	85.3	132.0	175.3	59.0	64.9	58.6	62.6

4.2   Application Result Analysis

The experimental environment for real applications is based on a cycle-accurate NoC simulator (GEMS/Simics [16] [17]). An NoC processor with 64 (8×8) nodes is simulated. Each NoC node consists of a dedicated router, an NI and a PE. The PE consists of a Sun UltraSPARCIII+ core with private L1 cache (split I + D, 16KB + 16KB, 4-way, 64-byte line, 3-cycle access delay) and a slice of the shared L2 cache (512KB per slice, totally 16MB). The cache/memory architecture of the system is static non-uniform [12] [22], and MOESI cache coherence protocol is used [1]. Orion2 is selected to evaluate the detailed power characteristics of routers and links [11]. Several workloads with 16 threads are chosen from [19]. All mapping algorithms are evaluated in the state where the aforementioned 10,000 tasks are mapped to the system with 90% network utilization, and first-in-first-out scheduling is used in case the available nodes are insufficient for the incoming application. Performance metrics are measured in terms of application execution time and power consumption of the routers and links. Here we only compare $P-SS8$ with other algorithms. The normalized results are illustrated in Figure 4a and 4b.

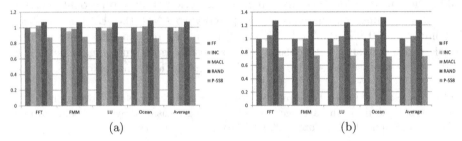

(a)   (b)

Fig. 4. Normalized average application execution time (a) and power consumption of the network (b) for different mapping algorithms

Experimental results from Figure 4a indicated that the proposed algorithm $(P-SS8)$ is the best among all algorithms in terms of average application execution time. Specifically, compared with FF and INC, the applications run 12.5% and 8% faster respectively. The performance of FF and $MACL$ are basically the same, where random mapping shows worst performance. The main reason is that, while INC considers continuity and compactness of the mapping region, the ACLs of nodes are neglected. Similarly $MACL$ is optimized for minimal ACL in all cases, while the continuity and compactness of the mapping region are ignored. We note that, in case of high system utilization, AIL is more important than ACL for multi-threaded applications since the available nodes left are usually those with higher ACL values. We also notice that, the selection of the first node is critical for choosing the mapping region. For example, INC selects the first node as close to the master node (i.e. node 0) as possible which can reduce fragmentation of the network, whereas the proposed algorithm starts from a node with minimal ACL. Obviously the strategy of the proposed algorithm is more effective compared with other algorithms. In terms of power consumption (Figure 4b), the improvement of $P - SS8$ is considerably higher than others. In comparison to INC and FF, the energy consumed by the on-chip network is reduced by 16.7% and 26.8%, on average for the applications, respectively. The improvement for execution time and power consumption differs from application to application, depending on the intensity of thread-thread communication and number of accesses to the shared-cache.

5 Conclusion

We proposed an application mapping algorithm for shared-cache multicore processors. Multiprocessing is a trend for modern data processing, more and more cores are integrated into a single chip to improve the performance of multiprocessing. We investigated the on-chip communication delays of shared-cache multicore processors. The delays were characterised as inter-application communication and shared-cache access. We explored an algorithm which optimizes both delays at the same time. A novel strategy is proposed to calculate the mapping region with low computation complexity. Experimental study compared theoretical and real world performances of our method with other algorithms under synthetic and application workloads. It is shown that the proposed algorithm consistently leads to reduction in the inter-application communication and cache access delays. Results from our algorithm also show 12.5% and 26.8% improvement of application execution time and network power consumption over the first fit algorithm, respectively.

References

1. AMD: Family 10th amd phenom processor product data sheet (November 2008), http://www.amd.com/us-en/assets/content_type/white_papers_and_tech_docs
2. Chen, Y.J., Yang, C.L., Chang, Y.S.: An architectural co-synthesis algorithm for energy-aware network-on-chip design. Journal of Systems Architecture 55(5-6), 299–309 (2009)
3. Choi, I., Zhao, M., Yang, X., Yeung, D.: Experience with improving distributed shared cache performance on tilera's tile processor. Computer Architecture Letters 10(2), 45–48 (2011)
4. Chou, C.L., Ogras, U., Marculescu, R.: Energy- and performance-aware incremental mapping for networks on chip with multiple voltage levels. IEEE Transactions on Computer-Aided Design of Integrated Circuits and Systems 27(10), 1866–1879 (2008)
5. Dally, W., Towles, B.: Principles and Practices of Interconnection Networks. Morgan Kaufmann Publishers Inc., San Francisco (2003)
6. Sharma, D., Pradhan, D.K.: Processor allocation in hypercube multicomputers: Fast and efficient strategies for cubic and noncubic allocation. IEEE Trans. Parallel Distrib. Syst. 6(10), 1108–1122 (1995)
7. Fattah, M., Rahmani, A.M., Xu, T., Kanduri, A., Liljeberg, P., Plosila, J., Tenhunen, H.: Mixed-criticality run-time task mapping for noc-based many-core systems. In: 2014 22nd Euromicro International Conference on Parallel, Distributed and Network-Based Processing (PDP), pp. 458–465 (February 2014)

8. Fleig, T., Mattes, O., Karl, W.: Evaluation of adaptive memory management techniques on the tilera tile-gx platform. In: 2014 27th International Conference on Architecture of Computing Systems (ARCS), pp. 1–8 (February 2014)

9. Hakem, M., Butelle, F.: Dynamic critical path scheduling parallel programs onto multiprocessors. In: Proceedings of the 19th IEEE International Parallel and Distributed Processing Symposium (IPDPS 2005), Workshop 8, vol. 9, pp. 203.2. IEEE Computer Society, Washington, DC (2005)

10. Hu, J., Marculescu, R.: Energy-aware communication and task scheduling for network-on-chip architectures under real-time constraints. In: Proceedings of the Conference on Design, Automation and Test in Europe, DATE 2004, vol. 1, pp. 10234. IEEE Computer Society, Washington, DC (2004)

11. Kahng, A.B., Li, B., Peh, L.S., Samadi, K.: Orion 2.0: a fast and accurate noc power and area model for early-stage design space exploration. In: Proceedings of the Conference on Design, Automation and Test in Europe, DATE 2009, pp. 423–428. European Design and Automation Association, 3001 Leuven, Belgium (2009)

12. Kim, C., Burger, D., Keckler, S.W.: An adaptive, non-uniform cache structure for wire-delay dominated on-chip caches. In: Proceedings of the 10th International Conference on Architectural Support for Programming Languages and Operating Systems, ASPLOS X, pp. 211–222. ACM, New York (2002)

13. Laudon, J., Lenoski, D.: The sgi origin: A ccnuma highly scalable server. In: The 24th Annual International Symposium on Computer Architecture, Conference Proceedings, pp. 241–251 (June 1997)

14. Lei, T., Kumar, S.: A two-step genetic algorithm for mapping task graphs to a network on chip architecture. In: Proceedings. Euromicro Symposium on Digital System Design, pp. 180–187 (September 2003)

15. Leutenegger, S.T., Vernon, M.K.: The performance of multiprogrammed multiprocessor scheduling algorithms. SIGMETRICS Perform. Eval. Rev. **18**(1), 226–236 (1990)

16. Magnusson, P., Christensson, M., Eskilson, J., Forsgren, D., Hallberg, G., Hogberg, J., Larsson, F., Moestedt, A., Werner, B.: Simics: A full system simulation platform. Computer **35**(2), 50–58 (2002)

17. Martin, M.M., Sorin, D.J., Beckmann, B.M., Marty, M.R., Xu, M., Alameldeen, A.R., Moore, K.E., Hill, M.D., Wood, D.A.: Multifacet's general execution-driven multiprocessor simulator (gems) toolset. Computer Architecture News (September 2005)

18. TGG: Task graph generator (July 2014), http://taskgraphgen.sourceforge.net/

19. Woo, S.C., Ohara, M., Torrie, E., Singh, J.P., Gupta, A.: The splash-2 programs: Characterization and methodological considerations. In: Proceedings of the 22nd International Symposium on Computer Architecture, pp. 24–36 (June 1995)

20. Xu, T., Guang, L., Yin, A., Yang, B., Liljeberg, P., Tenhunen, H.: An analysis of designing 2d/3d chip multiprocessor wit different cache architecture. In: NORCHIP 2010, p. 1–6 (November 2010)

21. Xu, T.C., Liljeberg, P., Plosila, J., Tenhunen, H.: Exploration of heuristic scheduling algorithms for 3d multicore processors. In: Proceedings of the 15th International Workshop on Software and Compilers for Embedded Systems, SCOPES 2012, pp. 22–31. ACM, New York (2012)

22. Xu, T.C., Liljeberg, P., Plosila, J., Tenhunen, H.: A high-efficiency low-cost het-erogeneous 3d network-on-chip design. In: Proceedings of the Fifth International Workshop on Network on Chip Architectures, NoCArc 2012, pp. 37–42. ACM, New York (2012)
23. Xu, T.C., Liljeberg, P., Tenhunen, H.: A Minimal Average Accessing Time Sched-uler for Multicore Processors. In: Xiang, Y., Cuzzocrea, A., Hobbs, M., Zhou, W. (eds.) ICA3PP 2011, Part II. LNCS, vol. 7017, pp. 287–299. Springer, Heidelberg (2011)
24. Yang, C.Q., Reddy, A.: A taxonomy for congestion control algorithms in packet switching networks. IEEE Network 9(4), 34–45 (1995)
25. Zhou, X., Chen, W., Zheng, W.: Cache sharing management for performance fair-ness in chip multiprocessors. In: 18th International Conference on Parallel Archi-tectures and Compilation Techniques, PACT 2009, pp. 384–393 (September 2009)

Applications

Parallelizing Convolutional Neural Networks on Intel® Many Integrated Core Architecture

Junjie Liu(✉), Haixia Wang, Dongsheng Wang, Yuan Gao, and Zuofeng Li

Tsinghua National Laboratory for Information Science and Technology,
Beijing 100084, China
{liujunjie12,g-y12}@mails.tsinghua.edu.cn,
{hx-wang,wds}@tsinghua.edu.cn,
leftlzf@gmail.com

Abstract. Convolutional neural networks (CNNs) are state-of-the-art machine learning algorithm in low-resolution vision tasks and are widely applied in many applications. However, the training process of them is very time-consuming. As a result, many approaches have been proposed in which parallelization is one of the most effective. In this article, we parallelized a classic CNN on a new platform of Intel® Xeon Phi™ Coprocessor with OpenMP. Our implementation acquired 131× speedup against the serial version running on the coprocessor itself and 8.3× speedup against the serial baseline on the Xeon® E5-2697 CPU.

Keywords: Convolutional neural network · OpenMP · Intel many integrated core architecture · Xeon phi

1 Introduction

Among various machine learning algorithms, convolutional neural networks (CNNs) have been proved to be state-of-the-art in many applications such as face detecting[1,2] and hand-writing digital recognition[3]. However, the training of CNNs is very time-consuming especially on large data sets. And this runtime can further increase exponentially with the networks' getting deeper and larger. Therefore, parallelization of the networks was widely applied as an effective approach to reduce the time cost, and it attracted strong research focus.

Multi-core CPUs and GPUs are two main platforms for the parallelization. Comparatively speaking, GPUs are more popular in the recent researches because of their rich floating point calculation power. With Nvidia® CUDA framework, developers are able to utilize the physical resources efficiently without learning a completely new language or a series of complex APIs. For example, [4] used two Nvidia GTX580 cards to build a super large convolutional neural network for the classification of 1.2 million high-resolution images and managed to train it in one week. More previously, [5] mapped a large scale CNN on a Nvidia GTX285 and acquired a speedup of about 100 times against its serial baseline. The keys to the high performance on GPUs are the efficient implementation of

© Springer International Publishing Switzerland 2015
L.M. Pinho et al. (Eds): ARCS 2015, LNCS 9017, pp. 71–82, 2015.
DOI: 10.1007/978-3-319-16086-3_6

convolution operation and using batch learning to improve the parallelism. On the other hand, multi-core CPUs provide even easier programming environment such as OpenMP, but the number of threads of a multi-core CPU is relatively low which limits the performance of parallelization. [6] showed that CPUs' implementation performed better for small neural networks than GPUs', while GPUs took back the advantage with the scale getting bigger.

In 2012, Intel published new Xeon Phi Coprocessors, codenamed Knights Corner (KNC in the rest of this paper), as its first commercial release of Many Integrated Core (MIC) Architecture for high performance computing. A typical model of KNC owns 60 cores on the single chip and provides 240 threads. The peak double precision floating point performance is up to over 1 TFLOPS. Like a GPU card, Xeon Phi is a PCIe device. It can be viewed as a coprocessor to the CPU as well as a host with its own operating system. Through the support of compiler, KNC can share the same programming environment with CPUs. Given a serial C/C++ program and provided it can be parallelized, it takes only a few efforts to map it to a KNC card (or cards) and acquire considerable speedup.

In this article, we accelerated the training process of a convolutional neural network on a KNC card as an alternative to the traditional platforms of multi-core CPUs and GPUs. We used OpenMP and SIMD to parallelize the network according to the hierarchy of KNC, and used some compiling skills to optimize the performance. The experiments showed our implementation acquired $131\times$ speedup against the serial version running on the new platform itself and it was $8.3\times$ faster than the serial baseline on Xeon CPU.

The rest parts of this paper are organized as follows. Section 2 gives details about the architecture of new Xeon Phi coprocessors. Section 3 introduces the structure of the convolutional neural network. Then in section 4, we discuss the technical points used in the parallelization process. Section 5 presents our evaluation results. Finally in section 6, we draw the conclusion and discuss the future work.

2   Intel® Xeon Phi™ Coprocessors

2.1   Architecture

Taking new Xeon Phi 5110P for example, it is equipped with 60 x86 cores that run at a low frequency for the consideration of power efficiency. Each one of these cores has an in-order dual-issue pipeline and supports 4 threads by Intel Hyper-Threading Technology to provide rich thread resources for parallelism. A bi-directional ring bus is used to connect them. The high-level overview of the KNC structure is given by Fig. 1.

For memory hierarchy, there are 32 KB private L1 caches for data and instruction and a sharing 512KB L2 cache in each core. All L2 caches are fully coherent by tag directories. As a PCI-E card, KNC has a quite big on-chip memory of up to 8GB and doesn't share memory with host CPU. There are 8 double-channel memory controllers on the ring bus, providing a bandwidth of up to 352 GB/s.

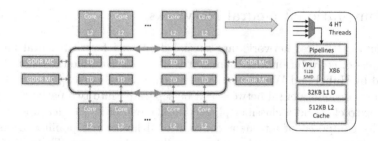

Fig. 1. Architecture Overview of KNC Coprocessors

KNC has a new designed 512-bit SIMD instruction set, which means the VPU(Vector Processing Unit) in each core can execute 16 single-precision(SP) or 8 double-precision(DP) operations per cycle. With multiply-add instruction, such long-width SIMD instruction set directly gives a 16x speedup in evaluating the FLOPS of double precision. Thus, it is of great importance to take full advantage of the SIMD when parallelizing applications on KNC.

2.2 Programming Modes

There are three programming modes for MIC: Native, Offload or Symmetric.

Native mode is the easiest by treating KNC who runs its own micro-Linux operation system to manage the on-chip resources as an independent many-core computer and directly running programs on it. However, the performance of serial parts of the code could be very bad because of the lightweight design of KNC cores. Symmetric mode is often used in MPI programming. It also treats KNC as an independent node and make it work together with host CPU and other KNC nodes. In fact, native mode can be a special case of Symmetric mode where there is only one KNC node.

In this paper, we parallelized the convolutional neural network on a KNC coprocessor by offload mode where KNC works in a quite similar way with GPU in GPGPU. The program runs on the host CPU until it comes to the parallel regions which are identified by developers with the compiler directive **#pragma offload**. These regions will be sent to the KNC card with necessary data blocks specified by clauses **in/out** through PCI-E and execute in parallel. The newest releases of Xeon Phi have supported PCI-E 2.0, but the offload bandwidth is still relatively low. Therefore, we should avoid too much communication between host CPUs and KNC cards.

2.3 Experiment Platform

We used a Xeon Phi 5110P for the parallelization task. It was installed on a dual-socket Intel Xeon E5-2697 server. The host CPU was responsible for handling serial part of the CNN algorithm such as reading data and constructing the network. What's more, the serial baseline of CNN was executed on it with SIMD option on. Detailed information of the platform is presented in Table.1.

3 Convolutional Neural Networks

Convolutional neural networks are special deep feed forward neural networks with layers of convolution filter banks. It is naturally suitable for vision tasks as inspired by Hubel and Wiesel's research on cat's visual cortex[7]

A convolutional neural network can be separated into two parts: a trainable feature extractor and a classifier plugged at the end of it. The feature extractor is usually composed of alternant convolutional layers and pooling layers, and each of them contains several sub-layers called feature maps. These layers imitate simple cells and complex cells in mammal visual area and together provide translation invariance for the network. When applied to tasks such as image recognition, CNNs are able to take images directly as input. Feature extraction is automatically learned by training rather than being designed manually beforehand. Fig. 2 shows the structure of our CNN for hand-writing digital recognition.

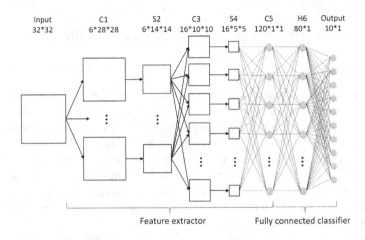

Fig. 2. Structure of our CNN, where C1 stands for the first layer being a convolutional layer, S2 stands for the second layer being a pooling layer, and so on. The two final layers are fully connected and serve as the classifier. All weight kernels in convolutional layers are 5 × 5.

Table 1. Platform Setup

	Host	Coprocessor
CPU Model	Xeon E5-2697	Xeon Phi 5110P
Sockets×core×SMT×SIMD:	2×12×2×4	1×60×4×8
Frequency:(GHz)	2.7	1.053
L1/L2/L3 Cache:(KB)	32/256/30,720	32/512/-
Memory:(GB)	64	8
Compiler:	Intel Composer_xe_2013.5.192	-

CNN is a machine learning algorithm. We need to train it with huge amount of labeled data before it can be used to get correct results as a classifier. The training process is consisted of forward propagation and then backward propagation, while the classification process only contains the forward. By parallelizing the training process, both forward and backward propagation are parallelized actually.

3.1   Convolutional Layers

Convolutional layers extract local features from the input maps by convolution of weight kernels and the corresponding patches of the input maps. The weight kernels are shared in an output feature map so that the number of trainable parameters is dramatically reduced. The kernels for an output feature map are 3D, i.e. $N_i \times K_y \times K_x$, where N_i stands for input feature maps, and K_y, K_x stand for the dimensions of kernels and patches. For each output neuron, convolution results are summed up to pass a non-linear function, a common choice of which is the sigmoid in [10]

$$f(x) = 1.7159 * tanh(2x/3) \tag{1}$$

3.2   Max Pooling Layers

Pooling layers play a crucial role in obtaining translation-invariant features by combining information in spatial neighborhood from inputs. The operation reduces the size of input feature maps at the same time. Unlike the convolutional layer, one feature map in a pooling layer connects to the only input feature map from the previous layer correspondingly in order. That means the number of feature maps in a pooling layer is exactly equal to the number in the previous layer.

Early CNN models such as LeNet 5[8] applied averaging operation for pooling layers. Later, [9] found that max pooling operation benefited in both convergence and generalization. After that, more and more implementation of CNNs chose max-pooling for their pooling layers, and so did ours. In max pooling layers, the output neuron equals to the max value in the receptive field of input map.

3.3   Back Propagation

Convolutional neural networks are trained by backward propagation (BP) algorithm under most of circumstances. Based on standard BP algorithm, there are three supplements.

The first one is the backward propagation of errors in convolutional layers, which can be implemented in two ways: by "Pushing" or by "Pulling"[11]. Fig. 3 illustrates the difference between these two implementation. For "Pushing", implementation is easier as we can treat the computation process in the same order of forward propagation. However, it may cause data writing competition when several neurons or feature maps conduct their back propagation at the same time, which is a disadvantage for parallelization. For "Pulling", there are no such competition, but we need to address all connections of a input neuron in an unnatural perspective which makes coding complex. We selected "Pulling" in our implementation for the sake of a better parallelization effect.

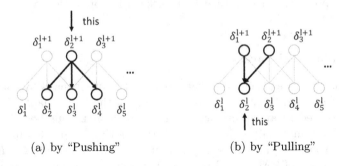

(a) by "Pushing"   (b) by "Pulling"

Fig. 3. Illustration of how "Pushing" and "Pulling" work in back propagation.

The second one is also in convolutional layers where each weight is shared by many connections of neurons. In this situation, the weight's gradient is calculated by summing up all gradients generated by those connections who share this weight.

Last but not least, each output neuron in max pooling layers only delivers the sensitivity to the input neuron from who this output neuron got its value, resulting in sparse sensitivity maps in the previous layer.

4   Parallelization

In this section, we describe main technical points in the parallelization. We used OpenMP to parallelize the network as it suits CNN algorithm which is consisted of multiple levels of loops well. It is also one of the most popular parallel models under multi-core environments. To take full usage of thread resources on MIC, we needed to divide the tasks into fragments which can be carried out at the same time independently and to make sure the parallelism scale is large enough. On the other hand, OpenMP runs in a join/fork model. The management of threads (creation and destroy) takes considerable time. So does the offloading through PCI-E as mentioned in section before. Therefore, the parallelism granularity of OpenMP should be relatively big to reduce the times of such additional cost. Parallelizing batch learning makes itself on top of the candidate list as it meets this two requirements well. Other points include threads affinity, nested parallelism, SIMD, and compiling skills like unrolling. They are presented in the following subsection in a top-to-bottom order.

4.1   Parallelizing Batch Learning

Batch learning can efficiently increase the parallelism. In batch learning, deltas of weights are temporarily stored instead of being used to update weights immediately as they are in stochastic learning so that the training of network can be parallelized by propagating many input images at the same time. After a certain number of propagation which is called batch size, the weights get updated by adding up those deltas stored in this batch. Therefore, batch size decides the maximum number of input images that can be propagated at the same time, in other word, the maximum number of parallel threads.

The updating of weights should be carried out every batch of propagation, making it a big time cost in training. Fortunately, these weights are completely independently from each other during this process. Therefore, we used all 240 threads on a KNC to parallelize it at the granularity of kernels of weights. After the parallelization, it takes only 6.25% time for updating in the whole training process.

Batch learning benefits parallelizing, but it also brings some problems as side effects. With bigger batch size, not only the convergency speed of training gets slower, but also the accuracy declines. Fig. 4 shows how growing batch size influences the training accuracy in 40 epochs in this application of handwriting digital recognition. Learning rates for different batch size were all picked heuristically to get better training effect. It's shown that the accuracy did decline by batch size getting larger. However, the decrease was not so dramatic in some range where batch size was not greater than 60 that it could be accepted in some degree. With some tricks in training CNNs such as image distortion, the accuracy would be compensated.

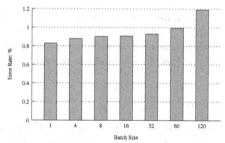

Fig. 4. Accuracy under different batch size after 40 epochs of training.

Taking both two factors of parallelism and accuracy into consideration, it was easy for us to set the batch size at 60 which is just equal to the number of cores on the KNC card. As an important side-effect, it made the mapping strategy very clear and efficient: each core be responsible for the propagation of one input sample at a time. This part of contents will be discussed in the next subsection.

4.2   Thread Affinity

The assignment of tasks was implemented by Thread Affinity, a mechanism in the Intel Compiler to bind OpenMP threads to physical's. It could greatly influence the speed of parallelized applications. Taking our case as an example, if we mapped four OpenMP threads in batch learning to four different KNC cores, it would be 2.05 times faster than mapping them to four threads on one core.

There are three interfaces provided to specify Thread Affinity. The most high-level and easiest one among them is through setting the **KMP_AFFINITY** environment variable. Each of its 7 optional values corresponds to a mode of assignment. Fig. 5 illustrates the difference between two typical modes: "Scatter" and "Compact" when mapping two OpenMP threads on a simplified topology where there are two cores in a CPU and each core supports two physical threads. In "Scatter" mode, two threads are allocated to Core0 and Core1, while they are both allocated to Core 0 in "Compact" mode. It's shown that setting **KMP_AFFINITY** to "Scatter" can satisfy our mapping strategy where each KNC cores be responsible for one threads in parallelizing batch learning.

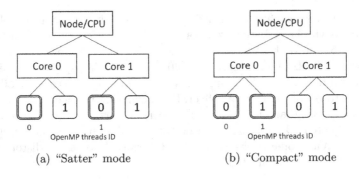

(a) "Satter" mode   (b) "Compact" mode

Fig. 5. Illustration of the difference between "Scatter" and "Compact" for KMP_AFFINITY. In "Scatter" mode, OpenMP threads would be assigned as evenly as possible across the cores as the mode's name suggests. "Compact" mode, on the contrary, tries to assign threads as close as possible to each other.

4.3   Nested Parallelism

Nested parallelism allows programmers to create parallel region within a parallel region itself. Therefore it can be used to fully utilize the hierarchy of threads on MIC. Through KMP_Affinity, we first mapped 60 OpenMP threads for batch learning to 60 MIC cores. Then we used the 4 threads per core to further parallelize the propagation of each sample. This is done at the level of each layer of the convolutional neural network where the propagation is carried out in the order of output feature maps independently. Note that the four threads in a MIC core doesn't mean they really run at the same time. They still run in order but are scheduled to avoid the time for fetching data.

4.4   Loop Unrolling

Loop unrolling is a basic compiling method to improve the performance. It can be done by compilers automatically. With appropriate guidance, Intel compilers nowadays can do perfect jobs. For the loops involving SIMD operation, we used **#pragma loop_account()** to inform the compiler of the most possible length and let it decide how to do the unrolling. For the loops with out SIMD on contrary, we can directly use **#pragma unroll** to tell the compiler to fully unroll the loops. For example, in the function of convolution calculation, we had the following code. By loop unrolling, the performance got further improvement.

```
#pragma loop_account(5)
for(int ky=0; ky < kernel_size_y; ky++)
{
    #pragma loop_account(5)
    for(int kx=0; kx < kernel_size_x; kx++)
        ...
}
```

4.5 SIMD Optimization

SIMD is at the bottom of parallelism hierarchy of MIC architecture and plays a great role in acquiring high performance. Here we used it to parallelize the convolution operation which is the innermost iteration in the CNN algorithm.

Just like loops unrolling discussed above, SIMD operation and optimization can be automatically done by the compiler with proper guidance. However, in our case, the 2D kernel size is relatively small by being 5 × 5. It means that the inner loop can't take full usage of 512-bit vector width of SIMD as the code above shows.

A native solution was to collapse the most inner 2-level loops into one so that the loop size would be big enough. However, the additional mod/div operation for computing arrays' reference brought really big harm and the performance got even worse. An alternative of using 1D arrays instead of 2D's for kernels and feature maps would bring the same problem in addressing for input neurons. Finally, we used an eclectic method by copying the involving data to temporary 1D arrays in advance and collapsing the inner 2-level loops for SIMD. In this way, there would be no additional mod/div operation, and the SIMD width would be utilized more efficiently in calculation. However, the performance would not be improved dramatically because the copy operation would take most of the time.

By now, three of the four main levels of loops in the CNN algorithms had been parallelized in a top-to-bottom order corresponding to the parallelism hierarchy of MIC architecture. They were the the iteration of input samples, the iteration of output feature maps in each layer and the iteration in convolution operation. The former two were parallelized by OpenMP and its nested parallelism, while the last one was parallelized by SIMD.

5 Evaluation

5.1 Accuracy

We used MNIST[8] as the benchmark for the evaluation. The data set contains 60,000 gray scale images of hand-writing digital for training and another 10,000 for testing. For the parallel version, we set the batch size at 60 as mentioned in

Section 4.1. The initial learning rate was 0.0001 and declined every other epochs until it became small enough(not less than 10^{-6}). Meanwhile, a serial baseline version was trained by stochastic learning as comparison. After 10 epochs of training, the parallel version achieved a 1.22% error rate for the test set. After 40 epochs, this value decreased to 0.993%, which was 0.113% higher than the baseline's. Therefore, the parallel version worked correctly and the accuracy didn't drop a lot.

5.2   Performance and Comparison

When parallelizing the network, we first directly mapped the serial version onto the KNC and then adopted those technical points described in section 4 in order. Fig. 6 shows how those methods improved the performance step by step. First, we used 60 cores to parallelize the batch learning and it brought 46.7× speedup. Based on that, nested parallelism improved the speedup by 1.55×. Loops unrolling further improved 1.43 times and SIMD optimization improved another 1.26 times. In the end, the parallelized version acquired 131× speedup against the serial version on the KNC.

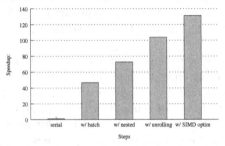

Fig. 6. Speedup brought by each technical point of parallelization.

On the other hand, as Fig. 7 shows, the serial performance on the KNC was much poorer than that on the Xeon CPU by over 15 times. It is because of the very lightweight cores on MIC. Intel uses long-width SIMD set to compensate for the floating point computing ability. However, the algorithm was not doing SIMD calculation all the time. And these non-SIMD parts magnified the weakness of KNC cores. Therefore, compared to the baseline on host CPU, the speedup was only 8.3 times.

Finally, we compared the performance with that on multi-core CPUs platform. Our parallelization implementation is for MIC architecture, but it also suits multi-core CPUs very well. The host CPU, Xeon E5-2679, is the top model among Intel Xeon family. We set the batch size to 24 and used 2 threads in each core for nested parallelism. Fig. 8 shows the results of comparison. The dual-socket E5-2697 acquired 11.2× speedup against the baseline and outperformed our KNC platform, although the KNC had a big advantage in peak computing ability.

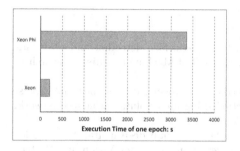

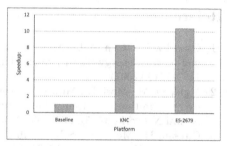

Fig. 7. Comparison of single-thread performance between KNC and Xeon CPU.

Fig. 8. Performance Comparison between KNC and multi-core platform.

6 Conclusion

We parallelized a classic convolutional neural network on Intel Xeon Phi coprocessor in a top-to-bottom order and showed the threads hierarchy of the MIC architecture is suitable for the parallelization of convolutional neural networks. The parallelized network running on a KNC card gained 131× speedup against the serial KNC version. Compared to serial baseline running on a Xeon E5-2697 CPU, the speedup dropped to 8.3× because of the low performance of MIC lightweight cores. We also showed the parallelized method suits well in traditional multi-core environments. The dual-socket E5-2697 on the motherboard acquired 11.2× speedup against the baseline and outperformed the KNC platform. Due to the lightweight-core design, the full usage of the 512-bit SIMD is of great importance to acquire high performance on MIC devices. While it greatly depends on developers' tuning as well as the features of applications themselves.

Anyway, Xeon Phi is a good supplement to multi-core CPUs. Programmers can map their code to Xeon Phi and get acceleration easily with lots of existing tools providing effective supports.

In future work, we will try to further improve the performance of our parallelization of CNN on Xeon Phi since the platform's great floating point computing ability is very potential. We will start from the following two points: improving the utilization of SIMD by merging convolutional layers and pooling layers, working on the cache issues. We will also try to improve the scalability of our parallelized CNN algorithm.

Acknowledgments. This work was supported by NSF of China(Grant No 61303002, 61373025), the National 863 High-Tech Program of China(Grant No 2012AA010905) and TNList cross-discipline foundation. The authors would like to thanks Prof. Wenguang Chen and Feng Zhang for helpful discussion and Prof. Wei Xue for providing experiment environment.

References

1. Osadchy, M., Cun, Y.L., Miller, M.L.: Synergistic face detection and pose estimation with energy-based models. The Journal of Machine Learning Research **8**, 1197–1215 (2007)
2. Matsugu, M., Mori, K., Mitari, Y., Kaneda, Y.: Subject independent facial expression recognition with robust face detection using a convolutional neural network. Neural Networks **16**(5), 555–559 (2003)
3. Ciresan, D., Meier, U., Schmidhuber, J.: Multi-column deep neural networks for image classification. In: 2012 IEEE Conference on Computer Vision and Pattern Recognition (CVPR), pp. 3642–3649. IEEE (June 2012)
4. Krizhevsky, A., Sutskever, I., Hinton, G.E.: Imagenet classification with deep convolutional neural networks. In: Advances in Neural Information Processing Systems, pp. 1097–1105 (2012)
5. Scherer, D., Schulz, H., Behnke, S.: Accelerating large-scale convolutional neural networks with parallel graphics multiprocessors. In: Diamantaras, K., Duch, W., Iliadis, L.S. (eds.) ICANN 2010, Part III. LNCS, vol. 6354, pp. 82–91. Springer, Heidelberg (2010)
6. Huqqani, A.A., Schikuta, E., Ye, S., Chen, P.: Multicore and gpu parallelization of neural networks for face recognition. Procedia Computer Science **18**, 349–358 (2013)
7. Hubel, D.H., Wiesel, T.N.: Receptive fields, binocular interaction and functional architecture in the cat's visual cortex. The Journal of Physiology **160**(1), 106 (1962)
8. LeCun, Y., Bottou, L., Bengio, Y., Haffner, P.: Gradient-based learning applied to document recognition. Proceedings of the IEEE **86**(11), 2278–2324 (1998)
9. Scherer, D., Müller, A., Behnke, S.: Evaluation of pooling operations in convolutional architectures for object recognition. In: Diamantaras, K., Duch, W., Iliadis, L.S. (eds.) ICANN 2010, Part III. LNCS, vol. 6354, pp. 92–101. Springer, Heidelberg (2010)
10. LeCun, Y.A., Bottou, L., Orr, G.B., Müller, K.-R.: Efficient BackProp. In: Montavon, G., Orr, G.B., Müller, K.-R. (eds.) Neural Networks: Tricks of the Trade, 2nd edn. LNCS, vol. 7700, pp. 9–48. Springer, Heidelberg (2012)
11. Simard, P.Y., Steinkraus, D., Platt, J.C.: Best practices for convolutional neural networks applied to visual document analysis. In: 2013 12th International Conference on Document Analysis and Recognition, vol. 2, pp. 958–958. IEEE Computer Society (August 2003)

Mobile Ecosystem Driven Dynamic Pipeline Adaptation for Low Power

Garo Bournoutian[1,2]($\boxtimes$) and Alex Orailoglu[2]

[1] Qualcomm Technologies, Inc., San Diego, CA 92121, USA
garo@cs.ucsd.edu
[2] University of California, San Diego, La Jolla, CA 92093, USA
alex@cs.ucsd.edu

Abstract. State-of-the-art mobile smartphone and tablet processors are beginning to employ fully speculative, out-of-order architectures with deep instruction pipelines. These processors often have pipeline lengths of 24 or more stages. Furthermore, to improve high-performance ILP, these processors provide multiple parallel pipeline paths for various instruction types. These architectures provide multiple execution clusters defined by instruction type, each with its own issue queue. Instructions are dispatched to one of the appropriate issue queues, and all issue queues are then scanned in parallel to identify instructions ready for execution. The goal of such a resource-intensive architectural design is to sustain peak processor performance. Unfortunately, applications oftentimes only leverage a small subset of these robust computation resources, and the excess hardware resources still consume power while idle. This paper proposes a novel methodology that leverages the unique characteristics of the mobile ecosystem to drive hardware adaptation for a power-efficient execution pipeline microarchitecture. The proposed architecture will monitor the run-time execution behavior in order to enable only those pipeline resources that are currently needed, allowing the system to rapidly respond to changing resource demands to ensure performance is maintained while reducing power consumption. The simulation results show that processor performance is maintained while achieving a significant reduction in execution pipeline power consumption.

Keywords: Mobile · Low-power · Dynamic · Adaptive hardware · Pipeline

1 Introduction

High-performance mobile processors are beginning to employ heterogeneous processor topologies in order to provide a continuum of computational resources that can handle the wide range of variability that occurs in the mobile domain. These heterogeneous processor topologies typically utilize a cluster of "Little" processor cores optimized for low-power, as well as a cluster of "Big" processor cores targeting higher performance at the cost of higher power dissipation. An example of

© Springer International Publishing Switzerland 2015
L.M. Pinho et al. (Eds): ARCS 2015, LNCS 9017, pp. 83–95, 2015.
DOI: 10.1007/978-3-319-16086-3_7

such a topology is the ARM big.LITTLE architecture, which incorporates high-performance Cortex-A15 "big" processors with low-power Cortex-A7 "LITTLE" processors [6].

In general, the "Little" processor leverages an in-order architecture with a simple pipeline. For example, the ARM Cortex-A7 has a pipeline length of 8–10 stages. On the other hand, the "Big" processor usually employs a fully speculative, out-of-order architecture with a deeper pipeline. For comparison, the ARM Cortex-A15 supports register renaming and has a pipeline length of 15–24 stages. Furthermore, to improve high-performance ILP the Cortex-A15 provides multiple, parallel pipeline paths for various instruction types. These microarchitectural differences are one of the main reasons for the large increase in energy consumption compared to the "Little" processor.

In this paper, we propose reducing the power consumption of these more power-hungry "Big" processor cores by dynamically adapting the instruction pipeline. Leveraging the unique characteristics of high-performance mobile processor architectures, a fine-grained adaptive hardware control mechanism is developed. The microarchitecture will automatically shut down individual pipeline paths during periods of reduced utilization. Upon subsequent demand, these pipeline paths can be re-enabled in a manner that avoids any performance penalties. Furthermore, the aggressiveness of shutting down pipeline paths will be guided by an application-specific code analysis. The result will be a significant reduction of wasted power from idle pipeline paths without any negative impacts to performance.

2   Related Work

A good amount of prior research has been done related to reducing execution pipeline power in general purpose processors while incurring a minor performance degradation. A common approach relies on resizing the issue queue in order to control the rate of execution of the processor pipeline.

The authors in [11] proposed an architecture allowing the sizes of the issue queue, reorder buffer, and the load/store queue to be dynamically adjusted. They employed periodic sampling of occupancy levels to determine when to increase or decrease capacity. Similarly, the authors in [5] present an issue queue design that allows for dynamic configurability of size and speed using transmission gate insertion. The circuit also gathers activity statistics during execution to allow on-the-fly adjustments to improve energy and performance. Both of these approaches rely on costly run-time profiling techniques that consume power to keep track of such statistical information.

The authors in [10] propose a mechanism to disable one or more processor pipelines based on dynamically monitoring the processor's performance. They focus on an Alpha 21264 processor with two integer pipeline clusters and a single floating-point pipeline. In a similar vein, *Pipeline Balancing* was proposed in [2], which dynamically monitors performance and adjusts the issue rate accordingly.

The implementation proposed by the authors necessitates that at least one cluster of functional units for each ISA type remain active, limiting the amount of power savings since the minimum issue rate will be 4 per cycle.

A proposal to power-gate execution units to abate leakage power was proposed in [8]. The authors provide analytical equations for determining break-even points, and then apply this information to put specific execution units to sleep based on elapsed time or branch misprediction events.

A software-assisted approach to dynamically resizing the issue queue was presented in [9]. Compile-time analysis provides information on the required number of issue queue entries. Unfortunately, the proposed static analysis does not handle inter-procedural dependence analysis, limiting the applicability of the algorithm in the presence of function calls.

3   Motivation

The larger, high-performance cores in the heterogeneous processor topology typically consist of an out-of-order architecture with a relatively deep pipeline. The incentive of having an out-of-order processor is to allow execution around data hazards in order to improve performance. The effectiveness of such an architecture is often limited by how far it can "look ahead" by placing decoded instructions into an issue queue used to identify those instructions whose dependencies are completely resolved. For high-end targets, having a window size of 40 or more instructions is often required to meet performance targets. Unfortunately, it is also common knowledge in the mobile industry that the issue queue size is frequency limited to about 8 entries, which severely limits the effectiveness of the architecture. The physical design of issue queues larger than 8 entries incurs longer critical path timing to concurrently scan all entries and route necessary data.

In order to overcome this limitation, it is common practice in mobile microarchitectures to employ multiple, smaller issue queues. The execution is broken down into multiple clusters defined by instruction type, each with its own issue queue. Instructions will be dispatched to the appropriate issue queue, and all

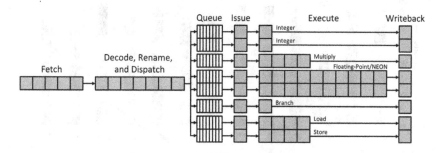

Fig. 1. Typical Mobile Out-of-Order Processor Pipeline

issue queues are then scanned in parallel to identify instructions ready for execution. A typical mobile out-of-order processor pipeline is shown in Figure 1, which is similar to that used in the ARM Cortex-A15 and Cortex-A57, Apple A6 Swift and A7 Cyclone, and Qualcomm Krait 400 and Krait 450 processors.

As one can see, after instructions are decoded, they will be dispatched into an issue queue for the appropriate instruction type. Once the instruction's dependencies are resolved, it will be issued and executed. Each pipeline has its own separate issue queue and can issue independently from the other pipelines. Certain instruction types can have more than one pipeline in order to increase parallelism by ameliorating structural hazards. For example, in the architecture shown in Figure 1, the *Integer* and *Floating-Point* instruction types are provided two parallel pipelines.

Under ideal circumstances, the instruction mix of an application will be well-balanced and essentially match the physically available pipeline functional units. In this case, the pipeline will deliver a substantial amount of ILP and hardware resources will be well utilized. Unfortunately, it is rare for an application to follow this ideal. For example, one may have an application that completely avoids using any floating-point instructions. Yet, the physical hardware for two entire floating-point pipelines is present. During the course of executing this application, a large portion of the hardware will be idle and wasting precious battery life. Even while nothing is executing within these pipelines a substantial amount of power is consumed by the issue queue logic checking for valid entries to issue, and the functional units themselves consuming power as they idle.

To demonstrate the possible skewed distribution of instruction types, the instruction mix of all SPEC CPU2000 [13] integer and floating-point benchmarks is shown in Figure 2 and Figure 3, respectively. As one would expect, the integer benchmarks very rarely make use of any floating-point operations. Thus, having some mechanism to disable the floating-point pipelines will clearly

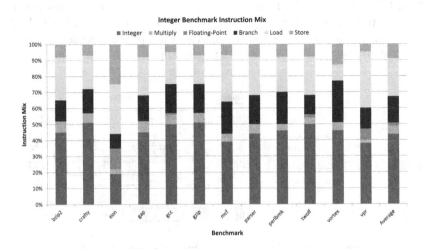

Fig. 2. SPEC Integer Benchmark Instruction Mix

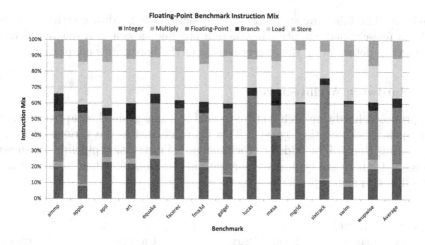

Fig. 3. SPEC Floating-Point Benchmark Instruction Mix

help to conserve power. Furthermore, for those instruction types with multiple parallel pipelines, a given application may be unable to actually exploit any ILP benefit of this additional hardware unless a sufficiently large amount of those instructions is present within the execution window.

Given these observations, it becomes clear that an adaptive approach is necessary to help tune the microarchitecture in order to conserve power. Each individual instruction pipeline should be monitored to determine if there is a sufficient demand for keeping it enabled. If these structures remain idle, an automated mechanism should exist to shut down the issue queue and execution logic in order to avoid both dynamic and static power dissipation.

As one would expect, there are trade-offs to such a dynamically reconfigurable microarchitecture. For instance, monitoring the pipeline activity patterns during run time to detect idleness requires additional hardware and power. Similarly, the process of disabling and re-enabling a pipeline path can incur both power and performance penalties. In particular, if the logic to re-enable a path is not accurately predicted, the pipeline will stall and waste even more power. Our goal is to intelligently exploit the unique characteristics of mobile processor architectures to minimize or completely eliminate these overheads.

4   Implementation

In order to conserve power, one would like to dynamically adapt the hardware pipeline to best match the computational needs of a specific application. This application-specific tailoring of the hardware microarchitecture needs to be fine-grained and able to efficiently respond to changes in the application's execution patterns. Furthermore, it is essential that any proposed additional hardware logic itself be frugal so as not to countermand the reductions in power we are trying to achieve. The following subsections will describe the hardware architecture to enable a fine-grained, adaptive instruction pipeline as well as a software-driven approach to determining the aggressiveness of the hardware's adaptation.

4.1   Hardware Architecture

The proposed hardware architecture to enable a fine-grained, adaptive instruction pipeline is shown in Figure 4. This figure illustrates the various hardware mechanisms that will be added to each individual instruction pipeline. As shown in Figure 1, there are typically 8 separate instruction pipelines, each of which will follow this same approach.

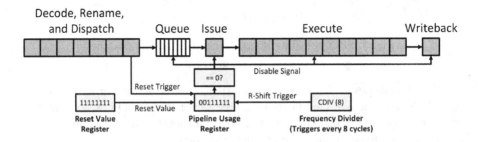

Fig. 4. Proposed Adaptive Pipeline Architecture

The first new hardware structure is a *Pipeline Usage Register*. The purpose of this register is to indicate the temporal utilization of a given pipeline path. This register will initially be populated with a non-zero value, and over time that value will decrease towards zero if the pipeline is idle. Once this register becomes zero, a *Disable Signal* will be asserted high, which will disable the issue queue, issue stage, execution stage, and writeback stage of the pipeline. These disabled hardware structures will have their supply voltage gated as described in [12], obviating both dynamic switching power and any static leakage power.

The *Pipeline Usage Register* is implemented as a shift register. Upon receiving the *R-Shift Trigger* signal, the *Pipeline Usage Register* is right shifted and fed a most-significant-bit (MSB) value of 0. The *R-Shift Trigger* signal will be generated by a *Frequency Divider* that will take the pipeline clock and divide it by 8. In this fashion, the *R-Shift Trigger* signal will occur every 8 pipeline cycles. This mechanism will be what determines that a given pipeline has been idle for a period of time and causes the *Pipeline Usage Register* to become zero, in turn shutting down the pipeline hardware structures.

The reciprocal logic that marks that a pipeline is actively in use is controlled by the *Reset Trigger* signal. This reset signal will be asserted during the decode stage four cycles before the instruction is dispatched into an issue queue. Upon the *Reset Trigger* signal going high, the *Pipeline Usage Register* will be reset to the value specified in the *Reset Value Register*. This logic not only handles the case of ensuring that an active pipeline is not turned off by keeping the *Pipeline Usage Register* non-zero, but it also handles re-enabling a disabled pipeline without causing any performance penalty. The decode stage typically takes multiple cycles (7 in our example architecture), since the instruction is not only decoded, but other logic like register renaming is done as well. Given this, the instruction type (i.e. integer, floating-point, branch, etc.) is determined rather early in the decode stage (based on the instruction opcode), and this information can be conveyed to the *Pipeline Usage Register* while things like register renaming are being done. Based on this observation, the *Reset Trigger* signal can be generated four cycles prior to the instruction being dispatched into an issue queue. This allows a possibly disabled issue queue to be fully re-enabled before a dispatched instruction is sent to it.

The *Reset Value Register* will possess the property of having a continuous run of 1's of some length L starting from the LSB. The longer the length L is, the longer the pipeline must remain idle before it will cause an automatic shutdown. This structuring of the *Reset Value Register* will minimize bit-flipping transitions within the *Pipeline Usage Register* (avoiding needless dynamic power consumption). Since the *Pipeline Usage Register* is right-shifted over and over, each right-shift will only incur a single bit-flip.

A further power reducing optimization is the circuitry to determine when the *Pipeline Usage Register* is zero. Instead of using a relatively expensive comparator circuit, all the bits within the *Pipeline Usage Register* can simply be fed into a NOR gate, which will become 1 only when all the input bits are 0.

Lastly, we can further optimize the instruction types with multiple pipelines (e.g. *Integer* and *Floating-Point*). In these cases, there may not be sufficient instructions to merit having two parallel pipeline paths. In order to gracefully account for this situation, the dispatch logic will be slightly updated. Instead of randomly selecting one of the issue queues to dispatch the instruction to, the multiple issue queues will be prioritized. Only when the first issue queue is full will the instruction be dispatched into the next queue. In this fashion, if one issue queue is able to support the instruction stream without becoming inundated, it will cause the second issue queue to remain idle, causing it to turn off. If the instruction demand increases and spills over the first issue queue, then the second issue queue can service the instructions as before. Performance will remain unaffected by this change. Rather, this prioritization of issue queues helps essentially defragment and compress the instructions into one queue before needing to expand into another, helping the second pipeline remain idle and thus be possibly turned off to conserve power.

To ensure any active executions have sufficient time to complete and exit before we shut down the pipeline, the *Reset Value Register* will be required to have at least two 1's in the LSBs. This will ensure at least two right-shift intervals occur before the pipeline is shut down, where each interval occurs after 8 pipeline cycles based on the *Pipeline Usage Register*'s clock divider. Given that the longest pipeline stage in our design is the *Floating-Point* pipeline, taking up to 12 cycles once leaving the issue queue, having two intervals of 8 pipeline cycles ensures that the last instruction in the pipeline has completed before the pipeline is disabled. This helps greatly simplify the shutdown logic, since no querying within the execution stages needs to occur before we turn off the pipeline. For pipeline stalls, the same stalling mechanism will cause the clock divider to also not move forward ensuring consistency in the timing.

4.2 Software-Driven Reset Thresholds

The prior section described the microarchitectural design to enable the adaptive instruction pipeline. However, instead of arbitrarily selecting the value for the *Reset Value Register* and hard-coding it across all the pipelines and even across different applications, one would like to make a more intelligent selection. Looking back at the instruction mixes shown for the benchmarks in Figure 2 and Figure 3, a logical extension would be to leverage this information to help guide the selection of the reset threshold value.

The general observation is that if the quantity of a particular instruction type is quite low, there is a higher probability that the pipeline for that instruction type will be idle. Furthermore, when the rare instruction type does occur, it most likely will be sporadic and shutting down the pipeline sooner rather than later can help maximize power savings. Thus, it is proposed to set the *Reset Value Register* to the following values based on the relative percentage of the instruction type (IT), where N is the size of the *Reset Value Register* in bits:

- If $IT < 5\%$, Reset Value Register $= \{\{(N-2)\{0\}\}, 1, 1\}$
- Else if $IT < 20\%$, Reset Value Register $= \left\{\left\{\frac{(N-2)}{2}\{0\}\right\}, \left\{\frac{(N-2)}{2}\{1\}\right\}, 1, 1\right\}$
- Else, Reset Value Register $= \{\{(N-2)\{1\}\}, 1, 1\}$

We examine two different software-based approaches to estimating instruction type density. The first approach is a pure compile-time code analysis to get static instruction type counts. In order to determine the instruction type distribution of a mobile smartphone application including all foundation libraries, an on-device code analysis framework is employed [3]. A simple post-processing script can then analyze and identify the opcodes for each instruction type. The second approach instead relies on profiling an actual execution of the application in order to garner dynamic instruction type counts. This latter approach will help identify hotspot patterns wherein loops may greatly increase the overall predominance of a small number of static instructions. In both of these approaches, the

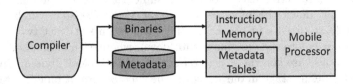

Fig. 5. Overview of Compiler and Hardware Interaction

pipeline-specific *Reset Value Register* number computed based on instruction type will be passed to the underlying hardware microarchitecture via metadata embedded within the software executable. Upon the application being loaded, the metadata will populate the values for the various hardware *Reset Value Registers* associated with each instruction type. An overview of this architecture is shown in Figure 5.

5   Experimental Results

In order to assess the benefit from this proposed architectural design, we utilized the SimpleScalar framework [1]. The stock code initially utilized a basic register update unit (RUU) structure, combining the reorder buffer (ROB) and reservation stations and provided no register renaming. In order to match the target architecture and fully exploit possible parallelism and instruction throughput, the default *sim-outorder* simulator was modified to implement a full speculative Tomasulo architecture [7], including register renaming and decentralized issue queues stations. Furthermore, the simulator is augmented with the adaptive instruction pipeline logic proposed in this paper and also incorporates a heavily customized version of the Wattch power analysis framework [4]. The size N of the *Pipeline Usage Register* and *Reset Value Register* was chosen to be 8 bits.

Table 1 summarizes the system configuration parameters, reflecting a typical high-performance mobile processor.

Table 1. Hardware Configuration Parameters

Fetch Stages	5
Decode Stages	7
Issue Stages	1
Execution Stages, INT	1
Execution Stages, MULT	4
Execution Stages, FP ADD/SUB	2
Execution Stages, FP MUL	6
Execution Stages, FP DIV	10
Execution Stages, BRANCH	1
Execution Stages, LD/ST	4
Writeback Stages	1
Issue Queue Entries	8
Instruction L1 cache	64 KB, 4-way set-associative
Data L1 cache	64 KB, 4-way set-associative
Unified L2 cache	2MB, 8-way set-associative
Number of Pipelines	2 INT, 1 MULT, 2 FP 1 BRANCH, 1 LD, 1 ST

The complete SPEC CPU2000 benchmark suite [13] is used, providing 12 integer and 14 floating-point real-world applications. The benchmarks are cross-compiled for the PISA instruction set using the highest level of optimization available for the language-specific compiler. The reference inputs are used for each benchmark, with each benchmark executed in its entirety from start to finish. For the approach of using profiled application information, the training inputs for each benchmark are used.

In order to assess the proposed architecture, the complete pipeline power utilization is analyzed, including both dynamic and static power. The additional power overhead incurred for enabling the adaptive pipeline, such as from registers, control logic, and transitioning pipelines off and on, are also incorporated into the results.

Figure 6 shows the power reduction across the pipeline logic observed for the integer benchmarks. The average power savings for integer benchmarks using pure static analysis is 27.11%, while execution profiling yields a slightly better average of 27.41%. In a majority of the integer benchmarks, the *Reset Value Register* threshold selected in both pure static analysis and execution profiling turns out to be the same. Additionally, while the execution profiling approach does better on average, in the *crafty* benchmark the improvement was actually worse than pure static analysis. In this case, it is likely that the training inputs used during profiling had a significantly different dynamic instruction distribution compared to the reference inputs used during actual benchmarking.

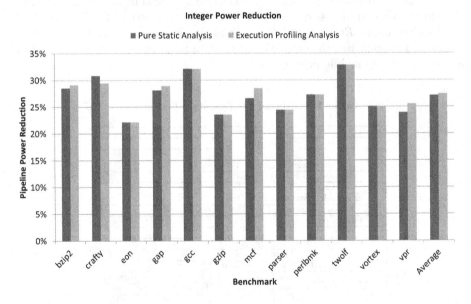

Fig. 6. Integer Benchmarks Pipeline Power Reduction

Similarly, the power savings for floating-point benchmarks are shown in Figure 7. The average power savings using pure static analysis is approximately 18.80%, while using execution profiling garners a 19.12% average reduction. Again, a majority of the benchmarks ended up having the same *Reset Value Register* threshold based on static analysis and execution profiling. The *lucas* benchmark was another exception to the execution profiling approach outperforming the pure static analysis approach. Additionally, as one would expect, the benefit for floating-point benchmarks is slightly less than the integer case, since the floating-point pipeline will need to be enabled much more often. However, the adaptive logic is still able to identify excess hardware resources that may occur throughout the execution lifetime and intelligently turn them off to save power.

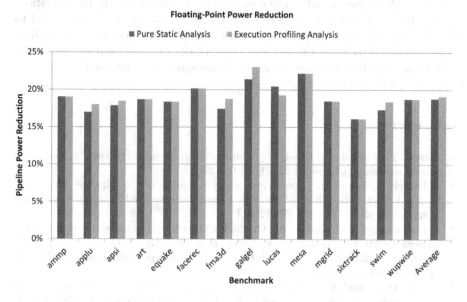

Fig. 7. Floating-Point Benchmarks Pipeline Power Reduction

As one can see, the proposed architecture is able to eliminate a substantial amount of power consumption by adaptively disabling portions of the pipeline when they are not actively needed. In particular, most of the integer benchmarks rarely, if ever, use the floating-point pipeline, which can account for approximately 20% of the energy in the pipeline logic. Furthermore, these power savings come at no cost to processor performance. Instruction throughput is not degraded using this proposal, since any time disabled pipeline resources are needed they will be immediately re-enabled four cycles ahead of time.

6 Conclusions

High-performance mobile processors typically employ more power-hungry out-of-order processors with deep pipelines in order to meet peak demands. However, not all applications possess the exact same instruction mix, leading to uneven physical resource allocations within the process pipeline. Given that power is a critical concern for mobile devices, conserving power without negatively impacting performance is a top priority.

A novel adaptive instruction pipeline architecture for mobile processors has been presented. This adaptive architecture leverages the unique characteristics of high-performance mobile processor microarchitecture design to propose a frugal dynamically adaptive mechanism to enable fine-grained pipeline gating. Based on run time utilization, idle pipelines and associated issue queues are turned off to reduce dynamic and leakage power. The proposed microarchitecture automatically shuts down individual pipeline paths during periods of reduced utilization. Upon subsequent demand, these pipeline paths are preemptively re-enabled to completely avoid any performance penalties. Application-specific code analysis is also leveraged to guide the aggressiveness of the pipeline gating. The results demonstrate a substantial amount of power savings can be achieved without any impact to performance.

References

1. Austin, T., Larson, E., Ernst, D.: SimpleScalar: An infrastructure for computer system modeling. Computer **35**(2), 59–67 (2002)
2. Bahar, R., Manne, S.: Power and energy reduction via pipeline balancing. In: ISCA 2001: Proceedings of the 28th Annual International Symposium on Computer Architecture, pp. 218–229 (2001)
3. Bournoutian, G., Orailoglu, A.: On-device objective-C application optimization framework for high-performance mobile processors. In: DATE 2014: Proceedings of the 2014 Design, Automation Test in Europe Conference Exhibition, pp. 85:1–85:6 (2014)
4. Brooks, D., Tiwari, V., Martonosi, M.: Wattch: a framework for architectural-level power analysis and optimizations. In: ISCA 2000: Proceedings of the 27th Annual International Symposium on Computer Architecture, pp. 83–94 (2000)
5. Buyuktosunoglu, A., Albonesi, D., Schuster, S., Brooks, D., Bose, P., Cook, P.: A circuit level implementation of an adaptive issue queue for power-aware microprocessors. In: GLSVLSI 2001: Proceedings of the 11th Great Lakes Symposium on VLSI, pp. 73–78 (2001)
6. Greenhalgh, P.: big.LITTLE processing with ARM Cortex-A15 & Cortex-A7, May 2013. http://www.arm.com/files/downloads/big_LITTLE_Final_Final.pdf
7. Hennessy, J., Patterson, D.: Computer Architecture: A Quantitative Approach. Morgan Kaufmann Publishers, Fifth edn (2011)
8. Hu, Z., Buyuktosunoglu, A., Srinivasan, V., Zyuban, V., Jacobson, H., Bose, P.: Microarchitectural techniques for power gating of execution units. In: ISLPED 2004: Proceedings of the 2004 International Symposium on Low Power Electronics and Design, pp. 32–37 (2004)
9. Jones, T., O'Boyle, M., Abella, J., Gonzalez, A.: Software directed issue queue power reduction. In: HPCA 2005: Proceedings of the 11th International Symposium on High-Performance Computer Architecture, pp. 144–153 (2005)
10. Maro, R., Bai, Y., Bahar, R.I.: Dynamically reconfiguring processor resources to reduce power consumption in high-performance processors. In: Falsafi, B., VijayKumar, T.N. (eds.) PACS 2000. LNCS, vol. 2008, p. 97. Springer, Heidelberg (2001)

11. Ponomarev, D., Kucuk, G., Ghose, K.: Reducing power requirements of instruction scheduling through dynamic allocation of multiple datapath resources. In: MICRO 34: Proceedings of the 34th Annual ACM/IEEE International Symposium on Microarchitecture, pp. 90–101 (2001)
12. Powell, M., Yang, S., Falsafi, B., Roy, K., Vijaykumar, T.: Gated-V_{dd}: a circuit technique to reduce leakage in deep-submicron cache memories. In: ISLPED 2000: Proceedings of the 2000 International Symposium on Low Power Electronics and Design, pp. 90–95 (2000)
13. SPEC: SPEC CPU2000 Benchmarks (2000). http://www.spec.org/cpu/

FTRFS: A Fault-Tolerant Radiation-Robust Filesystem for Space Use

Christian M. Fuchs[1,2(✉)], Martin Langer[2], and Carsten Trinitis[1]

[1] Chair for Computer Architecture and Organization,
Technical University Munich, Munich, Germany
{christian.fuchs,carsten.trinitis}@tum.de
[2] Institute for Astronautics, Technical University Munich, Munich, Germany
martin.langer@tum.de

Abstract. A satellite's on-board computer must guarantee integrity and recover degraded or damaged data over the entire duration of the spacecraft's mission in an extreme, radiated environment. While redundancy and hardware-side voting can protect Magnetoresistive RAM well from device failure, more sophisticated software-side storage concepts are required if advanced operating systems are used. A combination of hardware and filesystem measures can thus drastically increase system dependability, even for missions with a very long duration. We present a novel POSIX-compatible filesystem implementation offering memory protection, checksumming and forward error correction.

Keywords: Dependability · Data storage · Filesystem · Spacecraft · Satellite · Radiation · MRAM · Memory protection · Failure Tolerance · EDAC

1 Introduction

Recent small- and nanosatellite development has shown a rapid increase in available compute power and storage capacity, but also in system complexity. Cubesats [1], are currently the most popular nanosatellite form factor due to their cost efficiency and ever increased system performance. The authors are involved in developing such a satellite, MOVE-II, whose predecessor, First-MOVE, was launched into Low Earth Orbit (LEO) in 2013.

More challenging quality requirements, limitations in energy consumption, heat dissipation and the generally extreme environmental conditions result in spaceflight software and hardware evolution being considerably more time consuming and slower paced. Ultimately, nanosatellite computing will evolve away from federated clusters of specialized microcontrollers [2], a development that could also be observed with larger spacecraft over the past decades. Instead, more powerful, hardened, centralized general purpose computers will cover a wider range of responsibilities [3,4]. Thereby, overall spacecraft complexity can be reduced and efficiency improved, while each individual computer's complexity increases [2]. Certainly, an increased compute burden also requires more

© Springer International Publishing Switzerland 2015
L.M. Pinho et al. (Eds): ARCS 2015, LNCS 9017, pp. 96–107, 2015.
DOI: 10.1007/978-3-319-16086-3_8

sophisticated operating system (OS) software, which in turn results in increased code complexity and size [5].

For very simple computers, custom tailored OSs offer an excellent balance of size and functionality. However, development of proprietary OSs for unique custom computers has been abandoned in most of the IT industry, in favor of standard soft- and hardware reuse. This is still an ongoing process in spaceflight, though already producing a focus on a few types of radiation hardened processor platforms (i.e. LEON3, PPC750, RAD6000, see [6]) running common OSs [7,8]. The same evolution has begun in nanosatellite computing, albeit much faster.

OSs popular in spaceflight such as RTEMS can consume less than 256KB of non-volatile (nv) memory [9], whereas Linux requires at least 2MB. If such a larger OS is used aboard a satellite, more sophisticated storage concepts are needed. Data must be stored permanently and consistently throughout the mission lifetime. Space missions often last between 5 and 10 years [10], but can reach 25 years or longer like with the Voyager probes. Thus a satellite's command and data handling (CDH), the on-board computer, must guarantee integrity and recover degraded or damaged data (error detection and correction – EDAC) over a prolonged period of time in a hostile environment. We consider a filesystem (FS) the most resource conserving and efficient approach, which also allows dynamically adjustable protection for the individual data structures. As Magnetoresistive Random-Access Memory (MRAM) [11] is widely used for radiation resistant data storage in nanosatellites, FTRFS is applied FS to this technology.

This paper is organized as follows: Section 2 introduces the specific requirements and hazards to computing in orbit and deep-space, as well as the properties of different memories. Section 3 analyzes existing FSs and related research, to avoid implementation from scratch. Section 4 presents our FS, offering memory protection, forward error correction (FEC) and checksumming for both data and metadata. First results of our FS implementation are provided in Section 4.4 and its limitations are elaborated in Section 4.5. Finally, Section 5 contains potential solutions and our next steps in development.

2 Impact of the Spaceflight Use Case

Besides extreme temperature variations and the absence of atmosphere for heat dissipation, the impact of the near-Earth radiation environment must be considered in space computing. About 20% of all anomalies [12] aboard satellites can be attributed to high-energy particles from the sources depicted in Figure 1.

Particles originating from Earth's radiation belts, the Van Allen belts, consist mostly of trapped protons and electrons. Galactic Cosmic Rays from beyond our solar system are mostly protons [13,14], whereas various other high-energy particles are ejected by the Sun during Solar Particle Events (SPEs).

Therefore, depending on the orbit of the spacecraft and the occurrence of SPEs, an on-board computer will be penetrated by a mixture of high-energy protons, electrons and heavy ions. Physical shielding using aluminum or other material can reduce certain radiation effects. However, sufficient protection would require a spacecraft to dedicate unreasonable additional mass to shielding.

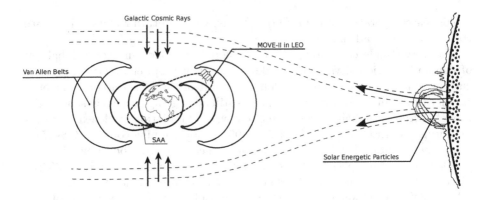

Fig. 1. The sources of radiation effecting a satellite. Figure is not to scale.

Furthermore, in LEO, the radiation bombardment will be increased while transiting the South Atlantic Anomaly (SAA). Earth's magnetic field experiences a local, height-dependent dip within the SAA, due to an offset of the spin axis from the magnetic axis. In this zone, a satellite and its electronics will experience an increase of proton flux of up to 10^4 times (energies $>$ 30 MeV) [14]. This flux increase results in a rapid growth of bit errors and other upsets in a satellite's CDH. In case of MOVE-II, the full functionality of CDH-subsystem is required at all time due to scientific measurements being conducted from one of the satellite's possible payloads, even though brief outages (e.g. reboots) are acceptable. This scientific payload should measure the anti-proton flux within the SAA, as its physical properties are subject of scientific debate.

Different storage technologies vary regarding the energy-threshold necessary to induce an effect and the type of effect caused. The most important radiation induced phenomena on memory are:

- Single Event Effects (SEE), local ionization from protons or heavy ions
- Total Ionizing Dose (TID), the cumulative effect of charge trapping in the oxide of electronic devices
- Displacement Damage due to structural displacement in crystalline components of electronic hardware.

Other types of SEEs, the destructive ones being the most relevant, are well described in [15]. Some novel memory technologies (e.g. MRAM [11], PCRAM [16]) have shown inherent radiation tolerance against bit-flips, Single Event Upsets (SEUs), due to their data storage mechanism [17,18].

Due to a shifting voltage threshold in floating gate cells caused by TID, commercial flash memories are more susceptible to bit errors. Highly scaled flash memories are also prone to SEUs causing shifts in the threshold voltage profile of one or more storage cells, referred to as Multiple Bit Upset [19].

All these memory technologies are sensitive to Single Event Functional Interrupts (SEFIs) [20], which can affect blocks, banks or entire circuits due to particle strikes in the peripheral circuitry.

3 Related Work and Preexisting File Systems

Filesystems often include performance optimizations like disk head tracking, utilization of data locality and caching. However, most of these enhancements do not apply to storage technologies used in spaceflight. In fact, such optimizations add significant code overhead, possibly resulting in a more error prone FS and may even reduce performance.

Next-generation FSs, e.g. BTRFS and ZFS, are designed to handle many-terabyte sized devices and RAID-pools. Silent data corruption has become a practical issue with such large volumes [21]. Thus, these FSs can maintain check-sums for data blocks and metadata. Due to their intended use in large disk pools, they do also offer integrated multi-device functionality.

Multi-device functionality would certainly be advantageous, but neither ZFS nor BTRFS scale to small storage volumes. Minimum volume sizes are far beyond what current nanosatellite CDHs can offer. Also, future development of these FSs will eventually result in design decisions not in favor of spaceflight application.

FSs for flash devices, like the memory technology itself, have evolved considerably over the past decade [22,23]. Upcoming FSs already handle challenges like potentially negative compression rates [24] or erase/write-block abstraction, offer proper wear leveling and interact with device EDAC functionality (check-summing, spare handling and recovery). UFFS even offers integrity protection for data and metadata using erasure codes.

Most new flash-FSs interact directly with memory [1], thereby are incompatible with other memory technologies unless flash properties are emulated. This introduces further IO and may result in unnecessary data loss, as flash memory is of course block oriented.

RAM filesystems are usually optimized for throughput or simplicity, often resulting in a relatively slim codebase. If designed for volatile RAM, these FS are optimized for simplicity and do not necessarily require a nondestructive unmount procedure. Non-volatile RAM FSs perform direct memory access to optimize for throughput, other utilize compression to increase storage capacity [25].

Except for *PRAMFS* [26], none of these FSs consider memory protection to increase dependability. *PRAMFS* offers execute-in-place (XIP) support [27] and is POSIX-compatible, but offers no data integrity protection.

In contrast to flash memories RAM filesystems are not block based, but benefit from the ability to access data arbitrarily. Thereby, no intermediate block management is required and read-erase-update cycles are unnecessary. While simple block-layer EDAC would certainly be possible, structures within a RAM filesystem can be protected individually allowing for stronger protection.

Open source space engineering and CDH research is directed mainly towards testing radiation related properties of memory technologies [20,28] and on NAND-flash in particular [29,30]. At the time of this writing, we are unaware of advanced software-side non-flash driven storage concepts for space use.

---

[1] In the case of Linux through the memory technology device subsystem (MTD).

4   FTRFS

FTRFS (fault-tolerant radiation-robust filesystem for space use) operates efficiently with small volumes($\leq$4MB), but also scales to larger volumes and is bootable.

Regarding the FS's threat model, ECC is applied to all CPU-caches and volatile SRAM, thus faults in these deceives are considered detectable and possibly correctable at runtime. A CPU running FTRFS must be equipped with a memory management unit with its page-table residing in volatile memory. All other elements (e.g. periphery and ALUs), other memories (e.g. registers and buffers) and in-transit data are considered potential error sources, see Section 2.

Memory protection has been largely ignored in RAM-FS design. In part, this can be attributed to a misconception of memory protection as a pure security-measure against malware. However, for directly mapped nv-memory, memory protection introduces the memory management unit as a safeguard against data corruption due to upsets in the system [32]. Thus, only in-use memory pages will be writable even from Kernel space, whereas the vast majority of memory is kept read-only, protected from misdirected write access i.e. due to SEUs in a register used for addressing during a store operation.

While data compression has been popular in size constrained FSs, it would offer low compression rates, as well-compressible data, e.g. log data, will not be kept in the same memory as the OS core components. Thus, it would offer little capacity gains but entail severe code overhead.

After a detailed OS evaluation, we chose the Linux kernel as the base for our FS due to its adaptability, extensive soft/hardware support and vast community. We decided against utilizing RTEMS mainly due to our limited software development manpower.

A loss of components has to be compensated at the software- or hardware level through voting or simple redundancy. Multi-device capability was considered for this FS, however it should rather be implemented below the FS level (e.g. via majority voting in hardware [33]) or as an overlay, e.g. RAIF [34].

The capability to detect and correct metadata and data errors was considered crucial during development. Based on the mission duration, destination or the orbit a spacecraft operates in, different levels of protection will be necessary. The protective guarantees offered can be adjusted at format time or later through the use of additional tools.

Our satellite's CDH offers 32MB of ECC-SRAM and is driven by an ARM Cortex-A5 CPU, however it could be upgraded to a Cortex-A7-MP. Due to the relatively restricted system resources aboard a nanosatellite, cryptographic checksums do not offer a significant benefit. Instead, CRC32 is utilized for performance reasons in tandem with Reed-Solomon encoding (RS) [31].

4.1   Metadata Integrity Protection

For proper protection at the FS level, in addition to the stored filesystem objects (inodes) and their data, all other metadata must be protected. Figure 2 depicts

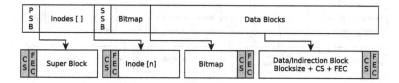

Fig. 2. The basic layout of the presented FS. EDAC data is appended or prepended to each FS structure. PSB and SSB refer to the primary and secondary super blocks.

the basic layout. Although similar to *ext2* and *PRAMFS* [26], data addressing and bad block handling work fundamentally different. We borrow memory protection from the *wprotect* component of *PRAMFS*, as well as the superblock and inode layout. *PRAMFS* is licensed under GPLv2 and based upon *ext2*.

The Super Block (SB) is kept redundantly, as depicted in Figure 2. An update to the SB always implies a refresh of the secondary SB, hence, hereafter no explicit reference of the secondary SB will be made. The SB also contains EDAC parameters for blocks, inodes and the bitmap.

The SB is the most critical structure within our FS, and is static after volume creation. Its content is copied to system memory at mount time, thus it is sufficient to assure SB consistency the first time it is accessed.

As the SB contains critical FS information, we avoid accumulating errors over time through scrubbing. Thereby, the CRC checksum is re-evaluated each time certain filesystem API functions (e.g. directory traversal) are performed.

A block-usage bitmap is dynamically allocated based on the overhead subtracted data-block count and is appended to the secondary SB. The bitmap EDAC is also dynamically sized and must be stored beyond the compile-time static SB, even though placing it there would be convenient. Thus, the protection data is located in the first block after the end of the bitmap, see Figure 2. In case the bitmap is extended, the new part of the bitmap is initialized and then the error correction data is recomputed at its new location. We refrain from re-computing and re-checking the EDAC data upon each access, instead FEC data is checked before and updated after each relevant operation has been concluded.

Inodes are kept as an array. Their consistency is of paramount importance as they define the logical structure of the filesystem. The array's length is determined upon FS initialization and can change only if the volume is resized. As each inode is an independent entity, an inode-table wide EDAC is unnecessary. Instead, we extend and protect each inode individually.

4.2   Data Consistency and Organization

To optimize the FS towards both larger (e.g. a kernel image, a database) and very small (e.g. scripts) files, direct and double indirect data addressing are supported, as depicted in Figure 3. The FS selects automatically which method is used. Data protection requirements vary depending on block size, and use case. Thus FTRFS allows the user to adjust the protection strength for data blocks, as will be described in the next section.

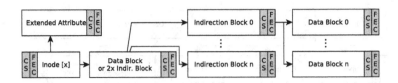

Fig. 3. Each inode can either utilize direct addressing or double indirection. Extended attributes are always addressed directly.

Data block size cannot be arbitrarily decreased, as some Linux kernel subsystems assume them to be sized to a power of two. Instead, the FS internally utilizes larger blocks to include EDAC data, see Figure 4.

Extended attributes (*xattr*) are deduplicated and referenced by one or more inodes, as depicted in Figure 3. Like in *PRAMFS*, *xattrs* are stored as data blocks, thereby we can treat these identically to regular data.

Nanosatellites, at least the non-classified ones, are not yet considered security critical devices. However, the application area of nanosatellites will expand considerably in the future [3]. An increasing professionalization will introduce enhanced requirements regarding dependability and security. Shared-satellite usage scenarios as well as technology testing satellites will certainly also require stronger security measures, which can be implemented using *xattrs*.

An *xattr* block's integrity is verified once its reference is resolved. Once all write access (in bulk) has been concluded, the EDAC data is updated.

4.3   Algorithm Details and Performance

Our primary goal was to develop an FS which could be used to store a full size-optimized Linux root FS including a kernel image safely over a long period of time within an 8MB volume. There are numerous erasure codes available that could be used to protect our FS. After careful consideration, RS was chosen mainly due to the following reasons:

- The algorithm is well analyzed, and widely used in various embedded scenarios, including spacecraft. Optimized software implementations, IP-cores and hardware accelerations is available.
- MRAM, while being SEU immune, is still prone to stray-writes, controller errors and in-transit data corruption. RS relies upon symbol level error correction, which is precisely the kind of corruption the FS must correct. Misdirected access within a page evades memory protection and corrupts the FS, thus corrupted single-byte, 2, 4 and 8B runs will occur.

RS decoding is computationally expensive, thus the protected data is subdevided into sub-blocks sized to 128B plus the user specified error number of correction-roots simplifying addressing and guaranteeing data alignment for power-of-two correction-root counts. Inodes and SBs can be fit into one single RS-code, while data block length does not result in extreme checking times.

To skip the expensive RS decoding step during regular operation, a CRC32 checksum allows high-performance checking. The RS-code is only read in case the checksum is invalid.

Data blocks are divided into subblocks so the FS can make optimal use of the RS code length. For common block-sizes and error correction strengths, 5 to 19 RS codes are necessary, see Table 1 for information on expected overhead. The correction data is accumulated at the end of the data block. Checksums across the entire block's data, each subblock and the error correction data are also retained. The resulting data format is depicted in Figure 4. Protection can be enhanced further by performing symbol interleaving for the RS codes and the block data, at the cost of performance.

FS traversal and data access will eventually slow down for strongly degraded storage volumes. As we immediately commit corrected data to memory, performance degradation is only temporary, assuming soft-faults.

4.4   Results and Current Status

FTRFS is currently undergoing testing and has been implemented for the Linux kernel. Due to its POSIX-compliance, it could easily be ported to other platforms. The memory protection functionality has been inherited from *PRAMFS*, the FS structure from *ext2*. We utilize the RS implementation of the Linux kernel, as its API also supports hardware acceleration.

Several components of the FS should undergo an optimization process, which will result in a drastic performance increase. Even though we have not yet conducted long-term benchmarking and performance analysis, the throughput degradation during regular operations is minimal. Modern CPUs can compute CRC32 within a few cycles due to hardware acceleration. We intend to publish additional performance and energy consumption metrics, once testing has been concluded and basic optimizations have been applied and the OBC computer has been finalized.

Data is read and written once per access. It is good practice in critical scenarios and especially spaceflight to read and write data multiple times, or deploy

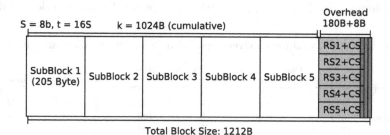

Fig. 4. A data block subdivided into 5 subblocks. Separate checksums for the entire data block, EDAC data and each subblock are depicted in red.

more advanced consistency checking techniques [35]. These changes could be applied in bulk, through a macro, or compiler side.

The level of protection offered by the FS can be adjusted at format-time, or later by using a proprietary FS-tuning tool. RS has a long record of space use in CDH and communications. Thus, we know the algorithm offers efficient protection regarding our threat scenario. Once testing has been concluded, we will perform long-term performance analysis in a degraded environment. To benchmark the FS, data degradation can be introduced using fault injection and we will be performed these tests after optimizations have been applied. However, artificial fault injection is usually not considered sufficient to prove the efficiency of a fault-tolerance concept for space-use. Our satellite's CDH computer including the FS will – and in general a satellite has to – undergo testing using various radiation sources before launch. Results will be made available once these tests have been carried out.

4.5   Conceptional Limitations and Restrictions

It is debatable whether journaling would increase FTRFS's reliability, as it usually helps safeguard FS consistency with slow storage media [36] due to power loss or disconnect. However, all access in our FS happens synchronously, and MRAM is only slightly slower than regular DRAM. Thus, journaling is currently not implemented.

Loss of power can also happen in our spaceflight use case, but depending on the event it can be handled differently. Spacecraft are battery backed and will utilize on-PCB components providing relatively abundant hold-back time after the electrical power subsystem (EPS) and the battery are disconnected due to latch-up protection. The FS can thus either conclude a pending write operation within the remaining active time, or the OS will have sufficient time to cancel pending writes in case the system has sufficient warning time.

The FS can not protect itself from device or memory bank failure. However, as MRAM access is deterministic, majority voting can be implemented in hardware to compensate for device failure [33]. This would also further increase protection against SEFIs, as upsets within one chip would be compensated by voting.

If data is stored with RS-symbol interleaving, a XIP mapping would technically be impossible. XIP could still perform mappings for non-interleaved data

Table 1. EDAC overhead for FS structures. Bitmap: 16MB FS, 5% inodes, 1024B BS

Data Structure	Size (B)	Correction Symbols/Code	# Codes	Correction Total (B)	Overhead (B)	Overhead (%)
Super Block	128	32	1	32	68	53.13%
Inode	160	32	1	32	68	42.50%
Data Blocks	1024	4	5	20	68	5.86%
	1024	16	5	80	188	17.58%
	4096	4	17	68	212	4.98%
	4096	16	19	304	692	16.70%
Bitmap	1773	32	10	320	688	38.80%

though, but thereby only the clear-text part of each RS code would be mapped and read. Via this memory mapping, integrity protection for stored file data would be ignored, unless we accept that a potential XIP mapping would allow program code to be loaded/executed without any integrity checking. Thereby, the integrity assumptions upon which FTRFS's concept is based would be violated and integrity could not be guaranteed for any executed program stored on the FS. Theoretically, data integrity could also be checked each time a mapping is established for a block. To perform these checks however, this data would have to be read in full, obsoleting the performance advantage and RAM conserving properties of XIP. XIP and FS-level data integrity protection can thus be considered mutually exclusive.

5   Outlook and Future Work

Permanent defects will require FEC upon every access to an object. If such a hard fault occurred in a frequently accessed object (e.g. the root inode or a populated directory), we would want to avoid future re-checks. In the current FS implementation, there is no functionality to avoid this behavior, however it could be added later on.

Bad-block relocation is already implemented within the FS, but only used during write, truncate and allocation operations, not during other access. The only exception hereby is the root inode, which currently is assumed to be in a fixed location, like in *PRAMFS*. This feature as well could be implemented in a future version and would certainly increase storage reliability, performance and reduce data degradation.

FTRFS could theoretically also operate on different memory technologies, however, most of its advantages are enabled through RAM properties. Protection at the FS layer would be rather complex, unwieldy and could still not offer proper protection against device failure. Thus, the authors are working on a different protective concept for flash memory.

In contrast to RAM, flash access times will vary depending on block integrity. Thus, full voting based majority decisions would require very complex control logic. If voting was conducted utilizing hardware-side flash controllers, a delayed response from one controller would stall access to the entire voting circuit. Even if the result has already been determined, the circuit would still be busy.

A transparent protective layer utilizing RAID1, FEC and checksuming could however be implemented as an MTD middleware layer. MTD-striping [37] has been proposed as a middleware function in the past, but has never been included in the Linux Kernel. However, the existence of the MTD-striping code proofs the feasibility of a mirroring and protection MTD-layer.

6   Conclusions

We presented a novel filesystem implementation enabling a software-side protective scheme against data degradation due to environmental effects introduced by the space environment as described in Section 2. We have shown the feasibility of a bootable, POSIX-compatible FS which can efficiently protect an OS image from device failure and software flaws according to the threat model outlined at the beginning of Section 4.

With respect to our use case in spaceflight, neither component level, nor hardware- or software-side measures individually can guarantee sufficient system consistency. Traditionally, radiation effects in space systems are compensated for with stronger hardware-EDAC and component-redundancy, which do not scale for complex systems and result in increased energy consumption. While redundancy and hardware-side voting can protect well from device failure, data integrity protection is difficult at this level. A combination of hardware and software measures can thus drastically increase system dependability, even for missions with a very long duration.

References

1. Heidt, H., et al.: Cubesat: A new Generation of Picosatellite for Education and Industry Low-Cost Space Experimentation. In: Proc. 14th AIAA/USU Conference on Small Satellites (2000)
2. Busch, S., Schilling, K.: UWE-3: a modular system design for the next generation of very small satellites. In: Proceedings of Small Satellites Systems and Services–The 4S Symposium, Slovenia (2012)
3. Evans, D., Merri, M.: OPS-SAT: An ESA Nanosatellite for Accelerating Innovation in Satellite Control. Spaceops (2014)
4. Bridges, C., et al.: Smartphone Qualification & linux-based tools for cubesat computing payloads. In: 2013 IEEE Aerospace Conference, pp. 1–10. IEEE (2013)
5. Stringfellow, M., Leveson, N., Owens, B.: Safety-Driven Design for Software-Intensive Aerospace and Automotive Systems. IEEE Proc. **98**(4), 515–525 (2010)
6. Ryu, K., Shin, E., Mooney, V.: A comparison of five different multiprocessor SoC bus architectures. In: Proceedings of the Euromicro Symposium on Digital Systems Design 2001, pp. 202–209. IEEE (2001)
7. McComas, D.: NASA/GSFC's Flight Software Core Flight System (2012)
8. Williams, J., Bergmann, N.: Reconfigurable linux for spaceflight applications. In: Proceedings of the Military and Aerospace Programmable Logic Devices (MAPLD 2004) (2004)
9. Atienza, D., et al.: Systematic Dynamic Memory Management Design Methodology for Reduced Memory Footprint. ACM-TODAES **11**(2), 465–489 (2006)
10. Saleh, J., Hastings, D., Newman, D.: Weaving Time into System Architecture: Satellite Cost per Operational Day and Optimal Design Lifetime. Acta Astronautica **54**(6), 413–431 (2004)
11. Katti, R., Stadler, H., Wu, J.: High Speed Magneto-resistive Random Access Memory, US Patent 5,173,873 (December 22, 1992)
12. Bourdarie, S., Xapsos, M.: The Near-Earth Space Radiation Environment. IEEE Trans. on Nuclear Science **55**, 1810–1832 (2008)
13. Xapsos, M., O'Neill, P., O'Brien, T.: Near-Earth Space Radiation Models. IEEE Transactions on Nuclear Science **60**, 1691–1705 (2013)
14. Schwank, J., Shaneyfelt, M., Dodd, P.: Radiation Hardness Assurance Testing of Microelectronic Devices and Integrated Circuits. IEEE Transactions on Nuclear Science **60**, 2074–2100 (2013)

15. ESA/ESTEC Requirements and Standards Division ECSS: Calculation of Radiation and its Effects and Margin Policy Handbook. ECSS-E-HB-10-12A (2010)
16. Chen, F.: Phase-Change Memory, US Patent App. 14/191,016 (February 26, 2014)
17. Tsiligiannis, G., et al.: Testing a Commercial MRAM Under Neutron and AlphaRadiation in Dynamic Mode. IEEE Trans. on Nuclear Science **60** (2013)
18. Maimon, J., et al.: Results of radiation effects on a chalcogenide non-volatile memory array. In: Proceedings of 2004 IEEE Aerospace Conference, vol. 4, pp. 2306–2315. IEEE (2004)
19. Gerardin, S., et al.: Radiation Effects in Flash Memories. IEEE Transactions on Nuclear Science **60**, 1953–1969 (2013)
20. Nguyen, D., Irom, F.: Radiation effects on MRAM. In: Radiation and Its Effects on Components and Systems, pp. 1–4. IEEE (2007)
21. Baker, M., et al.: A fresh look at the reliability of long-term digital storage. In: ACM SIGOPS Operating Systems Review, vol. 40, pp. 221–234. ACM (2006)
22. Engel, J., Mertens, R.: LogFS - finally a scalable flash file system. In: 12th International Linux System Technology Conference (2005)
23. Qiu, S., Reddy, N.: NVMFS: a hybrid file system for improving random write in NAND-flash SSD. In: 2013 IEEE 29th Symposium on Mass Storage Systems and Technologies (MSST), pp. 1–5. IEEE (2013)
24. Liangzhu, W.: The Investigation of JFFS2 Storage. Microcomputer Information **8**, 030 (2008)
25. Edel, N., et al.: MRAMFS: a compressing file system for non-volatile RAM. In: Proceedings of the IEEE Computer Society's 12th Annual International Symposium on MASCOTS 2004. IEEE (2004)
26. Stornelli, M.: Protected and Persistent RAM Filesystem. pramfs.sourceforge.net
27. Hulbert, J.: The Advanced XIP file system. In: Linux Symposium, p. 211 (2008)
28. Elghefari, M., et al.: Radiation Effects Assessment of MRAM Devices (2008)
29. Cassel, M., et al. : NAND-flash memory technology in mass memory systems for space applications. In: DASIA 2008, vol. 665, p. 25 (2008)
30. Herpel, H., et al.: Next generation mass memory architecture. In: DASIA (2010)
31. Wicker, SB., et al.: Reed-Solomon Codes and their Applications. Wiley & Sons (1999)
32. Suzuki, S., Shin, K.: On memory protection in real-time OS for small embedded systems. In: Proceedings of the Fourth International Workshop on Real-Time Computing Systems and Applications, pp. 51–58. IEEE (1997)
33. Su, S., et al.: A Hardware Redundancy Reconfiguration Scheme for Tolerating Multiple Module Failures. IEEE Transactions on Computers **100**(3), 254–258 (1980)
34. Joukov, N., et al.: Raif: redundant array of independent filesystems. In: 24th IEEE Mass Storage Systems and Technologies, MSST 2007, pp. 199–214 (2007)
35. Cagno, B., et al.: Verifying data integrity of a non-volatile memory system during data caching process. US Patent 8,037,380
36. Prabhakaran, V., Arpaci-Dusseau, A., Arpaci-Dusseau, R.: Analysis and evolution of journaling file systems. In: USENIX Annual Technical Conference, General Track, pp. 105–120 (2005)
37. Belyakov, A.: Linux-MTD Striping Middle Layer. Linux-MTD mailing list (March 2006)

CPS-Xen: A Virtual Execution Environment for Cyber-Physical Applications

Boguslaw Jablkowski$^{(\boxtimes)}$ and Olaf Spinczyk

Department of Computer Science,
Technical University of Dortmund, Dortmund, Germany
{boguslaw.jablkowski,olaf.spinczyk}@tu-dortmund.de

Abstract. The range of applications for virtualization technology grows continually. The possibility of workload consolidation, the facilitated system administration, the fault-tolerance properties and cost reduction are what renders this technique so interesting. Thus, it stands to reason to expand its field of application to the domain of Cyber-Physical Systems (CPSs). Unfortunately, the integration of multiple CPS on a single server by means of virtualization is not a straightforward task. In this domain, real-time constraints of critical tasks have to be satisfied, in order to avoid damage or even a catastrophe, and virtualization was initially not designed to cope with such requirements. In this article we present CPS-Xen, a platform for executing virtualized safety-critical CPS applications. CPS-Xen is based upon the Xen-Hypervisor - a popular open-source Virtual Machine Monitor (VMM). We extend the VMM with a real-time scheduler implementing the rate-monotonic (RM) scheduling policy and show that optimizing the VMM-scheduler alone is not enough, as the I/O-scheduling introduces delays and priority inversion in the scheduling of the VMs. In order to solve this issue, we propose an architecture that synergizes the work of both schedulers. Finally, throughout an extensive set of experiments the proposed architecture is shown to fulfill – even under high CPU load and up to 36 concurrent VMs – the hard real-time requirements of CPS applications.

Keywords: Virtualization · Cyber-physical systems · Power systems · Real-time systems

1 Introduction

Cyber-physical systems became a fundamental constituent of many different environments. They can be found in domains such as autonomous automotive and avionic systems, transportation, intelligent buildings, robotics, power systems and many more. Yet, despite their variety most CPS share a common

This work has been carried out in the course of research unit 1511 *Protection and control systems for reliable and secure operations of electrical transmission systems* funded by the German Research Foundation (DFG). The authors would like to thank the DFG for funding and all the project partners for the helpful discussions.

L.M. Pinho et al. (Eds): ARCS 2015, LNCS 9017, pp. 108–119, 2015.
DOI: 10.1007/978-3-319-16086-3_9

denominator, their complexity. This originates from their immanently heterogeneous and distributed character as well as the fact that modern CPS evolved into software-intensive systems composed of numerous software components. Considering the recent technological advancements in computing, sensing and communication, it stands to reason that in the future the use and importance of software in CPS will constantly grow, further increasing their complexity. This poses a challenge in the analysis and deployment of CPS. However, the issue of distributed heterogeneous components and complicated software is not exclusive to the area of CPS. There are other domains with similar challenges. A good example are large data centers. In this area similar issues could have been successfully tackled by the technique of virtualization. The fundamental features of virtualization are that it allows for a transparent integration and consolidation of the system components, thus significantly reducing its complexity and, at the same time, enables new management and fault-tolerance options. For instance, the high degree of fault-containment provided by this technology - both in space and time dimension - permits safety and security improvements. The software encapsulated in Virtual Machines (VM) is unable to propagate errors across the system or withhold crucial system resources. Therefore, an already compromised or erroneous VM is isolated and cannot affect the execution of other VMs. This property not only increases the dependability and security of the system but it is also one of the arguments in favor of using virtualization for the construction of mixed-criticality systems. Further, features like live migration, replication and checkpoint recovery enable dynamic system reconfiguration at runtime, facilitate administration and even allow for the implementation of high availability solution to transparently survive hardware failures. The list of benefits provided by virtualization is substantial, hence, it seems reasonable to try to expand its field of application to the domain of CPS. The integration of the computational subsystems into a one functional whole on a homogenous platform could not only result in a strongly reduced system complexity, raised dependability and availability, but also in a significant reduction of the procurement, operation, and maintenance costs. This article studies the feasibility of such an approach in the context of Cyber-Physical Energy Systems (CPES) by introducing CPS-Xen, an architecture for hosting virtualized CPS applications. In contrast to other works, CPS-Xen synergizes the scheduling of VMs with I/O-scheduling. Due to this, we can show throughout an extensive set of experiments that our architecture not only fulfills the hard real-time constraints of CPS applications but also exhibits minimal delay and jitter.

The rest of the paper is structured as follows. Section 2 describes the application domain of Cyber-Physical Energy Systems (CPES) and their typical real-time requirements. Section 3 presents our CPS-Xen architecture and discusses important implementation details. Section 4 elucidates the experiments setup and the measurements techniques. Section 5 provides the results for the conducted experiments. Finally, Section 6 discusses related works and the paper concludes in Section 7.

2   Cyber-Physical Energy Systems and Real-Time Constraints

Since modern power systems are good examples of large, distributed and complex cyber-physical systems they will serve in this article as the background for our research. In the last years, the circumstances in operating the electric power grid have changed substantially. The principal reasons for this change are the newly emerging technologies (e.g. electric mobility), the ongoing integration of renewable energy sources and - at least in Europe - the liberalization of the electricity markets. All of those change the expectations and therefore the requirements regarding the Information and Communication Technology (ICT) infrastructure and demand for new solutions. Particularly interesting for our research is the substation automation field. On the substation level of the power grid, new, interconnected and intelligent microprocessor-based controllers - Intelligent Electronic Devices (IED) - are being installed to meet the new requirements of monitoring, protection and control applications. Because these applications are commonly implemented on dedicated IEDs and - due to safety requirements - often redundantly the new solutions require a considerable number of devices to be installed and managed. Fortunately, in many of the cases, the computation logic from these devices can be abstracted and encapsulated in VMs. However, it has to be guaranteed that such an integrated, new system is fulfilling all functional and non-functional requirements. These have to be identified and verified. The functional aspects referring to, for example, the result correctness of the protection algorithm are beyond the scope of this article. The latter ones, we are interested in, are defined by appropriate standards and associations. Regarding the timing constrains for the domain of interest we will refer to the IEC 61850 Standard [3,4].

IEC 61850 is a bundle of standards for power system automation including substation automation and transmission grid protection. In short, the main protocols implementing the IEC 61850 specifications are Sampled Values (SV) used for the transmission of the measurements values, the Generic Object Oriented Substation Event (GOOSE) responsible for carrying the state changing commands (e.g. tripping commands) and the Manufacturing Message Specification (MMS) transmitting general purpose data for substation applications. The first two are layer-2 protocols, in contrast to the MMS which is a layer-3 protocol. The communication requirements for our studies imposed on the test system by the IEC 61850 specifications are summarized in Table 1. The transfer time limit comprises of the network communication delay and the communication processing time at the sender and receiver. The inter-arrival time describes the frequency at which the devices communicate with each other (e.g. a circuit breaker and an IED). In order to facilitate the evaluation of our architecture, for the purpose of this paper we assume that the computation delays for the algorithms executed inside the VMs are already included in the communication constraints for the different message types. Note that this approach introduces stricter timing constraints, as the transfer time requirements described in the standard do not include the computation delays. However, the computation time for our test

Table 1. Timing constraints

Protocol	Inter-Arrival Time	Transfer Time Limit
SV	0.250 ms	3 ms
GOOSE	5 ms	3-20 ms
MMS	50 ms	100 ms

implementation of a distance protection function - which is used for the overcurrent protection of power lines and is one of the most critical functions regarding timing constraints - never exceeded 40 s. In relation to the communication timing constraints including the computation latencies seems as an acceptable approach.

3   Architecture of CPS-Xen

The generic architecture for hosting virtualized safety-critical CPS applications is depicted in Figure 1. Our implementation is based on the Xen-Hypervisor [1], which is an open-source project with a large and active user community. Xen utilizes the technique of platform virtualization which allows for the concurrent execution of multiple Operating Systems (OS) on the same hardware. The OSs - including the applications running within - are encapsulated in VMs and are being managed by the hypervisor. The hypervisor also controls and assigns processor and memory resources to the VMs. In Figure 1, every physical host represents a server running the Xen-VMM. Each of the hypervisors is able to concurrently host a specific number of virtual machines - this number is bounded by the available hardware resources and the requirements of the applications to be run. A unique virtual machine created at boot time (Domain 0) holds the drivers for the underlying hardware and is responsible for the interaction between the other virtual machines, also known as guest operating systems, and the physical I/O resources. All of the remaining VMs encapsulate CPS applications. Figure 1 also depicts two physical communication interfaces, one for the virtualization management traffic (e.g. migrating VMs) and one for the communication between the physical part of the CPS (sensors and actuators) and the servers.

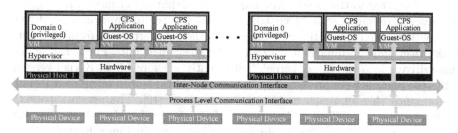

Fig. 1. Execution platform for virtualized CPS applications

3.1   Xen for Real Time

Xen 4.1.4 ships with two default VM-schedulers: the Credit and the Simple Earliest Deadline First (SEDF) scheduler. The Credit scheduler implements a fair share policy and for that reason it's not suitable for managing real-time applications that are encapsulated in VMs. In turn, the current implementation of the SEDF scheduler does not handle increased load situations and is not able to hold real-time constraints, as we show in Section 5. Therefore, we extended the Xen-Hypervisor with our own real-time scheduler.

Real-Time VM Scheduling. In the power systems domain, the safety-critical applications strictly depend on periodic sensor values which are being transmitted by computation-triggering network packets. A scheduling policy that provides optimal priority assignment in regard to these assumptions is the Rate Monotonic (RM) algorithm [5]. It is a dynamic preemptive scheduling algorithm based on static priorities where the highest priority is assigned to the task with the shortest period. We have implemented this policy in form of a VMM-scheduler. Our Xen-RM-scheduler takes the following parameters: a *slice*, a *period* and a *priority*. The *slice* denotes the maximum amount of CPU time a virtual machine may receive in a time interval that is specified by the cyclic consecutive requests for this VM and is called a *period*. The *priority* denotes the order in which an active VM, presumed it has not already consumed its whole slice for this period, will be scheduled on the processor and depends on its period. However, our implementation also allows for the explicit setting of the VMs priorities even if they differ from the RM policy priority assignment. This option was helpful in testing the influence of the network packet scheduler on the VMM-scheduler. Further, we enhanced the Xen tools for the possibility of adjusting the scheduler parameters at run time. The source code for CPS-Xen used in our experiments is available on our website: *http://ess.cs.uni-dortmund.de/EN/Software/index.html*.

Real-Time Networking. However, the response time of a real-time VM that is being triggered by a network packet depends not only on its workload and the hypervisor itself. Another crucial factor is the processing of the packets in the network driver domain - in our case Domain 0 (Dom0). One of the Xen features is that the virtualized OSs don't have to provide their own hardware drivers, this task is delegated to the Dom0. Xen implements a split driver model. In the case of network communication, a virtualized guest OS has to implement an driver abstraction called the netfront. Dom0 holds the counterpart in form of a netback driver and coordinates it with all of the guests netfronts. Further, it hooks these drivers into the Linux kernel. Till recently - before Linux Kernel version 3.12 - the packets were processed by a single kernel thread. In terms of real-time performance this approach had several limitations [10]. The network packets were scheduled regardless of the priority of the destined VM what directly led to priority inversion and an indeterministic behavior. In Linux Kernel 3.12, a new netback model has been implemented where the New API packet reception

mechanism (NAPI) [8] and multiple kernel threads are utilized for packet processing. The new model is called 1:1, since for every booted VM a dedicated
kernel thread (named *vif*) is being instantiated. The idea behind these changes
is to enable better scheduling fairness, yet we also use it to synergize the work
of the VMM-scheduler with the Linux scheduler in Dom0. Through the POSIX
interface (*chrt* command) in Dom0 we manipulate the real-time attributes of
the packet processing threads the way that the Linux scheduler performs as a
RM scheduler and corresponds with the VMM-scheduler priorities thus solving
the priority inversion issue. Section 5 provides the evaluation results for this
approach.

4   Experiment Setup

The main purposes of our experiments are to analyze the impact of the schedulers
synergy on the reactiveness of the system in regards to hard real-time constraints
and to investigate how well our architecture scales as load increases. For this, in
different scenarios we measure the response times of CPS applications that are
encapsulated in VMs.

We conducted our experiments on a Dell PowerEdge R620 machine consisting of two 8-core Intel Xeon E5-2650v2 processors running at a constant speed
of 2.6 GHz and an integrated Intel I350 1Gbit Ethernet network card. Domain
0 ran on a 64-Bit version of Ubuntu 14 Server with a para-virtualized kernel 3.13
and an exclusively dedicated core. As the VMM we used CPS-Xen based upon the
Xen version 4.1.4. The workloads representing the power system applications were
all embedded into the para-virtualized Mini-OS guest VMs. Further, we used additional computers to generate the network packets for the VMs under test.

4.1   VM Sets

The test VMs and their parameters were derived from the IEC 61850 standard,
which is elucidated in Section 2. The three VM types used in our experiments are:
the MMS-VMs – representing the soft or the non real-time load, the GOOSE-
VMs and SV-VMs – representing the workloads with hard real-time constraints.
Note that for the MMS-VMs we prepared a set of workloads, as we used them
in our CPU load scalability experiments for the iterative increase of the processor utilization. Further, in order to reduce the network load (for the scalability
experiments a total of 140 thousand packets had to be sent in less than a minute)
and, as it is a common practice for implementing SV-based protection functions,
we assumed a window of four SV-values for triggering the computation of the
protection algorithm running inside SV-VMs. Therefore, we set the period for
SV-VMs to 1 ms. The execution time for the workload of the SV-VM was determined on the basis of an implementation for a real distance protection function,
in turn, the other two are of synthetic nature. Table 2 summarizes the different
VMs and their parameters including the worst-case execution times (WCET).
The current design of our architecture assumes that each workload (task) runs

Table 2. VM types and their parameters

VM type	Period	WCET
SV-VM	1 ms	40 s
GOOSE-VM	5 ms	375 s
MMS-VM	50 ms	2.4 - 33.6 ms

in a separated VM. This approach has several advantage. It eases the formal timing analysis of the execution platform, as we don't have to assume a hierarchical scheduling architecture. It also allows for a higher utilization, due to the fact that the slice and the period of the VM can be chosen appropriately to its workload requirements. However, for test cases which employed a large number of instantiated VMs, simply applying the WCET values to the slices has proved to be an insufficient approach, as during long term experiments (10^6 requests) we witnessed rare outliers in our results. As the reason for the outliers we identified the context switch function inside the Xen-Hypervisor. During the conduction of our tests, the measured worst-case execution time for this function under RM reached 2122 ns and was 180 ns on average. Considering that the scheduling quantum of our scheduler is set to 10 µs then in worst-case the overhead of 2122 ns translates to a 21% resource loss. After appropriately adjusting the slice values we experienced no more outliers. Though, it has to be noted that calculating the worst-case context switch time into the slices leads to overly pessimistic assumptions about the required dimension of the system. However, in regards to the presented architecture the focus of this article lies on the fulfillment of real-time constraints and therefore we defer the optimization challenge of scaling the system appropriately as future work.

4.2   Measurements Techniques

For the purpose of this study we have implemented a UDP-based client-server benchmark in C. All of the servers (each representing a software function of a CPES) were running inside the VMs, the sensor values generating clients were instantiated on separate computers. During the conduction of our experiments we measured three different latency types. For estimating and monitoring of the execution times inside the VMs we implemented the approach suggested by Intel for clock cycle precise measurements [7]. This method provided us with a maximum measurement result deviation of only four clock cycles. Further, in Dom0 we collected data for the response times of each VM under test. In this article, we define the response time of a VM as the time interval between the moment when the network packet destined for that given VM arrives at the bottom of the Linux TCP/IP stack and the time-stamp at which it is delegated to the network adapter for a response transmission. Using systemtap[1] we hooked into the TCP/IP stack layer-2 kernel functions and logged the appropriate time-stamps. The focus of the subsequent experiments lies on the response times,

---

[1] At first we used tcpdump, yet we experienced significant measurement overheads.

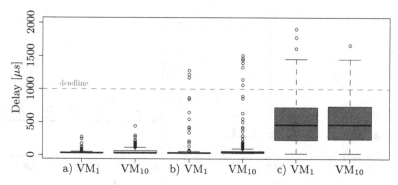

Fig. 2. Differences in the response times of real-time VMs under a) RM with synergyzed network packet scheduling, b) standard RM scheduling and c) standard SEDF scheduling

as they allow to characterize the impact of the I/O-scheduler on the VMM-scheduler as well as to gain insight into how the system would perform if it would to be deployed in a real industrial environment. Finally, on the machines generating the network packets with the sensor values we recorded the round-trip times (RTT) for every single packet. We used these values to additionally validate our execution and response time delays. In the subsequent experiments for each measurements and each of the presented figures - if not explicitly stated otherwise - a total number of 10,000 packets were sent to each of the VMs.

5   Evaluation

In this section, we describe the results from the conducted experiments with CPS-Xen. First, we show how the synergyzing of the network packet scheduler with the VMM scheduler impacts the response times of the real-time VMs. Next, we present the results of two scalability tests. The first one analyzes the real-time capabilities under increasing CPU load, the second scenario investigates the architecture in terms of a growing number of VM instances.

5.1   Scheduling Synergy

This experiment focuses on the interdependency between the network packet scheduler from Dom0 and the VMM scheduler with respect to the response times of real-time VMs. In order to analyze this relation, we instantiated ten VMs on a single core with no workload and measured the reaction latency of the VMs for three different scheduler setups. For each test and each VM the requests were send over a network from a sensor node with a constant period of 1 ms for a total number of 20,000 packets. All VMs were prioritized with VM_1 having the highest priority and VM_{10} the lowest. Figure 2 depicts the combined results in form of six boxplots merged into three VM pair blocks representing the different setups. Due to space limitations we only included the results for

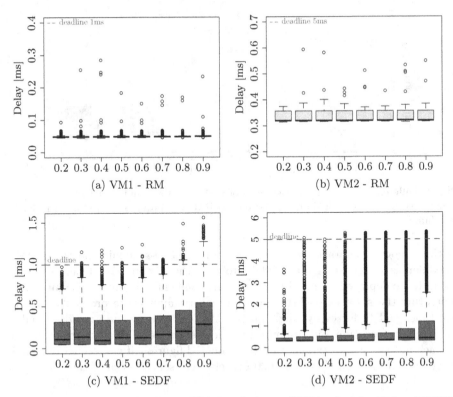

Fig. 3. Response times of real-time VMs in relation to CPU load under RM and SEDF

the highest and lowest priority VMs. Starting form the left, the pair of VMs in a) ran under the RM policy and the scheduling priorities for the kernel threads responsible for the processing of the network packets were set accordingly to the VMM scheduler priorities. In this test no deadlines were missed. The second pair b) represents the results for the setup were the packet processing threads were left unprioritized. In this case, the VMs again ran under the RM policy. However, here, several deadlines were missed. The differences in the results of a) and b) exemplify the impact of the I/O-scheduling on the VMM-scheduling. Finally, for the sake of completeness we also included the results for the Xen SEDF scheduler. These are depicted by the VM pair in c). In this setup the packets processing threads were left unchanged as in the case of b). The results for SEDF show hundreds of deadline violations.

5.2 Scalability

It is often the case that new and unknown issues emerge only after a certain load has been induced on an architecture under test. Therefore, in the subsequent experiments we evaluated CPS-Xen with respect to its scalability characteristics.

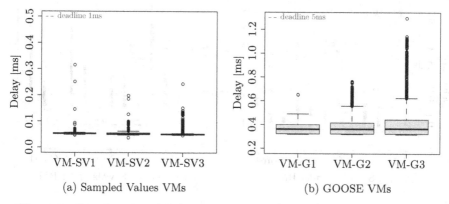

Fig. 4. Response times of six real-time VMs running on a single core under RM

CPU Load. This series of experiments relates to the behavior of our platform under increasing CPU load. All of the following tests include two real-time VMs (SV and GOOSE processing workloads) and one non real-time VM (MMS workload) scheduled on a single core. We used the non real-time VM for iteratively increasing the processor utilization. It has to be noted that the specified loads represent worst-case utilization values based upon the worst-case execution times of the workloads. During the execution of the tests the loads - on average - were about 15% lower. Figure 3 illustrates the response times of the two real-time VMs both for the RM and SEDF scheduling policies with respect to the rising CPU load. Figure 3 a) and b) present the respond latencies for VM_1 and VM_2 under the RM scheduler. We can observe that the worst-case response times for both VM_1 and VM_2 are far below their deadlines irrespective of the CPU load and that the response times manifest a deterministic behavior with a relatively small variance. Figure 3 c) and d) depicts the response times under SEDF. The results show that even under a low CPU load - starting at 30%- deadlines are being missed.

VM Instances. The following experiments address the scalability potential of CPS-Xen in respect to a growing number of VMs. The first test investigates the capability of the system to scale up in case of a single core. For this purpose we tripled the number of VMs used for the CPU load experiments and measured the response times of the 9 concurrently executed VMs - 6 real-time and 3 non real-time VMs. We additionally prioritized the VMs within each of the types, in order to clearly bring out the influence of the scheduler. Figure 4 shows the results for the a) SV- and b) GOOSE-workload processing VMs. We can observe that in both cases no deadlines were missed and the average and worst-caste response times are similar to the ones obtained in the CPU load experiments. It has to be noted that also all of the non real-time VMs completed their execution on time. The next experiment investigates the capability of our architecture to maintain its deterministic behavior in the case that additional VMs are being deployed on multiple cores. For this, we instantiated a total number of 36 VMs

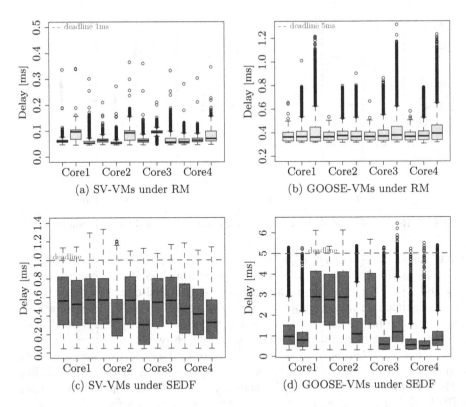

Fig. 5. Response times of 24 real-time VMs from a total of 36 VMs running on 4 cores under RM and SEDF

on four cores, 9 VMs on each core and each core hosting 3 SV-VMs, 3 GOOSE-VMs and 3 MMS-VMs. For the sake of completeness and better comparison we rerun the tests for the SEDF scheduler. Figure 5 depicts the measured response time values for both scheduler types and all four cores. For VMs scheduled under the RM policy no deadlines were missed and again the worst-case response times are in the region of the ones measured during the CPU load experiment. In the case of the SEDF scheduler none of the real-time constraints for the SV- or GOOSE-VMs have been fulfilled.

6   Related Work

There is still little literature on analyzing large-scale CPSs in the context of virtual execution environments. Till recently, virtualization has mainly been studied in terms of resource utilization. Nonetheless, some interesting work has been done in the context of virtualization and real-time systems. In [9] the authors propose a scheduling framework for analyzing compositional scheduling techniques in Xen and provide a suit of real-time VM scheduling policies. However, this work does not address the issue of I/O-scheduling or its influence on the VMM-scheduling.

In [6], a method for designing VM schedulers is being presented but also this analysis is burdened with priority inversion issues. A proposal for overcoming the I/O-scheduling related problems is being presented in [10], yet this approach restricts itself to local inter-domain communication. The communication-aware scheduling approach described in [2] improves the reactiveness of the I/O inten- sive VMs - scheduled under SEDF - by raising their priorities. Yet, this approach only alleviates the problem but does not solve it.

7   Conclusions

In this paper we presented CPS-Xen, an architecture for executing virtual- ized CPS applications such as those encountered in modern power systems. We showed that the default Xen SEDF real-time scheduler fails at fulfilling hard real-time constraints and therefore proposed a RM scheduler extension for Xen. Our scheduler performs within tighter response time bounds and achieves lower jitter. Nonetheless, our studies reveal that optimizing the VMM-scheduler alone is not enough, as the I/O-scheduling introduces delays and priority inversion to the system. Therefore, we assigned real-time priorities to the network packets processing threads and synergized the work of both schedulers. The results of the conducted series of experiments - including scalability studies - show that this is the right approach, as in none of the tests a deadline was ever missed.

References

1. Barham, P., et al.: Xen and the art of virtualization. SIGOPS Oper. Syst. Rev. **37**(5), 164–177 (2003)
2. Govindan, S., Nath, A.R., Das, A., Urgaonkar, B., Sivasubramaniam, A.: Xen and co.: communication-aware cpu scheduling for consolidated xen-based hosting platforms. In: VEE 2007. ACM, New York (2007)
3. IEC TC57: Iec 61850: Communication networks and systems for power utility automation
4. Ingram, D.M., Schaub, P., Taylor, R.R., Campbell, D.A.: Network Interactions and Performance of a Multifunction IEC 61850 Process Bus. IEEE Transactions on Industrial Electronics (September 2012)
5. Liu, C.L., Layland, J.W.: Scheduling algorithms for multiprogramming in a hard- real-time environment. J. ACM **20**(1), 46–61 (1973)
6. Masrur, A., Pfeuffer, T., Geier, M., Drössler, S., Chakraborty, S.: Designing vm schedulers for embedded real-time applications. In: CODES+ISSS, pp. 29–38. ACM, New York (2011)
7. Paoloni, G.: How to benchmark code execution times on intel ia-32 and ia-64 instruction set architectures (2010)
8. Salim, J.H., Olsson, R., Kuznetsov, A.: Beyond softnet. In: Proceedings of the 5th Annual Linux Showcase & Conference, ALS 2001, vol 5. USENIX Association, Berkeley (2001)
9. Xi, S., Xu, M., Lu, C., Phanm, L.T.X., Gill, C., Sokolsky, O., Lee, I.: Real-Time Multi-Core Virtual Machine Scheduling in Xen. EMSOFT 2014 (October 2014)
10. Xi, S., Li, C., Lu, C., Gill, C.D.: Prioritizing local inter-domain communication in xen. In: IWQoS, pp. 73–82. IEEE (2013)

Trust and Privacy

Trustworthy Self-optimization in Organic Computing Environments

Nizar Msadek[✉], Rolf Kiefhaber, and Theo Ungerer

Institute of Computer Science, University of Augsburg, 86135 Augsburg, Germany
{Msadek,Kiefhaber,Ungerer}@informatik.uni-augsburg.de

Abstract. In this paper, we present a self-optimization approach that does not only consider pure load-balancing but also takes into account trust to improve the assignment of important services to trustworthy nodes. Our approach uses different optimization strategies to determine whether a service should be transferred to another node or not. The evaluation results showed that the proposed approach is able to balance the workload between nodes nearly optimal. Moreover, it improves significantly the availability of important services, i.e., the achieved availability was no lower than 85% of the maximum theoretical availability value.

Keywords: Organic computing · Autonomic computing · Trust · Self-x properties · Self-optimization

1 Introduction

Organic Computing [1] is an initiative that brings together many fields of computing with the purpose of creating computing systems that self-configure [2], self-optimize, self-heal and self-protect (i.e., the so called self-x properties). Trust as a basic concept can be used to improve the robustness of such systems. In this paper we adopt the definition of trust [3] of the research unit OC-Trust of the German Research Foundation (DFG). In their research, trust covers different facets, as, for example, safety, reliability, credibility and usability. Our investigation focuses on the reliability aspect. Furthermore, we assume that a node can not realistically assess its own trust value because it may trust itself fully. Therefore, the calculation of the trust value for the self-x properties must be done with the following trust metrics:

- **Direct Trust** [4] is based on the own experiences a node has made directly with an interaction partner node. Typically, trust values are calculated by taking the mean or weighted mean of past experiences.
- **Reputation** [5] is based on the trust values of others that had experiences with the interaction partner. Reputation is typically collected if not enough or outdated own experiences exist.

This research has received funding from the research unit OC-Trust (FOR 1085) of the German Research Foundation (DFG).

© Springer International Publishing Switzerland 2015
L.M. Pinho et al. (Eds): ARCS 2015, LNCS 9017, pp. 123–134, 2015.
DOI: 10.1007/978-3-319-16086-3_10

When all the aforementioned values are obtained, a total trust value based on direct trust and reputation values can be calculated using confidence to weight both parts against each other [6]. This value can then be used to enhance the self-x properties with trust capabilities. In this paper, we primarily focus on self-optimization and note that our goal is to develop an autonomously trust-enhanced self-optimization algorithm that works in a distributed manner and also ensures global optimality. It uses at runtime the current information of nodes to perform an equal load distribution of services in the whole network as in a typical load balancing scenario.

2   Related Work

A lot of papers have been published to deal with the assignment problem of services on nodes, either to achieve a static or dynamic load balancing [7]. In most existing algorithms, the consideration of the trustworthiness of nodes has been neglected so far. For instance, the work of Rao et al. [8] proposes several methods for solving the load balancing problem in distributed systems. One of these methods, called one-to-one, is similar to our approach: two nodes are picked at random. Then, a virtual server transfer is initiated if one of the nodes is heavy and the other is light. Their method, however, does not consider how the availability of important services may be improved, and does not distinguish between trustworthy and untrustworthy nodes. Bittencourt et al. [9] presented an approach to schedule processes composed of dependent services onto a grid. This approach is implemented in the Xavantes grid middleware and arranges the services in groups. It has the drawback of a central service distribution instance and therefore a single point of failure can occur. In [10], two individual self-optimization algorithms for LTE networks are presented. One of these algorithms, called Load Balancing in Downlink LTE networks, is similar to our approach. The authors try to shift the virtual load of overloaded cells to less loaded adjacent cells by changing the virtual cell borders. The virtual load is modeled as the sum of resources needed to achieve a certain QoS for all active user equipments. In [11], the authors presented a receiver-initiated optimization algorithm that automatically balances the workload of nodes in service distributed environments. It is implemented in the $OC\mu$ middleware. In their algorithm, services can be relocated or transferred to other nodes to balance the resource consumption among nodes. Moreover, it takes into account the trust constraints of nodes to transfer important services only to trustworthy nodes. However, it is based on the unrealistic assumption that all nodes have the same resource capacity. Contrary to this work, our approach is able to work with heterogeneous capacities.

3   Basic Idea of the Self-optimization Algorithm

A distributed system consisting of a set of n nodes $\mathcal{N} = \{n_1, n_2.., n_n\}$ is considered, where each node can interact with each other through a set of application messages. They can optimize at runtime the assignment of services in the network by transferring their own services to other nodes. Suppose that node j at a certain point during runtime sends an application message to another node i. It appends onto the outgoing message (a) its trust in node i (b) its current workload and (c) some information (i.e., importance level and consumption) about services, which are running on it. Based on this information node i decides which of the following optimization strategies should be performed:

3.1 No Optimization

- **Description:** The workload between nodes is well balanced and their trust values are similar enough.
- **Discussion:** This is the simplest case that can happen between nodes. Both of them are well optimized in terms of trust and workload.
- **Solution:** Nothing will happen

3.2 Load Optimization

- **Description:** Trust of nodes is similar enough but their workload is unbalanced.
- **Discussion:** This strategy aims to find a pure load balancing between nodes since their trust is similar enough.
- **Solution:** Services are transferred to balance the workload between the nodes. Then, two cases are distinguished: (a) either the workload of i is higher or (b) the workload of j is higher. In the case of (a), node i balances the workload of the nodes by transferring a subset of its services to j. Otherwise, node i sends an alert message to j together with all information which are necessary for the optimization. Case (a) will be then triggered on side of j.

3.3 Trust Optimization

- **Description:** The workload between nodes is well balanced but their trust values differ significantly. In this case important services might run on untrustworthy nodes and are prone to fail.
- **Discussion:** This strategy aims to use particularly trustworthy nodes for important services. Therefore, important services have to be relocated to more trustworthy nodes and unimportant services to less trustworthy nodes. Furthermore, the overall workload resources between nodes should still be well-balanced.
- **Solution:** By this strategy, we distinguish between two cases: (a) either i is more trustworthy than j or (b) j is more trustworthy than i. If (a), then i swaps its unimportant services for important services of j. In the case of (b), node i swaps its important for unimportant services of j. Note that the load consumption between important and unimportant services should be similar to keep the load-balancing property in both nodes satisfied.

3.4 Trust and Load Optimization

- **Description:** Trust of nodes differs significantly and their workload is unbalanced.
- **Discussion:** This strategy aims at workload balancing with additional consideration of the services' priority, i.e. to avoid hosting important services on untrustworthy nodes.
- **Solution:** Four cases are distinguished: (a) either the workload of i is higher and i is more trustworthy than j, (b) the workload of i is higher but j is more trustworthy, (c) the workload of j is higher but it is less trustworthy than i, or finally (d), the workload of j is higher and it is also more trustworthy than j. In the case of (a), node i balances the workload of load by transferring only unimportant services to j. If there are no unimportant services available, then no optimization is done. The rationale for this step is that there is a trade-off between trust and workload. Improving one of these criteria will typically deteriorate the other. In the case of (b), node i balances the workload by transferring only important services to j. Just as the case of (b), no optimization is done, if there are no available unimportant services. In other cases (i.e., c and d), node i sends an alert optimization message to j to piggy-back information necessary for self-optimization. Depending on the situation, case (a) or (b) will be then triggered on side of j.

4 Metrics and Notations

Since it is very complex to address the self-optimization problem in its full generality, we make some simplifying assumptions. Firstly, we assume that the load of a service is stable (or can otherwise be predicted) over the time interval it takes for the self-optimization algorithm to operate. Secondly, we assume there is only one bottleneck resource we are trying to optimize for. Let w_i denote the workload of a node i, where w_i represents the sum of the resource consumptions of all services running on node i (see Formula 1).

$$w_i = \sum_{s \in S_i} c_s, \text{ with } 0 \le w_i \le C_i^{max}. \tag{1}$$

It is to note that c_s means the resource consumption of a service s. The maximum resource capacity of a node i is denoted by C_i^{max} and its set of services by S_i. Moreover, we divide services S_i into two sets based on their importance levels:

- S_i^{imp}: Set of important services (running on node i), which are necessary for the functionality of the entire system.
- S_i^{unimp}: Set of unimportant services (running on node i), which have only a low negative effect on the entire system if they fail.

Then, considering only the context of pure load optimization, our goal is to balance the workload between nodes. Let us assume two nodes, i and j: node i is underloaded. However, node j is overloaded and its task is to balance the workload by service transfers to i. Thus, as you can see in Figure 1, j transfers

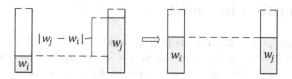

Fig. 1. Simple load optimization method

its services whose cumulative resource consumption is close enough to $\frac{|w_j - w_i|}{2}$ (optimal balancing). Although this simple idea seems to make a lot of sense, it has a big problem that does not operate with different resource capacities (see Figure 2).

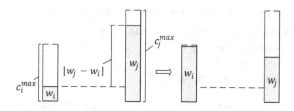

Fig. 2. Nodes still unbalanced

$$O_i = \frac{w_i + w_j}{c_i^{max} + c_j^{max}} c_i^{max} \qquad (2)$$

Therefore, we introduce a new optimal theoretical workload O_i, which should serve as a target reference point for every node. The node which surpasses this reference point ($w_i > O_i + \delta_{tol}$) is considered to be overloaded, otherwise it is underloaded ($w_i < O_i - \delta_{tol}$) or balanced ($|O_i - w_i| \leq \delta_{tol}$), where a δ_{tol} is a tolerable threshold and represents the quality to reach the perfect workload. The optimal theoretical workload of a node i is calculated using Formula 2. Since w_i is normalized in a different capacity than w_j, we must first divide the sum of workload $w_i + w_j$ by the sum of capacity $c_i^{max} + c_j^{max}$ to obtain the optimal theoretical workload per one unit capacity, which will be then multiplied by c_i^{max}. Furthermore, each node has an individual trust value calculated based on our previously developed trust metrics [6]. The trust value $t_i(j)$ represents the subjective trust of node i in node j and will always range between 0 and 1.

The value of 0 means that i does not trust j at all while a value of 1 stands for complete trust. Two nodes i and j are considered to have a similar trust behavior if $|t_i(j) - t_j(i)| \leq \gamma_{tol}$, where γ_{tol} is a tolerable threshold and reflects the quality to achieve a good trust similarity between nodes.

5   The Algorithm in Detail

The algorithm proposed in this section represents a best-effort approach to improve the assignment of services on nodes so as to satisfy both workload and trust constraints. It is used to solve this problem in a distributed manner. We assume that nodes of the network do not know about the workload of others until they receive a message from a node with information about that. The workload of nodes also might change over time. We further assume that a node can not assess its own trust value, but is rated by other nodes. Therefore, its trust value must be calculated from the neighbor nodes of the network (see [6] for more details). Note that the trust of nodes might also change over time.

Again we are considering two nodes i and j, where j sends an application message m_j to i, on which it piggybacks the following additional information:

- S_j^{unimp}: Set of less important services running on node j
- S_j^{imp} : Set of important services running on j
- $t_j(i)$: Current trust value of j in i
- w_j: Current workload value of j
- c_j^{max}: Maximum resource capacity of j

Based on this information node i decides which optimization strategy should be performed. In the following we consider all possible decisions a node i has to make:

5.1   No Optimization

- **Formal description:** $|t_i(j) - t_j(i)| \leq \gamma_{tol}$ and $|O_i - w_i| \leq \delta_{tol}$
- **Solution:** Nothing will happen

5.2   Load Optimization

- **Formal description:** $|t_i(j) - t_j(i)| \leq \gamma_{tol}$ and $|O_i - w_i| > \delta_{tol}$
  - **Case a:** $w_i > O_i$ and $w_j < O_j$
    Node i balances the workload by transferring some of its services to j, regardless of whether they are important or not since the trust of nodes is similar. Firstly, it determines Ψ (see Formula 3 and 4) as a set of services that could be selected to balance the workload of nodes. Note that $C(I_s)$ represents the consumption function of a set of services I_s and is calculated by the sum of all its service consumptions.
    If Ψ is empty, then no optimization is done. Otherwise i transfers Ψ to j.

$$\Psi = \{I_s \mid I_s \subseteq (\mathcal{S}_i^{imp} \cup \mathcal{S}_i^{unimp}) : max\, \mathcal{C}(I_s) \text{ and} \tag{3}$$
$$\mathcal{C}(I_s) \leq (O_j - w_j) \text{ and } 0 < \mathcal{C}(I_s) \leq (w_i - O_i)\}$$

$$\mathcal{C}(I_s) = \sum_{s \in I_s} c_s \tag{4}$$

- **Case b: $w_i < O_i$ and $w_j > O_j$**
  Since services are assumed not to be stolen from other nodes, node i sends an alert message to j to piggy-back information necessary for self-optimization as described above. Then, Case (5.2-a) will be triggered but on the side of j.

5.3   Trust Optimization

- **Formal description:** $|t_i(j) - t_j(i)| > \gamma_{tol}$ and $|O_i - w_i| \leq \delta_{tol}$
  - **Case a: $t_j(i) > t_i(j)$**
    In this case i determines Ψ (see Formula 5) as a set of unimportant services (i.e., with the maximum load consumption) that could be exchanged for important services of j so that the difference of their load consumption never exceeds $\mathcal{C}_{tol}$ to keep the load-balancing property in both nodes satisfied.

$$\Psi = \{I_s \mid I_s \subseteq \mathcal{S}_i^{unimp}, \exists J_s \subseteq \mathcal{S}_j^{imp} : max\, \mathcal{C}(I_s) \text{ and} \tag{5}$$
$$|\mathcal{C}(I_s) - \mathcal{C}(J_s)| \leq \mathcal{C}_{tol} \text{ and } (\mathcal{C}(I_s) + w_j) \leq c_j^{max}\}$$

   Then, after transferring Ψ, node i sends an alert optimization message to j (i.e., including all information which are necessary for the optimization) in order to trigger case (5.4-b) on side of j. Note that the execution of this step aims to balance again the workload between the nodes.
  - **Case b: $t_j(i) < t_i(j)$**
    In contrast to case (5.3-a), Ψ is determined only from important services (see Formula 6), since j is more trustworthy than i. Then, i sends an alert optimization message to j in order to trigger case (5.4-a) on side of j.

$$\Psi = \{I_s \mid I_s \subseteq \mathcal{S}_i^{imp}, \exists J_s \subseteq \mathcal{S}_j^{unimp} : max\, \mathcal{C}(I_s) \text{ and} \tag{6}$$
$$|\mathcal{C}(I_s) - \mathcal{C}(J_s)| \leq \mathcal{C}_{tol} \text{ and } (\mathcal{C}(I_s) + w_j) \leq c_j^{max}\}$$

5.4   Trust and Load Optimization

– **Formal description:** $|t_i(j) - t_j(i)| > \gamma_{tol}$ and $|O_i - w_i| > \delta_{tol}$
  - **Case a:** $w_i > O_i$ and $w_j < O_j$ and $t_j(i) > t_i(j)$
    Node i balances the workload only by transferring unimportant services
    to j (i.e., due to the fact that i is more trustworthy than j). It determines
    Ψ as a set of only unimportant services that could be selected to balance
    the workload of nodes (see Formula 7). Then, i transfers Ψ to j.

$$\Psi = \{I_s \mid I_s \subseteq \mathcal{S}_i^{unimp} : max\, \mathcal{C}(I_s) \text{ and } \mathcal{C}(I_s) \leq (O_j - w_j) \tag{7}$$
$$\text{and } 0 < \mathcal{C}(I_s) \leq (w_i - O_i)\}$$

  - **Case b:** $w_i > O_i$ and $w_j < O_j$ and $t_j(i) < t_i(j)$
    Since j is more trustworthy than i, Ψ will be determined only from
    important services (see Formula 8). Then, just as the case of (5.4-a), if
    Ψ is empty, no optimization is done. Otherwise i transfers Ψ to j.

$$\Psi = \{I_s \mid I_s \subseteq \mathcal{S}_i^{imp} : max\, \mathcal{C}(I_s) \text{ and } \mathcal{C}(I_s) \leq (O_j - w_j) \tag{8}$$
$$\text{and } 0 < \mathcal{C}(I_s) \leq (w_i - O_i)\}$$

  - **In other cases:**
    Node i sends an alert message to j (i.e., including all information which
    are necessary for the optimization). Depending on the situation, case
    (5.4-a or 5.4-b) will be then triggered on the side of j.

6   Evaluation

In this section an evaluation for the introduced self-optimization approach is provided. For the purpose of evaluating and testing, an evaluator based on TEM [12]
has been implemented which is able to simulate the self-optimization algorithm.
The evaluation network consists of 100 nodes, where all nodes are able to communicate with each other using message passing. Experiments with more nodes were
tested and yielded similar results, but with 100 nodes more observable effects
were seen. Each node has a limited resource capacity (memory) and is judged
by an individual trust value without any central knowledge. Furthermore, four
type of nodes are defined with different trust and resource values (see Table 1).

Then, a mixture of heterogeneous services with different resource consumptions are randomly generated for nodes. The sum of all node's service consumptions does not exceed a node's capacity (i.e., as defined in formula 1). If, for
example, a trustworthy node is already full, then the same procedure is repeated
for an untrustworthy node and so on until the average load of the system reaches

Table 1. Mixture of heterogeneous nodes

Node Type	Memory (MB)	Trust	Amount (%)
Type 1	500-1000	0.7-0.9	10
Type 2	500-1500	0.3-0.6	50
Type 3	2000-4000	0.4-0.8	30
Type 4	4000-8000	0.4-0.9	10

50% ($\overline{workload} = 50\%$). This means that some nodes may have many services and others none to unbalance the workload between nodes. Important services are created only for untrustworthy nodes and unimportant services for trustworthy nodes. Without the self-optimization techniques the workload of nodes are still unbalanced. Moreover, important services running on untrustworthy nodes are prone to fail. With the use of the trust metrics [6], the trust of a node can be measured and taken into consideration for the transfer of services.

Two rating functions are used to evaluate the fitness of a service distribution regarding trust and workload. The first rating function for workload $\mathcal{F}_{workload}$ aims to calculate the average deviation of all nodes from the desired workload $\overline{workload}$ (in our case, 50%). This is expressed by the formula 9, where $\mathcal{N}$ is the set of all nodes and $|\mathcal{N}|$ the cardinality of $\mathcal{N}$.

$$\mathcal{F}_{workload} = \frac{\sum\limits_{n \in \mathcal{N}} |workload(n) - \overline{workload}|}{|\mathcal{N}|} \tag{9}$$

$$\overline{workload} = \frac{\sum\limits_{n \in \mathcal{N}} workload(n)}{|\mathcal{N}|} \tag{10}$$

The main idea of the second rating function $\mathcal{F}_{trust}$ is to reward important services running on trustworthy nodes. This is expressed by the formula 11, where $\mathcal{N}$ is the set of all nodes, S_n is the set of services on a node n, $t(n)$ its trust value and p(s) the priority of a service s (i.e., if s is important, $P(s)$ has the value of 1, otherwise 0).

At the beginning of the simulation, the network is rated by using both $\mathcal{F}_{trust}$ and $\mathcal{F}_{workload}$. Then, the simulation is started and after each optimization step the network is rated again. Within one optimization step, 50 pair of nodes (sender/receiver) are randomly chosen to perform the self-optimization process. Senders send an application message to receivers to piggyback necessary information for the self-optimization, as described in section 3. Based on the extracted information the receiver determines whether it transfers its services or not.

$$\mathcal{F}_{trust} = \sum_{n \in \mathcal{N}} \sum_{s \in \mathcal{S}_n} p(s)t(n) \tag{11}$$

The goal is to maximize the availability of important services, which means that $\mathcal{F}_{trust}$ should be maximized (i.e., to an optimal theoretical point that we explain later in 6.2). Therefore, it is necessary to transfer the more important services to more trustworthy nodes. Furthermore, the overall utilization of resources in the network should be well-balanced, i.e., $\mathcal{F}_{workload}$ should be minimized near to zero.

6.1   Results Regarding the Rating Function $\mathcal{F}_{workload}$

As mentioned above, $\mathcal{F}_{workload}$ indicates the average workload deviation of all nodes from the desired workload $\overline{workload}$ (in our case, 50%). The lower the value of $\mathcal{F}_{workload}$, the better the performance of workload balancing.

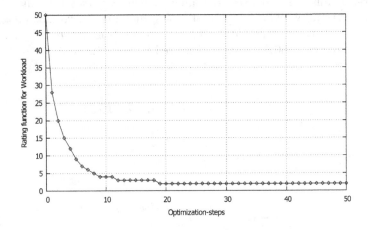

Fig. 3. Rating function for workload deviation($\mathcal{F}_{workload}$)

Figure 3 shows the result of this experiment, whereas the values on the x-axis stand for optimization steps and the average workload deviation of nodes is depicted on the y-axis. It can be observed that the proposed algorithm improves the workload balancing by about 93%. However, it does not reach the theoretical maximum rate of 100% due to the trade-off between trust and workload.

6.2   Results Regarding the Rating Function $\mathcal{F}_{trust}$

In the following, the service distribution for the proposed self-optimization algorithm is evaluated regarding $\mathcal{F}_{trust}$. Figure 4 shows the result of this experiment. The square line represents the result of $\mathcal{F}_{trust}$ using the proposed self-optimization algorithm. It can be observed that the algorithm improves during

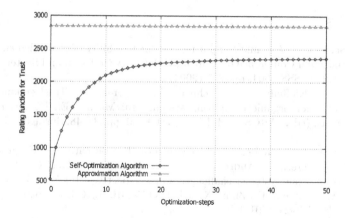

Fig. 4. Rating function for Trust ($\mathcal{F}_{trust}$)

runtime the availability of important services. This means that the consideration of workload does not prevent the algorithm to relocate important services to
trustworthy nodes. However, it remains to investigate how good is the obtained
result compared to an optimal theoretical result, when all important services
are hosted only on trustworthy nodes (pure trust distribution, i.e., regardless of
whether nodes are balanced or not). For this purpose we use an approximation
algorithm that sorts in decreasing order the trust values of nodes and relocates
all important services only to most trustworthy nodes until their capacity is full.
The triangular marked line in the figure illustrates the result of the approximation algorithm. As a conclusion to all simulations we have done so far (about
1000 runs were evaluated) we can state that the proposed algorithm greatly
improves the trust distribution of services. More precisely, it achieves 85% of the
theoretical maximum result. However, it stays by 15% behind the theoretical
maximum result due to the trade-off between trust and workload.

7   Conclusion

In this paper, we have presented a trustworthy self-optimization algorithm that
does not only consider pure load-balancing but also takes into account trust to
improve the assignment of important services to trustworthy nodes. More precisely, it uses different optimization strategies to determine whether a service
should be transferred to another node or not. The proposed algorithm has been
evaluated. The results show that for our model trust concepts improve significantly the availability of important services while causing a small deterioration
(i.e., by about 7%) regarding load balancing.

References

1. Müller-Schloer, C.: Organic computing - on the feasibility of controlled emergence. In: International Conference on Hardware/Software Codesign and System Synthesis, CODES + ISSS 2004, pp. 2–5 (2004)
2. Msadek, N., Kiefhaber, R., Fechner, B., Ungerer, T.: Trust-enhanced self-configuration for organic computing systems. In: Maehle, E., Römer, K., Karl, W., Tovar, E. (eds.) ARCS 2014. LNCS, vol. 8350, pp. 37–48. Springer, Heidelberg (2014)
3. Steghöfer, J.-P., Kiefhaber, R., Leichtenstern, K., Bernard, Y., Klejnowski, L., Reif, W., Ungerer, T., André, E., Hähner, J., Müller-Schloer, C.: Trustworthy organic computing systems: challenges and perspectives. In: Xie, B., Branke, J., Sadjadi, S.M., Zhang, D., Zhou, X. (eds.) ATC 2010. LNCS, vol. 6407, pp. 62–76. Springer, Heidelberg (2010)
4. Kiefhaber, R., Satzger, B., Schmitt, J., Roth, M., Ungerer, T.: Trust measurement methods in organic computing systems by direct observation. In: The 8th IEEE/IFIP International Conference on Embedded and Ubiquitous Computing (EUC 2010), pp.105–111, December 2010
5. Kiefhaber, R., Hammer, S., Savs, B., Schmitt, J., Roth, M., Kluge, F., André, E., Ungerer, T.: The neighbor-trust metric to measure reputation in organic computing systems. In: The 5th IEEE Conference on Self-Adaptive and Self-Organizing Systems Workshops (SASOW 2011), pp.41–46, October 2011
6. Kiefhaber, R., Jahr, R., Msadek, N., Ungerer, T.: Ranking of direct trust, confidence, and reputation in an abstract system with unreliable components. In: The 10th IEEE International Conference on Autonomic and Trusted Computing (ATC-2013) (2013)
7. Babak, H., Kit, L.Y., Lilja, D.J.: Dynamic task scheduling using online optimization. Journal IEEE Transactions on Parallel and Distributed Systems **11**(11) (2000)
8. Rao, A., Lakshminarayanan, K., Surana, S., Karp, R., Stoica, I.: Load balancing in structured P2P systems. In: Kaashoek, M.F., Stoica, I. (eds.) IPTPS 2003. LNCS, vol. 2735, pp. 68–79. Springer, Heidelberg (2003)
9. Bittencourt, L., Madeira, E.R.M., Cicerre, F.R.L., Buzato, L.E.: A path clustering heuristic for scheduling task graphs onto a grid. In: In 3rd International Workshop on Middleware for Grid Computing (MGC 2005) (2005)
10. Lobinger, A., Stefanski, S., Jansen, T., Balan, I.: Coordinating handover parameter optimization and load balancing in lte self-optimizing networks. In: 2011 IEEE 73rd Vehicular Technology Conference (VTC Spring) (2011)
11. Satzger, B., Mutschelknaus, F., Bagci, F., Kluge, F., Ungerer, T.: Towards trustworthy self-optimization for distributed systems. In: Lee, S., Narasimhan, P. (eds.) SEUS 2009. LNCS, vol. 5860, pp. 58–68. Springer, Heidelberg (2009)
12. Anders, G., Siefert, F., Msadek, N., Kiefhaber, R., Kosak, O., Reif, W., Ungerer, T.: Temas a trust-enabling multi-agent system for open environments. Technical report, Universität Augsburg (2013)

Improving Reliability and Endurance Using End-to-End Trust in Distributed Low-Power Sensor Networks

Jan Kantert[1]([✉]), Sergej Wildemann[1], Georg von Zengen[3], Sarah Edenhofer[2],
Sven Tomforde[2], Lars Wolf[3], Jörg Hähner[2], and Christian Müller-Schloer[1]

[1] Institute of Systems Engineering, Leibniz University of Hannover, Hanover,
Germany
{kantert,wildemann,cms}@sra.uni-hannover.de
[2] Organic Computing Group, University of Augsburg, Augsburg, Germany
{sarah.edenhofer,sven.tomforde,joerg.haehner}@informatik.uni-augsburg.de
[3] Institute of Operating Systems and Computer Networks,
Tu Braunschweig, Germany
{vonzengen,wolf}@ibr.cs.tu-bs.de

Abstract. Wireless Sensor Networks are characterised by a large amount of participating nodes. Considering attackers and malicious elements within such a network poses challenges for the network protocols in operation. Based on concepts from the Organic Computing domain, this paper introduces a novel approach to introduce reliability measures and establish End-to-End trust in WSNs. We evaluate our concepts using simulation by adding nodes which try to attack the system. The results show that these malicious nodes can be quickly isolated with low additional effort.

1 Introduction

Wireless Sensor networks (WSNs) describe a class of computing systems with special characteristics. They operate in highly dynamic environments and adapt their behaviour automatically to changing conditions while sensing the environment. Due to the potentially large number of participating nodes, the system architecture is spatially distributed over potentially large areas.

In standard WSNs, all nodes are assumed to belong to one authority and deliver their results to one or more sink nodes that are controlled in a centralised way. However, nodes may become compromised or broken during their lifetime. Current protocols and most installations do not take malicious behaviour or partially failures into account.

Based on insights from the domain of Organic Computing [18], we describe a novel concept for estimating the reliability of nodes in such WSNs. Taking this into account, we develop an artificial trust relationship between nodes to which we refer as *End-to-End trust* that improves the routing decisions within the network. We demonstrate the benefit of our approach using simulation and compare the results to standard approaches. Thereby, we demonstrate that the benefit of these measures come with only low additional effort.

© Springer International Publishing Switzerland 2015
L.M. Pinho et al. (Eds): ARCS 2015, LNCS 9017, pp. 135–145, 2015.
DOI: 10.1007/978-3-319-16086-3_11

This paper is organised as follows: Section 2 describes our application scenario in more detail. This is followed by the problem description in Section 3. Section 4 gives an overview to previous and related work. Afterwards, Section 5 introduces our novel approach of End-to-End trust, which is then evaluated in Section 6. Section 7 discussed the achieved results and derives research directions for current and future work. Finally, Section 8 concludes the paper.

2   Application Scenario

WSNs have a wide area of usage, from environmental [12] and industrial monitoring [1] to healthcare purposes [3]. Unlike normal wireless networks, WSNs often have special limitations, such as being battery powered or the limited processing power and memory size of the *Micro Controller* (μC) used on the nodes. Also, some use cases add other challenges, i.e. mobility of network nodes and, therefore, changing network topologies. Due to the limited power supply, nodes are equipped with low power transceiver chips for wireless communication standards, i.e. IEEE 802.15.4 [11]. Thus, WSNs belong to the group of low power and lossy networks. Another reason for the loss is the previously mentioned mobility and the resulting instability of links between nodes.

In most WSNs, the major traffic is directed to a more powerful node which is able to store the sensed data. This special node is called *sink* and typically has an uplink to the Internet or other large-scale networks.

Due to the instability, loss, and limitations mentioned above, standard protocols from the domain of mobile ad-hoc networks (i.e. AODV [16] or OLSR [5]) are not applicable. Therefore, the *Routing Protocol for Low power and Lossy Networks [20]* (RPL), an IPv6 Routing Protocol, was developed. It is a distance vector routing protocol designed for the limitations given by the hardware and the special environmental challenges in WSNs. To route packets, RPL constructs a *Destination-Oriented Directed Acyclic Graph* (DODAG). For most applications in WSNs, a DODAG is an appropriate routing assumption because most of the traffic is directed to the *sink* node. In RPL, this node is called *root*. A network can contain more than one RPL instance; every instance is serving goal of the network and may consist of more than one DODAG to fulfil the goal. Every DODAG can only have one *root*. To route a packet to the *root*, all intermediate nodes forward the packet to their parent nodes until the *root* is reached.

Contrary to the node-sink relation, packets have to be sent from the sink to nodes in certain cases. To be able to handle these cases, RPL has the ability to gather all nodes forwarding a packet to the *root*. Using this information, RPL is able to store the routing path into a packet and route it down to the desired node. However, this mode is optional and may be disabled to save memory on the nodes.

The way nodes select a parent inside the DODAG depends on the application's goal. It is influenced by different metrics, i.e. the required energy to transmit a packet to the next node. Furthermore, constraints such as the maximum number of forwards can influence the structure of the resulting DODAG. From all this information, the *Objective Function* (OF) generates the *rank* of a node. The *rank* influences the position of a node in the DODAG. Thereby, the *root* is always *rank* 0. Only nodes with a lower *rank* can be parents of a node. To forward a packet, a node does not necessarily take the parent with the lowest *rank*. This decision is left to the OF as well. The ability to construct an application-specific routing graph is a big advantage of RPL compared to AODV [16] or OLSR [5].

3 Problem

RPL is very efficient when building routing trees and recovering from node failures. However, it has major problems if nodes only fail partially or behave intentionally malicious. In standard RPL, all parent decisions are based on the *rank*. The *Minimum Rank with Hysteresis Objective Function [9]* (MRHOF) extension introduces metric containers and improves the parent selection. Most deployments use *Expected Transmission count [6]* (ETX) as a metric which derives the route with statistically the lowest count of transmissions. The ETX value is passed inside the DIO packets as a metric container. There exist two major problems: First, the ETX values for certain links could be fake; second, a node may not forward other packets than routing information. ETX is calculated based on the packets actually sent. Hence, it does not ensure any routing at all. This behaviour may be malicious or even unintended because of misconfiguration or failures.

In our experience with physical systems, the problem can have two reasons: first, because of broken software deployments to parts of the network; second, because overload happens on the bus to the wireless adapter. In both cases, one or more nodes practically performed a sink hole attack against the network and prevented significant portions of the network from communicating at all. Nodes with broken software behave like malicious nodes. However, this does not happen intentionally. Still, the routing protocol should be able to circumvent them and recover from this unintentional attack.

Overloading the bus to the wireless adapter happens frequently with cheap hardware on central nodes. As a result, we observe increasing packet loss, which is not represented in the ETX value for the links to the nodes. This effect is caused by the transceiver chip itself, because according to IEEE 802.15.4 it sends a link level acknowledgement after it successfully received a packet. The sending node considers the packets as successfully transmitted in its ETX calculation. However, when the bus to the transceiver chip is overloaded, the operating system of the receiving node may have never processed the packet. From the outside, this behaviour, which is done for power saving in the CPU, also looks like a (partial) sink hole attack.

4 Previous and Related Work

4.1 Sensor Networks

Typically, WSNs are designed as networks of dozens to thousands of small-scaled and cheap electronic sensing devices [2], called *sensor nodes*. Sensor nodes typically consist of at least one sensor to sense environmental variables, a wireless transceiver chip to communicate, and a *Micro Controller* (μC) to pre-process the gathered data and to handle the communication processing. These nodes are often battery powered, so, energy efficiency is one of the main objectives in the design of software for these devices. This objective is present in all layers of the network stack in such networks; starting down in the physical layer with low power communication standard such as IEEE 802.15.4 [11]. One of most active fields of research in energy preservation is the MAC-Layer [10] [15].

The routing of packets in such networks is not only challenging from the energy preservation objective, but also from the perspectives of packet loss and instability of links between nodes. Most sensor networks are deployed over an area which is larger than the transmission range of the sensor nodes. Thus, routing must be able to handle multi-hop transfer of packets. To be as cost-efficient as possible, every node in the network should be used as a forwarding node. This leads to multiple possible paths for packets to reach their destination. The way the path is chosen depends on the application the network is supposed to fulfil. For networks which have to deliver packets in a guaranteed time, approaches such as GINSENG [14] are available. Like GINSENG most routing protocols are specialised to meet one target, i.e. round trip time or the energy to transfer a packet to its destination. A more flexible approach regarding the objective function is RPL.

4.2 Trust and Reputation in Sensor Networks

In contrast to standard RPL, we do not assume any benevolence of nodes in the network [19]. To cope with this information uncertainty, we introduce a trust metric. A general overview about applying trust to distributed systems can be found in [4].

Ganeriwal et al. [8] implemented reputation in sensor networks. Every node rates its neighbours and malfunctioning nodes can be avoided. However, relay or wormhole attacks can not be prevented.

Another approach was presented by Leligou et al. [13]: They propose to use active traffic sniffing to defend against attacks and integrate encryption to fight most attacks. However, active sniffing costs a lot of energy, because the CPU has to read all packets on the air. Additionally, this approach can not ensure that packets are actually delivered to the *root*.

Zhan et al. [21] presented a *Trust Aware Routing Framework* (TARF), which can fight most attacks without much overhead. They use a very simple trust metric and no reputation. We adapted parts of their approach to RPL and extended them.

5   Approach

In RPL, nodes have only very limited knowledge about the topology to save power and memory. Since one of the main reasons for energy consumption is the use of radio, there should be as little communication as possible. Because of this constraint to minimise communication, there are no acknowledgements from the *root* about received packets. Unfortunately, this means that nodes can not know whether their packets were actually forwarded and delivered.

However, to detect malicious or broken nodes, we need to gain knowledge whether our packets actually reached the *root*. Normally, most communication is one-way in such networks, so, there is no feedback. In our approach, we introduce End-to-End Trust as an effective low-overhead measurement to fill the information gap about the delivery rate of a route.

5.1   End-to-End Trust

To achieve End-to-End Trust, we first add a sequence number to every packet from a node to *root*. This allows the *root* to determine if it missed packets. However, it still can not tell whether it got the last packet and, more important, the sending node does not know. Fortunately, the *root* periodically sends a DIO to all nodes. We add a header to all DIOs which contains the Trust Round (see Section 5.2) and the count of all received packets in this round. Additionally, we also trigger a DIO when the *root* sees a high count of missing packets. Nodes will receive a forwarded DIO from each of their neighbours. However, according to RFC 6550 [20], they shall ignore it from all but their parents. This ensures that every node knows about the last sequence number seen by the *root* and the amount of missing packets. An attacker can only prevent a node from receiving the correct DIO if it controls all neighbours of that node and in that case there would not be a working route anyway. In theory, the attacker would only have to control the parents, fortunately implementations (i.e. *Contiki*) also consider DIOs from non-parent neighbours.

5.2   Trust Rounds

Previous approaches had problems to determine whether a packet was actually sent before or after the DIO was generated since clocks are either not existent or not synchronised in sensor networks. To solve this dilemma, we introduce so called *Trust Rounds* (TR). Nodes attach TR and sequence number to every packet. When the *root* generates a DIO, it starts a new round. After nodes receive the DIO, they reset their sequence counter to zero and use the new round. The parent will only be reselected when a new round starts or when the old parent becomes unavailable. At the beginning of a TR nodes re-evaluate their parent selection and will select a better performing parent if available. This optimisation helps to save memory on all nodes since they only need to remember their sequence and the selected parent.

5.3   Trust Metric and Objective Function

With both sequence numbers and TRs, nodes will eventually know which packets reached the *root* and which did not. Based on this knowledge, a node calculates the delivery rate for the parent used in the last TR. This rate should be next to 100% in normal cases because a packet is resent if no link level acknowledgement was received by the radio.

We use a simple trust metric $T_{n,r}$ to calculate the trust for all neighbours n (see Equation (4)). In every round r, a node calculates the new Trust $T_{n,r}$ for its selected parent n_p based on the new experiences Ξ and the previous trust value $T_{n_p,r-1}$. The factor α decides how strong the new experiences are weighted compared to the previous ones (see Equations (3) and (4)). The initial trust value $T_{n,0}$ of every node is set to 0.5 (see Equation (2)).

$$T \in [0,1] \tag{1}$$

$$T_{n,0} := 0.5 \tag{2}$$

$$\Xi := \frac{\#\text{delivered}}{\#\text{sent}} \tag{3}$$

$$T_{n,r} := \begin{cases} \alpha \times T_{n,r-1} + (1-\alpha) \times \Xi & n = n_p \\ T_{n,r-1} & \text{otherwise} \end{cases} \tag{4}$$

When a node receives a DIO which starts a new TR, it will update the trust value for the current parent. We define an Objective Function (OF) which then uses this metric to select suitable parents. Initially, all nodes are equally trustworthy and the behaviour is equal to standard RPL with Objective Function OF0 according to RFC 6552 [17]. Every node increases its *rank* to be higher than those of the suitable parents. It then selects the best parent. If the trust value of the parent decreases, it will at some point no longer be considered as a good parent. The OF will select a better parent. Eventually, the node needs to adjust its *rank* to have more parents available.

5.4   Overhead

Sending additional information always causes overhead. However, we try to minimise the impact on power consumption. Therefore, we do not send additional packets to keep radio and CPU in power save mode as long as possible. Instead, we use existing messages which are sent anyway and add our data into the message. Additionally, we compress the data as much as possible: Since sequence number and TR are only two bytes they should fit inside the padding of most packets; in contrast, the DIOs which are sent by the *root* need an entry for every node in the network such that the amount of data is not negligible. One main concern is the size of IPv6 Addresses which are 16 bytes for every node. E.g. for a network with 400 nodes the DIO would grow to about 7 kB. However, most sensor networks use a common prefix for all nodes and we can exploit this to decrease the address size. We choose a prefix of 14 bytes, so, our addresses contain two bytes. Adding our one byte counter for the received packets, we result in a three byte entry per node. The resulting DIO for 300 nodes with about 1200 bytes still fits inside the standard MTU.

6   Evaluation

To measure the effectiveness of our approach, we implemented our RPL extension in *Contiki* [7] and ran simulations in *Cooja* [22]. *Cooja* allows us to use the same code which also runs on real hardware which similar restrictions to memory, cpu and radio. In this experiment, we set up a multi-hop sensor network with 26/27 *Tmote Sky* nodes (see Figure 1). Those sensor nodes run a Texas Instruments MSP430 microcontroller at 8 MHz. They control 10 kB of RAM and 48 kB of flash. Every node can reach its neighbours without packet loss to focus on malicious nodes only. We use a single DODAG in which nodes periodically send data to the *root*. When simulating broken or malicious nodes, we disable the forwarding of data packets. However, they still send out routing informations (i.e. DIOs), so, they remain inside the network. Indeed, routing information may be stale or wrong since RPL does not validate this information.

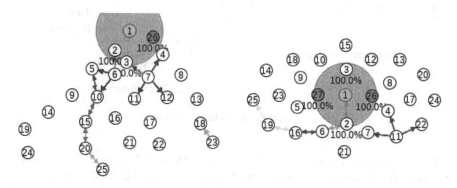

(a) Scenario A: One attacking node   (b) Scenario B: Two attacking nodes

Fig. 1. Evaluation scenarios with attackers coloured in red

To compare our approach with state-of-the-art RPL we consider three scenarios: first, we simulated an undisturbed scenario to compare our approach to standard RPL. This will be considered as the reference experiment later on. Second, we construct a scenario with one attacking node next to *root*. Only three nodes can reach *root* directly and one of those is malicious (see Figure 1a). To increase the attack, we provide a third scenario with two attackers next to *root*. They are two out of four nodes with direct link to *root* (see Figure 1b).

6.1   Undisturbed Case

In the undisturbed case we compare RAM, ROM and DIO size between our approach and the reference RPL implementation in *Contiki*. ROM and RAM usage is measured statically for the *Tmote Sky* build (see Figure 2a). Our implementation uses about 1.2 kB of additional ROM, which brings this particular sensor node to its limit. RAM is allocated at compile time and the usage increases by 1.6 kB, which is surprisingly high. The reason for this increase it that a Contiki node stores the last received DIO for every direct neighbour in RAM - even for neighbours which are not currently parents. Unfortunately, *Contiki* preallocates memory for every possible neighbour (maximal neigbour count is configurable; 20 is default for *Tmote Sky*) and we increased the size of DIOs by 65 bytes. However, a node only needs to remember the latest metric container and the memory usage could be reduced by optimising DIO storage.

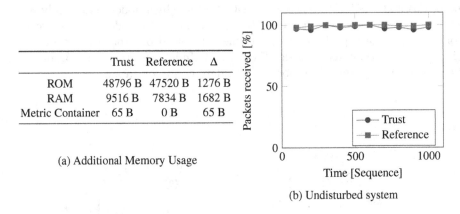

	Trust	Reference	Δ
ROM	48796 B	47520 B	1276 B
RAM	9516 B	7834 B	1682 B
Metric Container	65 B	0 B	65 B

(a) Additional Memory Usage

(b) Undisturbed system

Fig. 2. System in undisturbed case

We also compared the packet delivery rate between reference and our implementation. As shown in Figure 2b, both behave similarly. Minimal packet loss is happening in both cases and delivery rate is about 99%. However, in our implementation the delivery rate is slightly lower in simulation due to higher CPU usage and more radio inference due to bigger DIOs. In Future Work, we present some ideas to reduce the size of the DIOs to prevent this effect.

6.2   Under Attack

To evaluate our approach under attack we added one or two malicious nodes to the network (see layout in Figure 1). Those malicious nodes do not forward any data packets. However, they still send out RPL Routing packets so other nodes still may use them as parents. For both attacks we compare standard RPL with *rank* as metric and our implementation with Trust as metric. We placed attackers direct next to *root* to maximise their impact on the system.

In Scenario A with one attacker the reference implementation only achieves a delivery rate of constant 79% (see Figure 1a and 3a) This effect is caused by a single attacker which is one out of three nodes which can directly reach *root*. In contrast, our trust-enhanced RPL performs improves over time: At the beginning it reaches 86% delivery rate and eventually it recovers to over 99% deliver rate.

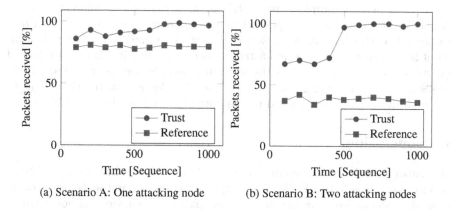

(a) Scenario A: One attacking node   (b) Scenario B: Two attacking nodes

Fig. 3. System under attack

We add a second attacker in Scenario B and repeat our measurements (see Figure 1b and 3b). In the reference experiment the delivery rate dropped to an average of 38,5%. About 60% of the nodes are unable to communicate with *root*. In comparison, our approach reaches a delivery rate of about 70% initially. After about 400 packets it improves to nearly 100%. The improvement happens quite abrupt because RPL requires nodes to change their *rank* if they do not have any suitable parents. However, the *rank* also influences the topology of the network and thereby the attackers move out of the routes for most nodes.

7   Discussion and Future Work

Our approach adds resilience against most kinds of attacks against RPL by verifying that packets actually reach their target. The routing will recover in case nodes are not forwarding packets correctly to the *root* by isolating broken or malicious elements. However, this produces some overhead which can be reduced. The sequence numbers added to every packet only account for very little additional data and can be neglected. Unfortunately, this does not hold for the list of sequence numbers in the DIO: first, depending on the count of nodes in the network, the size increases linearly; second, DIOs are resent by each node to all neighbours. So, if we consider transmitted bytes the amount increases at least quadratic by the count of nodes. Our approach to compress the length of the addresses reduces this effect.

To save more energy, the distribution of sequence numbers from *root* to all nodes should be optimised: RPL is able to build routes back from the *root* to all nodes, which can be used to distribute the sequence numbers. However, the Trust Round should stay inside the DIO to ensure that nodes can always determine the start of a new round. This allows them to notice when their parent intercepted the packet with sequence numbers and change the route.

We used a very simple trust metric to rate routes via different parents. Despite its effectiveness, this approach causes some unwanted side-effects: First, it does not matter how many packets were sent in a round. This makes the timing of the packets important and attackers can determine if it is save to discard a certain packet. Second, when the attacking node is very near to the *root*, it causes a cascade of routing changes because all nodes will switch the parent at the same time. This effect should be mitigated by a more advanced OF.

8 Conclusion

This paper introduced a novel approach to add reliability and End-to-End trust to Wireless Sensor Networks (WSNs). Typically, standard protocols for the operation of WSNs do not consider bad or even malicious behaviour of nodes which can be the result of an attack. Our approach is able to estimate the reliability of nodes during operation. Based on observing the behaviour, we establish End-to-End trust relationships that help to isolated malicious elements.

We evaluated the protocol by comparing the results to other related techniques. Thereby, we demonstrate that our approach is able to quickly isolate malicious elements with only low additional effort, since WSN nodes are typically characterised by restricted resources and low power supply. In current and future work, we are trying to improve the trust metric. The current approach utilised a simplified metric – taking the number of packets of a round into account will help to make it harder for the attacker to adapt to the protocol. Furthermore, we need techniques to avoid a cascading effects in route changes.

Acknowledgments. This research is partly funded by the research unit "OC-Trust" (FOR 1085) of the German Research Foundation (DFG).

References

1. Busching, F., Pottner, W., Brokelmann, D., Von Zengen, G., Hartung, R., Hinz, K., Wolf, L.: A demonstrator of the GINSENG-approach to performance and closed loop control in WSNs. In: 2012 Ninth International Conference on Networked Sensing Systems (INSS), pp. 1–2 (June 2012)
2. Büsching, F., Kulau, U., Wolf, L.: Architecture and evaluation of inga - an inexpensive node for general applications. In: 2012 IEEE Sensors, pp. 842–845. IEEE, Taipei, Taiwan (oct (2012)
3. Busching, F., Bottazzi, M., Pottner, W.B., Wolf, L.: DT-WBAN: Disruption tolerant wireless body area networks in healthcare applications. In: the International Workshop on e-Health Pervasive Wireless Applications and Services (eHPWAS 2013). Lyon, France (October 2013)
4. Castelfranchi, C., Falcone, R.: Trust Theory: A Socio-Cognitive and Computational Model, vol. 18. John Wiley & Sons (2010)
5. Clausen, T., Jacquet, P.: RFC3626 Optimized Link State Routing Protocol (OLSR) (2003)
6. Couto, D.S.J.D.: High-Throughput Routing for Multi-Hop Wireless Networks. Ph.D. thesis, Massachusetts Institute of Technology (2004)

7. Dunkels, A., Gronvall, B., Voigt, T.: Contiki - a lightweight and flexible operating system for tiny networked sensors. In: LCN 20'04 Proceedings of the 29th Annual IEEE International Conference on Local Computer Networks, pp. 455–462. IEEE Computer Society, Washington, DC, USA (2004)

8. Ganeriwal, S., Balzano, L.K., Srivastava, M.B.: Reputation-based Framework for High Integrity Sensor Networks. ACM Trans. Sen. Netw. **4**(3), 15:1–15:37 (2008)

9. Gnawali, O., Levis, P.: The Minimum Rank with Hysteresis Objective Function. RFC 6719 (Proposed Standard) (September 2012). http://www.ietf.org/rfc/rfc6719.txt

10. Guo, C., Zhong, L.C., Rabaey, J.: Low power distributed MAC for ad hoc sensor radio networks. In: GLOBECOM 2001 IEEE Global Telecommunications Conference, vol. 5, pp. 2944–2948 (2001)

11. IEEE: IEEE Standard for Local and metropolitan area networks- Part 15.4: Low-Rate Wireless Personal Area Networks (LR-WPANs) (2011)

12. Lazarescu, M.: Design of a WSN platform for long-term environmental monitoring for IoT applications. IEEE Journal on Emerging and Selected Topics in Circuits and Systems **3**(1), 45–54 (2013)

13. Leligou, N., Sarakis, L., Trakadas, P., Gay, V., Georouleas, K.: Design Principles of Trust-aware Routing Protocol supporting Virtualization (2011), Deliverable D4.1

14. O'Donovan, T., Brown, J., Büsching, F., Cardoso, A., Cecelio, J., do O, J., Furtado, P., Gil, P., Jugel, A., Pöttner, W.B., Roedig, U., sa Silva, J., Silva, R., Sreenan, C., Vassiliou, V., T. Voigt and, L.W., Zinonos, Z.: The GINSENG System for Wireless Monitoring and Control: Design and Deployment Experiences. ACM Transactions on Sensor Networks (TOSN) **10**(1) (November 2013)

15. Papadopoulos, G., Beaudaux, J., Gallais, A., Noel, T.: T-AAD: Lightweight traffic auto-adaptations for low-power MAC protocols. In: 2014 13th Annual Mediterranean Ad Hoc Networking Workshop (MED-HOC-NET), pp. 79–86 (June 2014)

16. Perkins, C., Royer, E.: Ad-hoc on-demand distance vector routing. In: Proceedings of the WMCSA 1999 Second IEEE Workshop on Mobile Computing Systems and Applications, pp. 90–100 (February 1999)

17. Thubert, P.: Objective Function Zero for the Routing Protocol for Low-Power and Lossy Networks (RPL). RFC 6552 (Proposed Standard) (March 2012). http://www.ietf.org/rfc/rfc6552.txt

18. Tomforde, S., Prothmann, H., Branke, J., Hähner, J., Mnif, M., Müller-Schloer, C., Richter, U., Schmeck, H.: Observation and Control of Organic Systems. In: Organic Computing - A Paradigm Shift for Complex Systems, pp. 325–338. Birkhäuser (2011)

19. Wang, Y., Vassileva, J.: Trust-Based Community Formation in Peer-to-Peer File Sharing Networks. In: Proc. on Web Intelligence, pp. 341–348 (September 2004)

20. Winter, T., Thubert, P., Brandt, A., Hui, J., Kelsey, R., Levis, P., Pister, K., Struik, R., Vasseur, J., Alexander, R.: RPL: IPv6 Routing Protocol for Low-Power and Lossy Networks. RFC 6550 (Proposed Standard) (March 2012). http://www.ietf.org/rfc/rfc6550.txt

21. Zhan, G., Shi, W., Deng, J.: Design and Implementation of TARF: A Trust-Aware Routing Framework for WSNs. IEEE Transactions on Dependable and Secure Computing **9**(2), 184–197 (2012)

22. Österlind, F.: A Sensor Network Simulator for the Contiki OS. Tech. rep, Swedish Institute of Computer Science (May 2006)

Anonymous-CPABE: Privacy Preserved Content Disclosure for Data Sharing in Cloud

S. Sabitha[1]([✉]) and M.S. Rajasree[2]

[1] Department of Computer Science and Engineering,
College of Engineering, Trivandrum, India
sabitha@cet.ac.in
[2] IIITM-K, Trivandrum, India
rajasree.ms@iiitmk.ac.in

Abstract. Healthcare Providers are widely using Cloud Computing to securely share Electronic Health Record(EHR). Entire EHR data cannot be disclosed to all the users with different privilege level, since it is more privacy sensitive. So Healthcare Provider has to enforce a privacy preserved access control mechanism to efficiently share EHR. Privacy preserved secure data sharing is one of the most challenging issues in cloud environment. Existing access control mechanisms for data sharing do not consider the privacy of individuals, who are the subjects of data which is being shared while preventing user revocation problem. To address these problems, we are proposing a novel idea in which, users whose attributes satisfy the access policy and access rights are effective in access time can recover the corresponding data. Proposed scheme is able to ensure security, integrity, privacy preserved fine-grained access control and prevent data mining attacks on shared data. Even though this paper focuses on EHR sharing, it can be generalized to privacy preserved data sharing.

Keywords: Cloud computing · Ciphertext-policy attribute-based encryption · Re-encryption · Anonymization

1 Introduction

Cloud computing is an emerging technological computing paradigm and a novel business model. It enables users to remotely store their data. Cloud providers are now claiming that cloud computing is in compliance with HIPAA(Health Insurance Portability and Accountability Act). Hence organizations are entrusting cloud providers [16] to host their sensitive data to the cloud. HIPAA was designed to protect the privacy of patient medical record and restrict access to the data, which are essential for healthcare industry. Healthcare industry now begins to migrate EHR and other data to the cloud due to its outstanding characteristics such as scalability, mobility and data sharing. Breach of medical record could lead to identity theft, which can destroy a person's finance, credit, reputation and violate privacy. So health care industry and professionals should take

© Springer International Publishing Switzerland 2015
L.M. Pinho et al. (Eds): ARCS 2015, LNCS 9017, pp. 146–157, 2015.
DOI: 10.1007/978-3-319-16086-3_12

care of maintaining security, privacy and access control for outsourced medical data in cloud. Major threat that hinders the wide adoption of cloud is the fear of losing privacy and security of the data stored on the cloud. Proper security mechanism not yet fully implemented in the cloud environment. It is still vulnerable to attacks. Thus privacy preserved data sharing becomes an important concern for cloud users.

Cryptographic methods are being used to ensure the security of data at rest and transit. In traditional cryptographic methods, only authorized users with decryption key would be able to recover data from an encrypted information [1], it cannot provide fine-grained access control and scalable user revocation. Data owner cannot exert any access control on the ciphertext. By the introduction of attribute based encryption, without knowing the exact identities of the recipient [2], data owner determines who can decrypt the data, then encrypt it using defined access policy. Recipients whose attributes satisfies the access policy would be able to decrypt the corresponding data. Hence we are proposing a novel idea to provide privacy preserved fine-grained access control for EHR sharing. Proposed system make use of CP-ABE [11,13] and K-anonymity to achieve fine-grained access control and privacy of EHR. User revocation problem is also resolved by proxy re-encryption.

The paper has been organized as follows. Section 1 gives the introduction and motivation for the proposed research work. Section 2 describes the related work relevant for data sharing and privacy preservation. System model discussed in Section 3. Proposed system described in section 4. Implementation and performance evaluation reviewed in section 5. Section 6 concludes the work and proposes the idea for future work.

2   Related Works

Losing privacy is one of the threat towards the wide adoption of cloud computing. Traditional way of data sharing among the requested users is either by symmetric or asymmetric cryptosystem in which security depends on the key used for encryption. Key compromise and absence of access control mechanism are the vulnerabilities exist in those types of cryptosystem. Following sections describe various data sharing and privacy preservation schemes for sensitive data.

2.1   Sharing of Encrypted Data

Kallahala et. al. [4] proposed a symmetric key cryptosystem to encrypt the data and protect it from untrusted server. Overall security only relies on key used for encryption. Key compromise leads to the unauthorized access to the encrypted data. Encryptor cannot decide what kind of receivers will be able to decrypt the information. Fine grained access control cannot be ensured by the symmetric key encryption. Number of Keys grows linearly with the number of file groups. Key management exerts more workload on the data owner. Goh el. al. [1] describes a combination of symmetric and public key cryptosystem. In order to recover the data, user has to get symmetric key by decrypting the message using his secret key. Main drawback of the system is that the number of Keys used in the system grows linearly with the number of users.

Identity of individual is disclosed to the public in Identity Based Encryption(IBE) [3]. This scheme is not able to preserve the privacy and fine-grained access control. Attribute based encryption is one of the solution for this problem. In Attribute Based Encryption(ABE) [2], Data Owner needs to use access policy to encrypt the information. Two variations of ABE are key-policy attribute-based encryption(KP-ABE) and ciphertext-policy attribute-based encryption (CP-ABE). Policies are built into the user's keys and attributes are used to encrypt the data in KP-ABE. Wang and Luo [17] proposes a constant sized ciphertext with KP-ABE scheme. Attributes are used to describe user's credentials, and data owner determines the policy on who can decrypt the data in CP-ABE. Key revocation problem still exists in CP-ABE.

HABE [7,10] is introduced to prevent the key revocation problem; once the user is revoked from the system, data owner should send proxy re-encryption (PRE) keys to the cloud service provider(CSP), then the CSP will be delegated to execute re-encryption. Data owner should be online to send the PRE keys is one of the problem to this approach. Delay in issuing PRE keys may cause security problems. In time based proxy re-encryption, each attribute of the user is associated with time to enable user's access right to be effective in a predetermined time and enable CSP to re-encrypt ciphertext automatically based on the time [9]. Time to be updated to renew the access right of the user.

2.2 Privacy Preservation

Health related data is highly sensitive and outsourcing it to the cloud is more prone to privacy violation. Disclosing a version of private data in its original form to all the requested users with various privilege level would violate the privacy of individuals who are the subjects of data stored in the shared document [8]. So healthcare provider has to guarantee the privacy of individual while maintaining the data practically useful [15]. Sweeney et. al. proposed K-anonymity [5] in which, information of a person contained in the release version of data cannot be distinguished from at least k-1 individuals whose information also appears in the release. It is achieved by make use of Quasi-Identifiers; attributes whose values when linked with external information can potentially identify an individual.

Ciphertext policy attribute based encryption is not able resolve the user revocation problem and not considering the privacy of individuals who are the subjects of data which is being shared. Anonymization can be used to preserve the privacy of data [6]. But it is not able to ensure security and access control of shared data. So we are proposing a novel idea to preserve the privacy of data and ensure access control, while sharing the data among the requested users. The scheme is also able to resolve the user revocation problem. It is achieved by combining CP-ABE with El-Gamal re-encryption. Privacy of shared data is achieved by K-anonymization technique. In the proposed system, CSP is delegated to re-encrypt and share data among the requested users.

3   System Model

Consider the scenario in which doctor, researcher, pharmaceutical company and insurance department needs same EHR which has been oursourced in the cloud. Doctor needs the data to prescribe the medicine. Researcher wants to analyze the rate of some contagious disease in some locality. Pharmaceutical company has to analyse the effect of certain drug to prevent disease and which can also be used for manufacturing drugs. Insurance department has to identify the patients to disburse the insurance claim. Sharing entire data to all communicating parties will adversely affect the privacy of an individual. According to this scenario, attributes which are more prone to privacy violation needs to be delinked from other information based on the privilege level of users while sharing the data among the authenticated users. Figure 1 describes the architecture of our proposed system, which guarantee fine-grained access control and privacy preservation on EHR data outsourced by the healthcare provider.

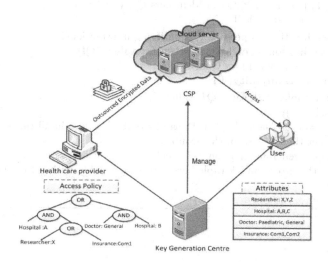

Fig. 1. System Architecture

4   Proposed Approach (Anonymous-CPABE)

Anonymous-CPABE allows healthcare provider to discloses data to the communicating agents only if their attributes satisfied with the access policy embedded in the message. It can also preserve the privacy of individuals by delinking the individual's identity from the sensitive attributes. The scheme is divided into three modules such as Optimized K-Anonymization, Fine-Grained Access Control and Re-encryption are described in the following sections.

4.1 Optimized K-Anonymization

We are adopting an optimized K-anonymization technique to delink the individual's identity from the sensitive attributes in the message. Anonymization of original data is done by the algorithm 1. In order to preserve the privacy of individual, personally identifying information(PII) is converted to an unidentified form by applying the hash function thereby delinking of PII from the sensitive attribute is achieved. In the proposed algorithm, anonymization is applied on each subgroup of k tuples, thereby efficiency is improved. By repeatedly applying generalization we are able to achieve k-anonymity without additionally including more number of tuples. Sample data shown in Table 1 describes the anonymization done by the healthcare provider using Optimized K-Anonymization algorithm.

Algorithm 1. Optimized K-Anonymization

Input: Table T, parameter k, Quasi Identifiers QI_i (i= 1 to n)
Output: k-anonymized table T'
1: Apply Hash function on personally identifying information(PII)
2: Apply generalization on each Quasi Identifier values (QI)
3: Perform K-Anonymity(T) on Quasi Identifiers
4: **Function K-Anonymity(T)**
   1: Group k tuples with same QI_i value
   2: **for** each group **do**
   3:   $QI' = QI$ - Discard QI_i with same attribute values in all tuples
   4:   Select the QI' within the group.
   5:   Apply generalization on QI' such that identifier values are generalized within the group and k-tuples are indistinguishable within the group based on QI.
   6: **end for**

Table 1. Original data and k-anonymized data (k=3)

	Key Atr.		Quasi Idfr.		Stv.Atr.		Key Atr.		Quasi Idfr.		Stv.Atr.
Idx	SSN	Name	Zipcode	Age	Disease	Idx	SSN	Name	Zipcode	Age	Disease
1	p100	Bob	47677	29	HIV	1	H(p100)	H(Bob)	476**	2*	HIV
2	p103	John	47602	27	Cancer	2	H(p103)	H(John)	476**	2*	Cancer
3	p110	Ancy	47678	47	Fever	3	H(p110)	H(Ancy)	476**	2*	Fever
4	p111	Julie	47909	53	Cancer	4	H(p111)	H(Julie)	479**	5*	Cancer
5	p113	Alice	47905	22	HIV	5	H(p113)	H(Alice)	479**	5*	HIV
6	p115	Wion	47906	36	Fever	6	H(p115)	H(Wion)	479**	5*	Fever

4.2   Fine-Grained Access Control

Healthcare provider determines access policy based on what kind of the recipient group is able to decrypt the shared data then anonymizes and encrypt the EHR by the decided policy and outsource it to the cloud. Key generation center(KGC) is responsible to distribute relevant keys required for data encryption and recipients' secret key. CP-ABE used for fine-grained access control over the shared data has 4 phases of execution such as Setup, KeyGen, Encrypt and Decrypt. Bilinear pairing is the basis of CP-ABE. Setup and KeyGen phases are executed by the trusted Key Generation Center(KGC). Encryption phase is executed by healthcare provider. Users are able to decrypt the message in Decrypt phase only if the attributes of users are satisfied with the access policy embedded in the cipher text.

Highly privileged users are authorized to get original data, so original data is encrypted using the access policy of the highly privilged recipient, which is the subset of the original access policy and re-encrypted data is made available only to those user by the proxy server. Information required for deanonymization is re-encrypted and shared by the proxy server to the user. User has to do the intersection of anonymized data and original encrypted data using the index of each tuple. Then replace anonymized data with original data. Only highly privileged user will get all the data in its original form. Personally identifying information will not be disclosed to lesser privileged user. Most of the users do not have the privilege to access the entire data in its original form, so that no need of deanonymization is required for those user groups.

4.3   El-Gamal Re-encryption

CP-ABE is still vulnerable to key revocation problem. In order to avoid this problem, El-Gamal re-encryption is performed on the EHR by the CSP to share the data among the requested users without the intervention of data owner. Message sequence chart of re-encryption of ciphertext is described in the figure 2. CSP is not be able to decrypt the data outsourced in the cloud, since it is encrypted using the CP-ABE by the specified access policy . Whenever user request data, proxy server re-encrypt the ciphertext using El-Gamal re-encryption key($RK_{A \to B}$). Key generation center is still responsible to distribute the re-encryption key($RK_{A \to B}$) to the proxy server. Genuineness of the user is verified at the key generation center by the shared symmetric key k and the time stamp shared in advance. Whenever the revoked user's request comes, KGC will not provide the re-encryption key to the proxy server to share the data. Thereby key revocation problem is resolved. Healthcare provider intervention is not needed to share the data among the requested users, so that workload exerted on the data owner is minimized. Otherwise data owner should be always online to share the data. Operations done on each agent is described as follows:

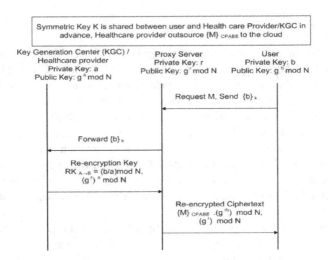

Fig. 2. Message Sequence Chart of El-Gamal Re-encryption

1. **Key Generation Center(KGC)**

   Setup, KeyGen and Re-encryption phase executes at KGC to distribute relevant keys. Let G_0 be a bilinear group of prime order p, g be a generator of G_0. Let $e : G_0 \times G_0 \to G_1$ denote a bilinear map.

   Setup(k) $\longrightarrow$ (PK, MK):- In Setup phase, KGC chooses public parameters (G_0, g, H, H_1) according to the security parameter k. Using public parameters and random exponents, it generates public key PK and master key MK. Health care provider make use of public key PK to encrypt the data to be shared and the master key MK is kept as secret to create the secret key for requested users.

   $$PK = (G_0, g, h = g^{\beta}, f = g^{1/\beta}, e(g,g)^{\alpha}), \quad MK = (\beta, g^{\alpha}) \qquad (1)$$

   KeyGen(PK, MK, S) $\longrightarrow$ SK:- Set of attributes S is used to authenticate a user u_t. KeyGen phase generates secret keys corresponding to the secret value r_t, $r_j \in_R Z_p^*$ where r_j is the random number corresponds to each attribute $j \in S$. It computes personalized secret key and a set of attribute keys for user u_t. Then secret key SK distributes to the requested user.

   $$SK_{u_t} = (D = g^{\frac{(\alpha + r_t)}{\beta}}, \forall j \in S : D_j = g^{r_t}.H(j)^{r_j}, D_j' = g^{r_j}) \qquad (2)$$

   Re-encryption(a, b) $\longrightarrow$ $(RK_{A \to B})$:- KGC generates and send re-encryption key $(RK_{A \to B})=(b/a)modN$ to the proxy server. where N is the large prime number, a is the healthcare provider private key, b is the user private key.

   $$(RK_{A \to B}) = (b/a)modN \qquad (3)$$

2. **Healthcare Provider**

   Healthcare Provider performs following operations and generates ciphertext corresponding to anonymized EHR based on access policy shown in the equation(4). Then outsource ciphertext $[M]_{CPABE}$ to the cloud and send $(g^r)^a modN$ to proxy server.

$$[M]_{CPABE} = (A, C', C, \forall y \in Y : C_y, C'_y) \quad \text{where}$$
$$C' = Me(g,g)^{\alpha s}, \ C = h^s, \ C_y = g^{q_y(0)}, \ C'_y = H(att(y))^{q_y(0)} \ . \tag{4}$$

(a) Encrypt(PK, M, A)$\longrightarrow [M]_{CPABE}$; where A- Access policy, M- EHR to be shared
(b) send $([M]_{CPABE}, (g^r)^a modN)$ to proxy server; where $g^r modN$ - public key of the proxy server, a and $g^a modN$ - private key and public key of healthcare provider

Access policy represented as access tree, which is to be embedded in the ciphertext for access control. Interior nodes of the tree is a threshold gates and leaf nodes are associated with attributes. Ciphertext is computed for the message M by giving the access structure A and the public key PK, which is described in algorithm 2. Let y be the set of leaf nodes in A.

Algorithm 2. Encrypt(PK, M, A)

1: **for** each node x in the *tree* from root node **do**
2:     Choose polynomial q_x
3:     set degree of polynomial $d_x = k_x - 1$, where $k_x = 1$ for OR gate and $k_x = num_x$ for AND gate
4: **end for**
5: Choose random $s \in Z_p$
6: **for** root node R **do**
7:     set $q_R(0) = s$
8: **end for**
9: C'= $Me(g,g)^{\alpha s}$; C = h^s
10: **for** all leaf nodes y in Y **do**
11:     $C_y = g^{q_y(0)}$; $C'_y = H(att(y))^{q_y(0)}$
12: **end for**

---

3. **Proxy Server**
Proxy server is used to re-encrypt and share the data to the requested users by using re-encryption key obtained from key generation center. Proxy server operations are listd below:
(a) Get re-encryption key from KGC: $(RK_{A \to B}) = (b/a) modN$
(b) Re-encrypt the ciphertext: $([M]_{CPABE} \cdot g^{ra})^{b/a})$
(c) send re-encrypted ciphertext to the requested user: $([M]_{CPABE} \cdot g^{rb}, g^r)$

4. **User**
Secret key b is made available only to the intended recipient so that he is able decrypt the re-encrypted ciphertext using the received g^r. Attributes of recipients' are to be satisfied with the access policy, to decrypt the data. Otherwise recursive DecryptNode algorithm returns a null and the corresponding user cannot decrypt the ciphertext. Decrypt operations are described by

---

Algorithm 3. Decrypt(PK, SK, $[M]_{CPABE}$)

1: DecryptNode($[M]_{CPABE}$, SK, y)
2: **if** access policy satisfied by S **then**
3:     $A = DecryptNode([M]_{CPABE}, SK, r) = e(g, g)^{rs}$
4:     $C' = M.e(g, g)^{\alpha s}; e(C, D) = e(g^{\beta s}, g^{\frac{(\alpha+r)}{\beta}})$
5:     $M = C'/(e(C, D)/A)$
6: **end if**
7: **Function DecryptNode($[M]_{CPABE}$, SK, y)**
    1: **for** each leaf node y **do**
    2:     set $j = att(y)$
    3:     **if** $j \in S$ **then**
    4:         DecryptNode $= \frac{e(D_j, C_x)}{e(D'_j, C'_x)} = \frac{e(g^{rt}.H(j)^{rj}, g^{q_y(0)})}{e(g^{rj}, H(j)^{q_y(0)})}$
    5:         return ($e(g, g)^{rq_y(0)}$)
    6:     **else**
    7:         return(null)
    8:     **end if**
    9: **end for**

---

algorithm 3. User performs the following operations to retrieve the original message. Proposed Anonymous-CPABE scheme can be efficiently utilized for sharing the information through the google drive. It provides the properties such as Scalability, Data Confidentiality, Fine-Grained Access Control, User Accountability, Collusion Resistant, Privacy Preservation and Resolve User Revocation Problem.

(a) Decrypt re-encrypted ciphertext and creates attribute-based ciphertext

$$[M]_{CPABE} = [M]_{CPABE}.g^{rb}/(g^r)^b \qquad (5)$$

(b) Decrypt $[M]_{CPABE}$ to obtain M; $C' = M.e(g, g)^{\alpha s}, A = e(g, g)^{rs}$

$$e(C, D) = e(g^{\beta s}, g^{\frac{(\alpha+r)}{\beta}}) = e(g, g)^{s(\alpha+r)} = e(g, g)^{\alpha s}.e(g, g)^{rs} \qquad (6)$$
$$M = C'/(e(C, D)/A)$$

5   Implementation and Performance Evaluation

All the experimentations are done on 2.2GHz intel core-i7 processor with 8GB of RAM running 32-bit Linux Kernel version 3.2.0. Proposed Anonymous-CPABE scheme implemented using CP-ABE tool kit and PBC library [14]. All pairing operations are done by the pbc library. The implementation uses a 160-bit elliptic curve group based on the supersingular curve $y^2 = x^3 + x$ over a 512-bit finite field.

Optimized K-anonymization algorithm anonymizes the data and thereby preserve the privacy of shared data. Then data is encrypted by deciding the access policy using CP-ABE. Healthcare provider outsource the EHR to the

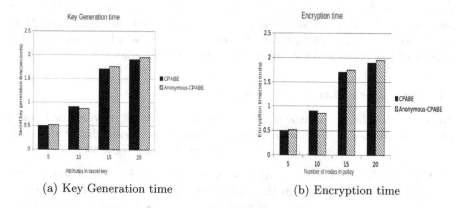

(a) Key Generation time   (b) Encryption time

Fig. 3. Performance of Anonymous-CPABE

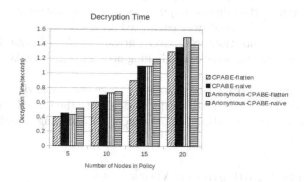

Fig. 4. Decryption time with various level of optimization

cloud. Whenever user request data, CSP re-encrypt the data using El-Gamal re-encryption by receiving the re-encryption key from the KGC. We have experimented the proposed system using 46MB census data. Cloud storage implemented using Openstack-Swift environment for the storage of data. The Proposed Anonymous-CPABE has been analyzed with the CP-ABE. Analysis has been done for key generation time, encryption time and decryption time on the basis of various policy attributes. Different optimization techniques has been tested for decryption. In all the cases system performs well as that of CP-ABE. Performance analysis is specified graphically. Figure 3(a) shows secret key generation time required by running CP-ABE KeyGen phase. It exerts workload only on KGC since it is executed at the KGC. Figure 3(b) displays encryption time required by running CP-ABE Encrypt phase, which is executed by the healthcare provider. Figure 4 describes decryption time for various access policy.

Decryption time has been analysed for various optimized algorithms. Decryption time for "naive" represents the time for running recursive DecryptNode algorithm and arbitrarily selecting nodes to satisfy each threshold gate. More optimized results are obtained for "flatten" algorithm, which reduces the final number of leaf nodes and thereby reduces the exponentiations.

5.1   Security of Encrypted Contents

Proposed data sharing scheme is provably secure and it can provide fine-grained access control, data confidentiality, integrity, and privacy in any distributed environment. Proposed system is also free from any data mining attacks.

1. **Fine-Grained Access Control-** Access control is maintained by the embedded access policy in the ciphertext. Since the CP-ABE is based on bilinear mapping and it is provably secure, it is infeasible to break the scheme. Nobody is able to modify/recreate the key required for maintaining access control.
2. **Data Confidentiality-** Encryption/Decryption is based on public/secret key generated by the bilinear mapping. So it is provably secure and infeasible to violate the confidentiality of encrypted data.
3. **Privacy-** Anonymization preserve the privacy of shared data. K-anonymity is able to prevent the attacks like linking attacks, which leads to the privacy violation.
4. **Data Mining Attack Prevention-** By make use of knowledge base, adversary is able to retrieve valuable information from the shared data. Since the shared data is encrypted and anonymized, data mining attack is also preventing.

6   Conclusion and Future Work

Anonymization technique preserve the privacy of shared data while disclosing the data to a set of users. This technique enables us to share the same data in different form to a set of users by delinking the sensitive information from the PII. CP-ABE allows the data owner to decide the access control mechanism for the message to be shared to a group of users. This mechanism can be efficiently utilized for fine-grained access control based data sharing in cloud environment. The shared data can be directly used for analysis and data mining. As a future work, we are trying to eliminate single point of vulnerability at the key generation center. Analyze the effect of outsourcing the decryption phase partially to the cloud. Then we have to elaborate the work by including security proof.

References

1. Goh, E.J., Shacham, H., Modadugu, N., Boneh, D.: Sirius: securing remote untrusted storage. In: Network and Distributed Systems Security Symposium (NDSS), pp. 131–145 (2003)

2. Goyal, V., Pandey, O., Sahai, A., Waters, B.: Attribute-based encryption for fine-grained access control of encrypted data. In: ACM Conference on Computer and Communications Security (CCS), pp. 89–98 (2006)

3. Green, M., Ateniese, G.: Identity-based proxy re-encryption. In: Katz, J., Yung, M. (eds.) ACNS 2007. LNCS, vol. 4521, pp. 288–306. Springer, Heidelberg (2007)

4. Kallahalla, M., Riedel, E., Swaminathan, R., Wang, Q., Fu, K.: Plutus: scalable secure file sharing on untrusted storage. In: USENIX Conference on File and Storage Technologies (FAST), pp. 29–42 (2003)

5. Sweeney, L.: k-Anonymity: A Model for Protecting Privacy. International Journal on Uncertainty, Fuzziness and Knowledge-Based Systems **10**(5), 557–570 (2002)

6. Sedayao, J.: Enhancing cloud security using data anonymization. Intel white paper on Cloud computing and information security, June 2012

7. Wang, G., Liu, Q., Wu, J.: Hierarchical attribute-based encryption for fine-grained access control in cloud storage services. In: ACM Conference on Computer and Communications Security (CCS), pp. 735–737 (2010)

8. Gentry, C., Silverberg, A.: Hierarchical ID-based cryptography. In: Zheng, Y. (ed.) ASIACRYPT 2002. LNCS, vol. 2501, pp. 548–566. Springer, Heidelberg (2002)

9. Liu, Q., Wang, G., Wu, J.: Time-based proxy re-encryption scheme for secure data sharing in a cloud environment. Information Sciences, pp. 355–370 (2014)

10. Wang, G., Liu, Q., Wu, J., Guo, M.: Hierarchical attribute-based encryption and scalable user revocation for sharing data in cloud servers. Computers and Security **30**(5), 320–331 (2011)

11. Bethencourt, J., Sahai, A., Waters, B.: Ciphertext-policy attribute-based encryption. In: IEEE Symposium on Security and Privacy, pp. 321–334 (2007)

12. Boneh, D., Boyen, X., Goh, E.-J.: Hierarchical identity based encryption with constant size ciphertext. In: Cramer, R. (ed.) EUROCRYPT 2005. LNCS, vol. 3494, pp. 440–456. Springer, Heidelberg (2005)

13. Ostrovsky, R., Sahai, A., Waters, B.: Attribute-based encryption with non-monotonic access structures. In: ACM Conference on Computer and Communication Security, pp. 195–203 (2007)

14. The Pairing-Based Cryptography Library (2012). http://crypto.stanford.edu/pbc/

15. Fung, B.C.M., Wang, K., Chen, R., Yu, P.S.: Privacy Preserving Data Publishing: A Survey of Recent Developments. ACM Computing Surveys 42(4), Article 14 June (2010)

16. Jansen, W., Grance, T.: Guidelines on Security and Privacy in Public Cloud Computing. NIST Special Publication, December (2011)

17. Wang, C-J., Luo, J.F.: A Key-policy Attribute-based Encryption Scheme with Constant Size Ciphertext. In: 8th International Conference on Computational Intelligence and Security, pp. 447–451, November (2012)

Best Paper Session

A Synthesizable Temperature Sensor on FPGA Using DSP-Slices for Reduced Calibration Overhead and Improved Stability

Christopher Bartels$^{(\boxtimes)}$, Chao Zhang,
Guillermo Payá-Vayá, and Holger Blume

Institute of Microelectronic Systems,
Leibniz University of Hanover, Hanover, Germany
{bartels,czhang,guipava,blume}@ims.uni-hannover.de

Abstract. Current research on synthesizable temperature sensors, using the reconfigurable logic of the FPGA to measure temperature anywhere on the FPGA, ueses an oscillating, temperature dependent route on the FPGA. These LUT-based routes require a complex calibration process and have a large footprint on the die. The proposed synthesizable temperature sensor uses DSP-slices to reduce the calibration overhead and the footprint as well. The sensor can achieve a resolution of up to 0.12°C, depending on configuration. A sample rate of up to 1040 samples per second is feasible, in the fastest configuration. The sensor was evaluated and compared. The sensor is more stable, easier to calibrate and features a smaller footprint. This allows a higher density of temperature sensors than before. It uses 45 FF, 69 LUTs, 6 Shift-Registers (SRL32) and 4 DSP-slices to realize a fully digital, synthesizable temperature sensor, including a calibration circuit, a reading circuit and a buffer structure to save multiple data samples.

Keywords: FPGA · Temperature sensors · Routing · LUTs · DSP-slices

1 Introduction

Temperature sensors are used in many integrated circuits. Apart from providing temperature data, they are also used as safety guard to prevent irreversible and functional failures. The power dissipation can also be estimated using these sensors. A circuit with a high temperature drives a higher current than the same circuit at a lower temperature, therefore, the power dissipation is temperature dependent. While miniaturisation moves forward and integrated circuits become even smaller, power dissipation becomes a more and more important issue. By observing the temperature, parts of the FPGA could be dynamically reconfigured to reduce the power dissipation. For example, the clock could be adjusted in hotter parts, creating locale, temperature dependent frequency variations.

The temperature sensors should produce a minimal dissipation loss themselves, ensuring the energy saved by dynamically reconfiguring the FPGA, is

© Springer International Publishing Switzerland 2015
L.M. Pinho et al. (Eds): ARCS 2015, LNCS 9017, pp. 161–172, 2015.
DOI: 10.1007/978-3-319-16086-3_13

greater than the dissipation loss by the sensors. Analysing hotter and colder parts of the FPGA requires a complete temperature profile. The temperature sensors should be evenly distributed over the FPGA to measure the temperature profile more accurately. Most commercially available FPGAs feature only a single temperature sensor in the middle of the die, which is not enough for a complete temperature profile. To distribute as many temperature sensors as possible on the die, the sensors should be very small. The temperature sensor should therefore use only few resources, to minimize the power loss and reduce the footprint, the required physical area on the FPGA. In this paper, a fully digital, synthesizable temperature sensor is presented. A comprehensive evaluation is shown and the sensor is compared to other FPGA-based temperature sensors. In section 2, related work is presented. Section 3 discusses the proposed temperature sensor design in detail. In section 4, an evaluation is shown, including evaluation environment and the implemented sensor types used. Section 5 concludes this work.

2   Related Work

Many integrated circuits feature onboard temperature sensors, the most common type being the band-gap sensor. The sensor type is based on band-gap reference voltage circuits, like the Brokaw band-gap reference, for example [1]. For example, one of these sensors is integrated in the center of the Virtex 6 FPGA on the Xilinx ML605 Development Board [2], which is used during the evaluation. These sensors are very low-cost and need only a couple of bipolar transistors. The sensors also provide an accurate measurement without extensive calibration, but their position is fixed during fabrication. Unfortunately, there is only one of these sensors available on most FPGAs impeding the implementation of a spatial temperature profile.

To measure a spatial temperature profile, flexible temperature sensors are needed. It should be possible to realize the sensors anywhere on the FPGA. For this purpose, the reconfigurable logic on the FPGA can be used. Chen et al. proposed a fully digital time domain sensor which can be implemented on the reconfigurable logic available in typical commercial FPGA devices [3]. The basic design is shown in Fig. 1. This sensor implements a delay line, which consists of several cascaded logic elements. Without any registers in between, the route starts to oscillate. The number of oscillations in a given time-frame, in this context called cycles, is proportional to temperature. By counting these cycles, a temperature sensor can be realized anywhere on the FPGA. The design must be calibrated every time the design is synthesized because of the routing algorithms in current EDA tools.

Syed et al. proposed a calibration circuit and a different delay line, using LUTs instead of cascaded logic blocks [4]. This sensor needs even fewer resources than the proposed design by Chen et al, the overall structure is shown in Fig. 2. The sensor uses look-up tables for the delay line, but the slices and LEs between these LUTs must not be used. The resource cost is therefore much higher due to

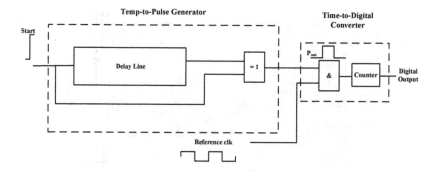

Fig. 1. Basic temperature sensor structure [3]

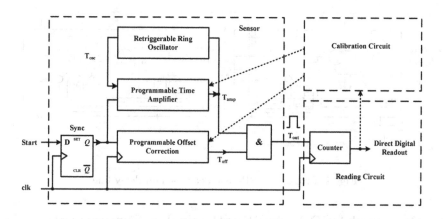

Fig. 2. Look-up table based temperature sensor structure [4]

the unused LUTs. One sensor configuration in [4] needs 16 slices horizontally and 40 slices vertically, blocking 640 slices by allocating just ten LUTs. The width and height of the delay line can be configured, but this has a direct impact on the resolution, accuracy and sampling frequency [4]. The last part of this sensor design, the calibration circuit, transforms the measured cycles into temperature, but an initial calibration is still needed.

Ring oscillator structures for temperature sensors are currently state-of-the-art, using either logic delay or LUTs [3–9]. Both variants provide a high degree of flexibility. The main problem with these sensors is the high overhead for calibration due the high variance in routing each time a bitstream is generated. The LUT approach has, compared to the used resources, a rather large footprint, rendering it less useful. A new sensor should reduce the effort on calibration and provide a small footprint, blocking less logical units. This paper proposes a temperature sensor based on DSP-slices instead of LUTs to match these requirements.

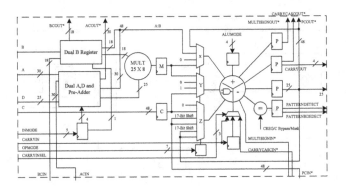

Fig. 3. DSP48E1 slice, taken from [11]

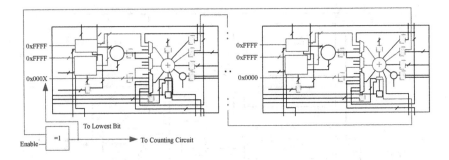

Fig. 4. Proposed DSP-based carry-chain delay line

3   Proposed DSP-Based Synthesizable Temperature Sensor

The main reason for the instability and therefore the need for an extended calibration, are the routing algorithms of current EDA tools like the Xilinx ISE Suite. While it is possible to constrain the placement of the implemented logic blocks, the routing itself can't be directly constrained. DSP-slices are pre-routed for maximum performance and minimal dissipation loss. The routing inside the slices can't diversify because it is set prior to production. The proposed design uses multiple cascaded DSPs to create a time-domain temperature sensor similar to [3] and [4]. The design is nearly identical to Syed et al., but exchanges the LUTs with DSP-slices. The design was implemented on a Xilinx ML605 development board, featuring a Virtex 6 FPGA [10]. The Virtex 6 series FPGA features vertical rows of DSP-slices, each DSP is connected to the DSP above and below with a minimum of routing. Each DSP can be configured individually by a number of configuration registers [11]. By utilizing this structure, the degree of freedom in the routing is reduced, which results in a higher degree of stability and performance.

Fig. 3 shows one DSP48E1 slice; these were used in the design of this sensor. It is possible to deactivate all registers in the DSP-slice. Most inputs and outputs of the DSP slice are not used and all internal registers are deactivated. Since a cascade of DSP-slices is used for the delay line, each slice is connected to the next one via the CARRYCASCIN and CARRYCASCOUT signal ports. This carry-chain is depicted in Fig. 4. Each slice uses three inputs, A, B and C. While A and B are driven completely by logical high levels, C is driven by logical low levels. By connecting the lowest bit of port C of the first DSP-slice to the enable bit, it is possible to generate a carry-out signal for the following steps of the cascade. It is not possible to connect the CARRYCASCIN of the lowest DSP-slice to the enable signal, due to routing and configuration restrictions.

An XOR gate is connected to this cascade and the enable signal. The output of this gate is connected to the last bit at signal port C of the first DSP in the carry chain. The carry-out signal of the last DSP-slice is fed to the clock port of a counter circuit and also back to the XOR gate. When the carry-out signal from the last DSP reaches the XOR gate, it is inverted as long as the enable signal is still driving a logical high level. The logical low level, which is now driven through the carry-chain, generates no carry-out signal, which is also inverted, as long as the enable signal is still driving a high level. This continues as long as the enable signal is still driving a high signal. Each time the delay line generates a rising edge this way, the number of counted cycles is increased. Because of the temperature dependency, the number of counted cycles is higher when the temperature is high and vice versa. By using a basic counter to count down from a pre-defined value, the enable signal can be set at high, Ensuring fixed time intervals for each measurement performed. The counting circuit is identical to [4].

This design also reduces the footprint of the proposed temperature sensor. The minimum number of needed DSP-slices is four. The combinatorial delay generated by each DSP-slice depends on the speed grade of the FPGA. The delay ranges from 1.64 ns up to 2.6 ns. Since the system clock is set to 100 MHz, four cascaded slices generate a combinatorial delay of at least 6.56 ns up to 10.4 ns. Less DSP slices would also oscillate, but the shift-register, which counts the oscillations, couldn't keep up [12]. The design was successfully tested with up to 10 DSP slices, but could be expanded to use up more. The number of DSP-slices affects resolution and sampling rate and is covered in the following section.

4   Evaluation

4.1   Emulation Environment and Climate Chamber

The evaluation was performed in an automatic climate chamber to provide a stable and reproducible environment for testing. The climate chamber and the ML605 inside are depicted in Fig. 5. The climate chamber can drive temperatures as low as -40 °C up to 180 °C while controlling the humidity. For each test, the same temperature range was driven, starting with 10 °C up to 40 °C room temperature whilst the humidity was held for stable at 40%. The temperature

Fig. 5. The device under test inside the climate machine

rose in steps of 0.5 °C. The temperature was hold a moment after reaching the set value before the actual measuring took place, to let the temperature propagate properly. After collecting at least 5000 samples, the temperature was increased again. Each temperature curve was driven multiple times to eliminate measurement error as much as possible.

To evaluate the proposed sensor, it was integrated in an emulation framework. The framework offers modules for memory access, a Master/Slave bus interface and Ethernet register transfer to name a few. The sensor was integrated in the framework as a module. A hardware monitor module [13] was instantiated, which accesses the on-board temperature sensor and provides a reference temperature for each measurement. The result of each sensor and the reference temperature is stored in a central register structure which can be accessed via Ethernet by a PC client.

The temperature increase has an impact on the current, therefore the effect on power, voltage and current should be monitored as well. To measure this effect, a USB interface adapter by Texas Instrument was used [14]. The results were calculated in the same way as the temperature samples, using at least 5000 samples per temperature step to minimize the measurement error.

4.2   Implemented Sensor Types

To validate the proposed approach, the design by Syed et al. [4] was used as a reference. In total, 16 sensors were placed on the FPGA in a grid, each sensor using 10 LUTs for the delay line. This design was evaluated for multiple configurations, including different amounts of shift registers in the divider and different word lengths in the integrator. The design was evaluated on three Xilinx ML605 evaluation boards, featuring the same hardware specifications. These boards were selected for comparability reasons and to evaluate the impact of fabrication differences. The results of this evaluation are not in the scope of this document. The configuration chosen for the evaluation offers an acceptable

a) Reference Sensor Design [4]

b) DSP-based sensor (10 DSP-slices)

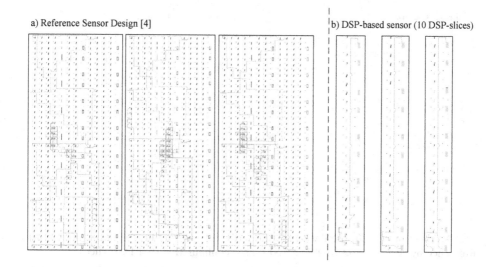

Fig. 6. Routing variations of the same design on the same FPGA; a) Reference by Syed [4] and b)DSP-based sensor configured with 10 DSP-slices

trade-off between accuracy and sampling rate. To compare both sensors objectively, the same amount of sensor modules were implemented. In total, 16 sensors were instantiated evenly on the FPGA and evaluated. These proposed sensors were placed in the same physical regions on the FPGA as the referenced sensors. The use-cases for the evaluation differ for the number of used DSP slices, ranging from four to ten. This design was also evaluated on the same three ML605 evaluation boards.

4.3   Evaluation and Comparison

The routing differences between both designs were evaluated. Fig. 6 shows the differences due to the routing algorithms of the EDA tools. The graphs were created with the FPGA Editor by Xilinx. For better viewing, the images were inverted afterwards. The routing from the delay line can be seen highlighted in blue. Fig. 6 a) shows the sensor by Syed et al., Fig.6 b) shows the proposed DSP-based sensor. The routing is shown for the same design, but for different synthesis runs. Additional to these global differences, local routing variances for the same design can be observed as well. The sensor by Szed et al. shows a higher deviation, compared to the proposed DSP-sensor.

Since the hardware monitor module was used as a golden reference, the error of this sensor must be noted as well. The sensor uses an analogue-to-digital converter with a precision of 0.5 °C. The temperature sensor has a maximum measurement error of 4 °C over a range of -40 °C to 125 °C [13].

Fig. 7a) shows the results of the temperature sensor by Syed et al. [4]. The depicted mean values were calculated by multiple measurement runs as described

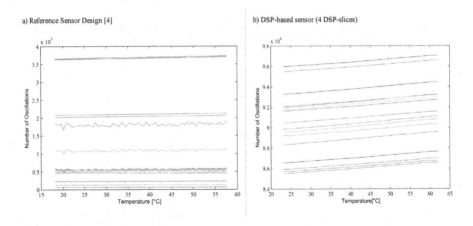

Fig. 7. Mean number of oscillations for 16 individual sensors in a given timeframe; a) Reference by Syed [4] and b)DSP-based sensor configured with 4 DSP-slices

before and at least 5000 samples per measured temperature. The x-axis depicts the temperature, the y-axis shows the number of oscillations per given time-frame. This time-frame is defined by a counter, driven by the regular clock. This results in a sampling frequency of 250 samples per second for the evaluation. The counter can be modified and the maximum sample rates are presented later on. Fig. 7b) shows the mean values of each sensor configured with 4 DSP-slices. All sensors with the proposed DSP-structure have nearly identical gradients, but an offset which differs. This offset varies and depends mainly on the number of used DSP-slices. A shorter delay line results in a higher oscillation count per measured segment. Compared to the sensor by Syed et al., lower offset values can be seen.

To compare the values to each other, the gap between the highest and lowest value is used as an indicator. A wide gap is an indication for instability and displays the need for a two point calibration to accurately measure the gradient for the fitting curve. The gap in Fig. 7a) ranges from 6729 to 365980, a factor of 54.39. The gap pictured in Fig. 7b) ranges from 85527 to 95977, which is a factor of 1.12. The width of this gap varies, depending on board and sensor type. For the referenced sensor the factor for this gap ranges from 52.97 to 55.63, while the factor for the proposed sensor ranges from 1.05 to 2.24. The proposed sensor shows smaller gaps and is therefore more stable, even with longer delay paths.

Fig.8b) shows the gradients for the referenced sensor by Syed et al., Fig.8b) shows the gradients of the proposed sensor design. The x and y-axes represent the relative position on the FPGA, while the z-axis represents the gradient for each sensor. The colours bear no meaning and are only for ease of viewing.

The instability at the referenced sensor can be observed very clearly, each sensor should have roughly the same gradient. Instead, some sensors have huge gradients, while others have very low gradients. By measuring only one sensor and applying the resulting calibration on every sensor, huge errors would be

a) Reference Sensor Design [4]   b) DSP-based sensor (4 DSP-slices)

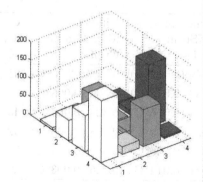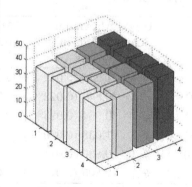

Fig. 8. Gradient for each sensor on the FPGA; a) Reference by Syed [4] and b)DSP-based sensor configured with 4 DSP-slices

introduced into the measurement. This graphical representation of the proposed design shows no significant hotspot, but individual sensors with slightly different gradients. High offsets and gradients are not necessarily at the same position on the FPGA. The highest offset can be found in sensor (4,4) while the lowest is in sensor (1,4); the highest gradient is in sensor (3,4), while the lowest is in sensor (4,1) for example. The values for gradient and offset are not coupled. The highest offset can always be found in the same physical region of the same FPGA, regardless of design differences, but constant with used board. This makes calibration even more important. The difference on each gradient is small and by inducing a small error, it is possible to calibrate each sensor by measuring only one sensor and using the data for each sensor.

The same bitstream produced different results on the three available boards, which can be seen in Table 1. As the boards and the FPGAs have the the same specifications, these differences are due to the manufacturing process. A higher number of DSP-slices reduce the gap between the maximum and the minimum root mean square error, the sensor gets more stable with increasing DSP-slice count. A longer delay line results in a longer oscillating path and therefore fewer oscillations in the same given time-frame.

The equivalence between sampling rate, resolution and accuracy per °C depends on the length of the delay line and can be seen in Table 2. The table lists much larger resource requirements than the original paper by Syed et al. This is due to an included buffer structure. This buffer structure stores the last temperature samples to provide temporal temperature information. The sensor evaluation is shown for 4, 5, 6, 7 and 10 DSP slices. Regarding resolution, the sensor is theoretically better than other research. Realistically, this value must be greater or equal to 0.5 due to the on-board temperature sensor. The accuracy was calculated by analysing the residuals of the mean values of each sensor. The mean values were fitted using a two point calibration. Afterwards, the

Table 1. Overview sensor configuration vs root mean square error on three different Xilinx ML605 boards

Sensor Configu- ration	Used Board	Maximum RMSE in Cycles	Minimum RMSE in Cycles	Difference Max/Min in Cycles	Cycles per °C
4 DSP	# 1	1.284 (0.042°C)	0.508 (0.017°C)	0.776 (0.025°C)	31
5 DSP	# 1	0.842 (0.022°C)	0.536 (0.014°C)	0.306 (0.008°C)	38
6 DSP	# 1	0.964 (0.023°C)	0.634 (0.015°C)	0.329 (0.008°C)	43
7 DSP	# 1	1.038 (0.020°C)	0.629 (0.012°C)	0.408 (0.008°C)	52
10 DSP	# 1	0.839 (0.011°C)	0.450 (0.006°C)	0.389 (0.005°C)	76
Syed et.al.	# 1	0.805 (0.016°C)	0.681 (0.014°C)	0.125 (0.003°C)	49
4 DSP	# 2	0.801 (0.019°C)	0.522 (0.013°C)	0.279 (0.007°C)	42
5 DSP	# 2	1.138 (0.023°C)	0.786 (0.016°C)	0.352 (0.007°C)	51
6 DSP	# 2	0.806 (0.014°C)	0.544 (0.010°C)	0.262 (0.005°C)	57
7 DSP	# 2	0.680 (0.010°C)	0.532 (0.008°C)	0.148 (0.002°C)	68
10 DSP	# 2	0.614 (0.007°C)	0.420 (0.005°C)	0.194 (0.002°C)	84
Syed et.al.	# 2	0.920 (0.020°C)	0.705 (0.015°C)	0.217 (0.005°C)	47
4 DSP	# 3	2.345 (0.057°C)	1.942 (0.047°C)	0.403 (0.010°C)	42
5 DSP	# 3	2.598 (0.056°C)	2.166 (0.047°C)	0.432 (0.009°C)	47
6 DSP	# 3	2.822 (0.053°C)	2.396 (0.045°C)	0.426 (0.008°C)	54
7 DSP	# 3	2.806 (0.045°C)	2.489 (0.040°C)	0.318 (0.005°C)	63
10 DSP	# 3	2.867 (0.038°C)	2.520 (0.034°C)	0.349 (0.005°C)	75
Syed et.al.	# 3	1.793 (0.027°C)	1.399 (0.021°C)	0.394 (0.006°C)	67

maximum and minimum values for these residuals were analysed. The presented values show the worst case, classified by the largest gap between minimum and maximum residual. The last column shows the maximum number of possible samples. This value decreases with increasing DSP-slice count, due to the longer delay line.

Finally, the power dissipation of the FPGA was monitored in the climate chamber as well. An adapter by Texas Instruments was used to evaluate the power dissipation [14]. This adapter reads available registers on the FPGA. These registers store information from on-chip sensors, including Voltage, Current and many more. Table 3 summarizes the results of the measurements. The current rose about ten percent, while the voltage didn't change much. The additional current was expected, due to the temperature dependency of the transistors on the FPGA. Overall, an additional power dissipation of about nine percent can be noticed over a span of 30°C. Compared to each other, there was no significant increase in power due to replacing the LUT-based temperature sensors with the DSP-based temperature sensors.

Table 2. Overview synthesizable sensor design configurations

Sensor Configuration	Used Resources	Resolution [°C]	Accuracy [°C][1]	Samples per sec[1]
[3]	140 LE	0.06	-1.5 to 0.8	3000
[5]	48 LE	0.13	-0.7 to 0.6	4400
[4]	7 FFs, 16 6-LUTs, 7 SRL32	0.5	0.5	1000
From [4] [2]	42 FFs, 74 6-LUTs, 6 SRL32	0.021	±1.0	869
4 DSP[2]	45 FF, 69 6-LUTs, 6 SRL32, 4 DSP-Slices	0.032 [1]	-1,16 to 1,15	1040
5 DSP[2]	45 FF, 69 6-LUTs, 6 SRL32, 5 DSP-Slices	0.026 [1]	-0,48 to 1,22	879
6 DSP[2]	45 FF, 69 6-LUTs, 6 SRL32, 6 DSP-Slices	0.018 [1]	-0,36 to 0,87	754
7 DSP[2]	45 FF, 69 6-LUTs, 6 SRL32, 7 DSP-Slices	0.015 [1]	-0,70 to 0,82	671
10 DSP[2]	45 FF, 69 6-LUTs, 6 SRL32, 10 DSP-Slices	0.012 [1]	-0,49 to 0,78	517

[1] Worst Case

[2] Includes the buffer structure and the calibration circuit

Table 3. Power analysis with different temperatures

Sensor Configuration	Current [A] @55°C	Current [A] @25°C	Voltage [V] @55°C	Voltage [V] @25°C	Power [W] @55°C	Power [W] @25°C
4 DSP	2.0104	1.8128	1.0185	1.0172	2.0155	1.8525
5 DSP	1.9777	1.7813	1.0185	1.0175	2.0198	1.8674
6 DSP	2.026	1.8426	1.0181	1.0175	2.0491	1.8963
7 DSP	1.998	1.837	1.0188	1.0176	2.0362	1.8789
10 DSP	2.0043	1.8098	1.0247	1.0224	2.0539	1.8555
Syed et.al.	1.8799	1.6992	1.0212	1.0205	1.9289	1.7383

5 Conclusion

The proposed sensor uses a configurable amount of DSP-slices to implement a stable and easy to calibrate temperature sensor on a FPGA. Using DSP-slice-based routing showed improved stability, with smaller gaps in oscillation counts compared to LUT-based routing, making calibration more easy. The accuracy of the proposed sensor is about the same as other research; the resolution proves to be better than LUT-based temperature sensors. The sensor has acceptable hardware requirements, using 45 FF, 69 6-LUT, 6 SRL32 and a varying number of DSP-slices. These hardware resources can be packed more densely compared to other research and include a buffer structure. The power analysis with the measurement tool by Texas Instrument showed no significant increase or decrease in power dissipation.

References

1. Paul Brokaw, A.: A simpe three-terminal ic bandgap reference. IEEE Journal of Solid-State Circuits (1974)
2. Xilinx: ML605 Hardware User Guide, October 2012
3. Chen, P., Shie, M.-C., Zheng, Z.-Y., Zheng, Z.-F., Chu, C.-Y.: A fully digital time-domain smart temperature sensor realized with 140 fpga logic elements. IEEE Transactions On Circuits And Systems (2007)
4. Ha, Y., Veeravalli, B., Syed, R., Zhao, W.: A low overhead temperature sensor for self-aware reconfigurable platforms. In: Self-Awareness in Reconfigurable Computing 2012 (2012)
5. Chen, P., Chen, S.-C., Shen, Y.-S., Peng, Y.-J.: All-digital time-domain smart temperature sensor with an inter-batch inaccuracy of -0.7c -+0.6c after one-point calibration. IEEE Transactions On Circuits And Systems (2011)
6. Lopez-Buedo, S., Garrido, J., Boemo, E.: Dynamically inserting, operating, and eliminating thermal sensors of fpga-based systems. IEEE Transactions On Components And Packaging Technologies (2010)
7. Boemo, E., Lopez-Buedo, S.: Thermal monitoring on FPGAs using ring-oscillators. In: Luk, W., Cheung, P.Y.K., Glesner, M. (eds.) FPL 1997. LNCS, vol. 1304, pp. 69–78. Springer, Heidelberg (1997)
8. León Franco, J.J., Boemo, E.: Ring oscillators as thermal sensors in fpgas: experiments in low voltage. In: Programmable Logic Conference (SPL) (2010)
9. Zick, K.M., Hayes, J.P.: On-line sensing for healthier fpga-systems. In: Proceedings of the 18th Annual ACM/SIGDA International Symposium on Field Programmable Gate Arrays (2010)
10. Xilinx: Virtex 6 FPGA Configuration User Guide, November 2013
11. Xilinx: Virtex 6 FPGA DSP48E1 Slice User Guide, February 2011
12. Xilinx: Virtex 6 FPGA Data Sheet: DC and Switching Characteristics, May 2014
13. Xilinx: Virtex 6 FPGA System Monitor User Guide, June 2010
14. Texas Instruments: USB Interface Adapter Evaluation Module User's Guide, August 2006

Virtualized Communication Controllers in Safety-Related Automotive Embedded Systems

Dominik Reinhardt[✉], Maximilian Güntner, and Simon Obermeir

BMW AG, Munich, Germany
{dominik.reinhardt,maximilian.guentner,simon.obermeir}@bmw.de

Abstract. Meeting non-functional requirements, like safety according to ISO26262, is gaining rising importance in the automotive industry along with the reuse and migration of existing applications. Embedded virtualization is a promising technology to isolate software and its possible faults. In a virtualized system shared communication devices constitute a bottleneck and require special treatment for safety-related systems.

In this paper, we evaluate the emulation of CAN and Ethernet hardware drivers in virtualized automotive software systems of BMW. We show a methodology how to relocate and isolate safety-related drivers within a large scale software integrated virtualized system. For our analysis we use the Infineon AURIX TriCore TC27x controller. To encapsulate our software, we use a research-based hypervisor supported by ETAS Ltd.

Keywords: Automotive · Embedded multicore · Embedded hypervisor · Virtualization · Emulated communication controller · CAN · Ethernet

1 Introduction

In the next decade, many new features and technologies, like Advanced Driver Assistant Systems (ADAS), will be integrated in our cars [3], [4]. The trend to develop bigger and more complex software systems on capable Electronic Control Units (ECUs) is rising. To tackle such always increasing amount of vehicle functionality, Electric and Electronic (E/E) architectures, using the example of BMW [12], were reordered in a domain-oriented manner. To reduce the amount of ECUs, automotive software is consolidated onto comprehensive hardware platforms. This methodology is illustrated in figure 1 and is called Large Scale Software Integration (LSSI) [12].

Virtualization technology could be a proper methodology to integrate software components in a transparent and flexible way, protected from each other [12], [14]. To be prepared for safety-related systems, the ISO26262 demands freedom from interference between vehicle software and functionality [8]. The isolation features between Virtual Machines (VMs) could achieve that requirement

© Springer International Publishing Switzerland 2015
L.M. Pinho et al. (Eds): ARCS 2015, LNCS 9017, pp. 173–185, 2015.
DOI: 10.1007/978-3-319-16086-3_14

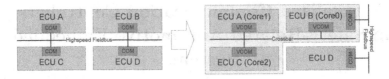

Fig. 1. Repartitioning of ECUs in automotive E/E systems

for separation of safety-related software parts from the rest of the system. The Hypervisor (HV) acts as the smallest instance related to all VMs in the system. For safety-related systems, the HV must be qualified to the highest Automotive Safety Integrity Level (ASIL) assigned to any application within the system. In any case, real-time capabilities, deterministic behavior and hard deadlines must be fulfilled to achieve required properties of an automotive embedded system.

In this paper, we focus on the emulation of communication controllers for Controller Area Network (CAN) and Ethernet in a paravirtualized automotive software system by using an embedded HV, closely developed to the AUTOSAR standard. We discuss how to permit peripheral access to VMs and how to deal with limited memory protection ranges. To run mixed-integrity automotive functionality, we suggest an approach to integrate the Communication Hardware Abstraction within the AUTOSAR Microcontroller Abstraction Layer (MCAL) in a decentralized manner, encapsulated in a unique VM. This method is analyzed for timing overheads of the information flow between VMs and interconnected automotive fieldbuses. For our analysis, we use an embedded HV with real-time capabilities. The hypervisor (called *RTA-HV*) is supported by ETAS Ltd. [13] and is ported to the Infineon AURIX TriCore microcontroller which fulfills our needs for paravirtualization [2].

The next sections are organized as follows: Section 2 outlines the related work on hardware emulation by using embedded HVs for real-time systems. Section 3 outlines methods to integrate systems in a paravirtualized environment. In section 4 we summarize the implementation to build virtual gateways for information routing. The results and performance evaluations are discussed in section 5. Section 6 summarizes the paper and its results.

2   Related Work

To achieve performance advantages, paravirtualization is already used in data centers supported by Virtual Machine Monitors (VMMs) like Xen [1]. Embedded real-time VMMs like XtratuM [9] or Sysgo's PikeOS are available and able to encapsulate safety-related functionality. But these HVs are not available for controllers without a Memory Management Unit (MMU) [2], which is mostly not integrated in state-of-the-art automotive devices. These are mostly equipped with only a Memory Protection Unit (MPU) to realize spatial protection.

Chip vendors like Intel or AMD feature their controllers with virtualization extensions like Intel VT or AMD-V. These chips are applied in data centers, where software applications are massively consolidated on from server systems decoupled from the hardware. For I/O virtualization, extensions like Intel VT-c (Virtualization Technology for Connectivity) come into consideration [7].

Research based solutions for self-virtualized CAN and Ethernet controllers for embedded real-time systems is shown in [6] and [11]. No hardware emulation is necessary and message arbitration is processed controller internally. An approach without a full HV for CAN virtualization with safety aspects is presented in [14].

The architecture of our work is derived from Xen [1]. Front- and backend drivers called *Netfront* and *Netback* were used to pass information between the master VM called *dom0* and other guest VMs called *User Domains (DomUs)* (see figure 3). The *dom0* runs all device drivers needed from other *DomUs*.

3   Methods to Integrate Virtualized Peripherals Using the Infineon AURIX TriCore

The HV represents a Type-1 VMM which runs bare-metal in supervisor mode on the Infineon AURIX microcontroller. No hosting Operating System (OS) is needed. Every VM operates in a one-to-one mapping per core in user mode and implements its core local HV instance. Additional Virtual Device Emulators (VDEs) run in the context of the HV and have kernel access rights. VDEs allow the emulation of peripherals or the implementation of communication channels between VMs. Each VDE implementation exists once for the overall system and is re-entrant for any core and VM. A trap class 6 (System Call) is used to trigger the HV. Every VDE implements its own *request()* function, where incoming service requests are processed. VDEs possess the highest interrupt priority levels in the system. If the core is handling a trap routine or executing HV code, all interrupts for VMs are blocked.

3.1   Granting Access to Peripheral Space

For the Infineon TriCore AURIX microcontroller, three different privileged modes exist. In supervisor mode there are no restrictions for memory or peripheral access. In user mode, two distinctions exist between User-0 mode, where peripheral access is generally restricted and User-1 mode which basically grants access to I/O controllers. Any register call of a VM which runs in User-0 or 1 mode is either allowed due to the Instruction Set Architecture (ISA) or must be executed by the HV which runs in Supervisor (SU) mode itself. For the latter, the HV verifies such calls on software level. If they are not allowed, they will be restricted by the MPU. To grant access to communication controllers or to other peripherals, we identified the following three use cases. To operate virtual communication controllers, all three approaches are applicable and must be analyzed depending on the project situation and hardware resources.

1. **Direct Device Assignment (DDA)**: DDA is a well proven technique like for server systems in data centers. Peripherals like CAN or Ethernet controller must not be shared between multiple virtual machines. The VM has

to run in User-1 mode and affected peripheral address space must be registered additionally in the MPU per core. For sure, this method is restricted by given MPU protection ranges and by given hardware resources.

2. **Paravirtualization of non-shared devices**: If the MPU's protection address ranges are insufficient to grant access to peripheral space, hardware accesses must be paravirtualized. In this case, every call from VMs must be wrapped by HV and forwarded to the HV and its VDEs. This is mandatory if the virtual machine runs in User-0 mode. Unfortunately, this approach will increase the timing overhead due to trap and emulation due to the HV.

3. **Emulation of shared devices**: In this case, more than one virtual machine needs access to a particular peripheral. The access must be controlled and arbitrated by the HV. There are identical timing overheads as in use case 2 and besides additional efforts for routing, concurrent accesses and blocking times must be taken into account. To arbitrate messages within the HV an additional VDE must be developed.

3.2   Relocating Hardware Drivers to Allow Safe and Secure Accesses

Every peripheral needs its individual hardware drivers for operation located in the AUTOSAR MCAL. Typically, software instances should have exclusive access to peripherals. Within LSSI systems probably some peripherals must be shared. For mixed-integrity systems it is problematic to introduce unqualified software and its communication channels into a safety-related system. The uncontrolled sharing of peripherals between software partitions without any controlling instance can lead to malfunctions [8], [14]. Especially, in case of VM shutdown or restart, hardware drivers for other VMs must always be available for safety-related software parts. Therefore, we list identified approaches for paravirtualized automotive E/E systems, illustrated in figure 2.

1. **Driver modules integrated within each VM**: All drivers are integrated within a VM and run completely in user space. Either the VM has direct access to peripherals, due to the AURIX' User-1 mode granted by the MPU, or all attempts to register access have to be executed within kernel space by the HV. In any case, the VM needs exclusive access to peripherals (DDA). All SU only registers must be handled from the HV by using hypercalls. We use a

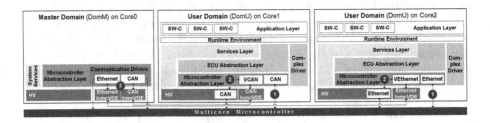

Fig. 2. Possible relocation for hardware drivers in an AUTOSAR system

paravirtualized approach where trapping and emulation of register calls are reduced as much as possible and routed to the HV.

2. **Driver modules integrated within the HV**: Relevant MCAL modules are located within the HV and operate in kernel space in SU mode. They have direct access to the hardware and all privileges. In this configuration, malicious drivers can jeopardize the overall system (single point of failure), even the HV itself. All attempts to have access to peripherals must be routed to and arbitrated by a VDE. This will increase the timing overheads because of trap and emulation to reach the HV.

3. **Driver modules relocated to a privileged VM**: This approach differs between guest VMs called DomUs and a unique VM called Master Domain (DomM). This method is very similar to Xen's *dom0* approach [1], where all drivers run in a special domain. DomM integrates drivers in a special VM. Only DomM routes frames to the fieldbus and has exclusive access to the communication controller. All attempts to exchange data of DomUs must be transmitted to DomM and routed to another DomU or fieldbus. The DomM must not run in supervisor mode. To gain performance advantages, exclusive access to peripherals (DDA) which run in User-1 mode is necessary. The DomM runs as an encapsulated VM and implements a bridge for incoming attempts to peripheral access. It routes I/O information to VMs or fieldbuses.

4   Building Virtual Gateways

Sharing peripherals during run-time will cause interference to arbitrate frames (time) and protect peripheral access (space). We focus on the supervised emulation of communication controllers in safety-related systems. DDA needs no special routing mechanism because all devices are assigned exclusively to VMs. But this method is only possible if no peripheral must be shared. If drivers are relocated to the HV, its Trusted Computing Base (TCB) will increase. Due to the timing limitations and arbitration overheads within HV withdraws that method, as well. Therefore, we analyze the relocation of drivers to an independent, priviledged VM called DomM, as described in section 3.2. To grant peripheral access for hardware drivers (see section 3.1), MPU regions can be used exclusively for that purpose. Because of exclusive access to peripherals in DomM there is no need for hardware emulation (DDA).

4.1   Information Exchange Between Virtual Machines

To guarantee a safe and secure way to interact between VMs and cores, we implement a special VDE interface called Inter-Virtual-Machine-Communication VDE (IvmcVDE) which acts as a generic communication channel to transfer data [10]. Every information flow between VMs is under the control of the HV itself. The HV forwards incoming service requests to its IvmcVDE. Either polling or interrupt-driven communication mechanisms are possible to exchange information between VMs. Both strategies implement an event channel between VMs. All data is exchanged by using HV mechanisms like IvmcVDE.

In case of polling strategies, the VM has to notify new information by observing global data memory sections in the Local Memory Unit (LMU) of the AURIX. No traps or interrupts are needed to activate other cores. If there is new information available in the LMU, the dedicated VM will fetch that information periodically. In case of interrupt-driven strategies, we use a notification mechanism supplied by the HV, to trigger other cores and VM instances to re-enter the context of IvmcVDE. The sender core stores data in the global data RAM and triggers the receiver core by using an interrupt. The *request()*-function of IvmcVDE is reached to process new data.

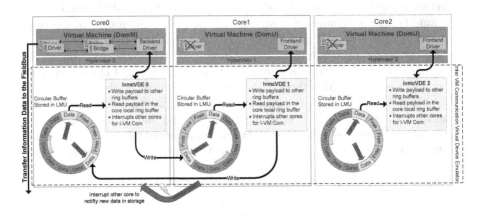

Fig. 3. Inter virtual machine communication mechanism build in a VDE

To avoid blocking accesses or starvation we implement three ring buffers (see figure 3) by using the *Circular Buffer Addressing Mode* of the AURIX TriCore. This feature supports atomic load and store operations including circular pointer shifting. They are supplied hardware features of the AURIX microcontroller. For each buffer we choose a size of 4096 byte located in the global data RAM of the LMU. All DomUs write messages to the DomMs ring buffer where they are retrieved and routed (FIFO). Two types of event channels are implemented: The polling (a flag signals new data) and interrupt-driven mechanisms.

Figure 4 describes the base frame-formats in our system. The Protocol Control Information (PCI) of every frame is stored in an additional header. The *Request Mode* controls the IvmcVDE operation and distinguishes between transmission modes like polling or interrupt-driven strategies. The *Destination* and *Source Core* field directs the information exchange between VMs. Because we support dynamic package length to efficiently support variable frame length in IEEE 802.3 Ethernet, the *Length* field stores the overall payload size. The *Payload* includes a wrapped communication frame e.g. CAN or Ethernet. Since we are in a safe environment where data corruption is very unlikely due to ECC-RAM and lock-step cores, we can omit check-summing the payload. They are

Table 1. Exemplary routing table to direct CAN frames

ID	Port($DomM_{core0}$)	Port($DomU_{core1}$)	Port($DomU_{core2}$)
0x1F	TRUE	FALSE	TRUE
0xA2	FALSE	TRUE	TRUE
...	...	...	...

calculated and inserted within the hardware driver or the controller itself and must not be transmitted in that layer.

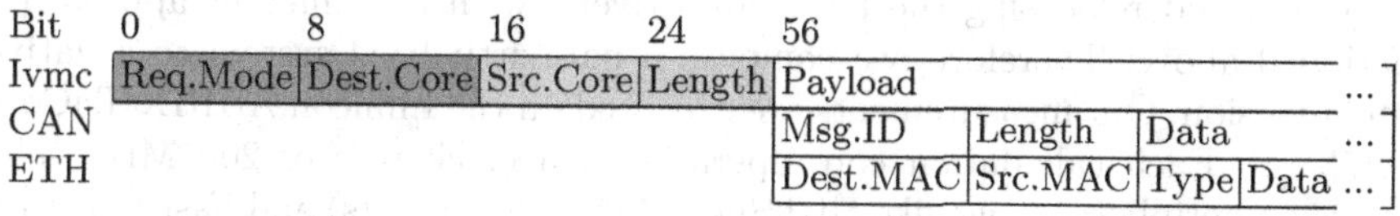

Bit	0	8	16	24	56			
Ivmc	Req.Mode	Dest.Core	Src.Core	Length	Payload			...
CAN					Msg.ID	Length	Data	...
ETH					Dest.MAC	Src.MAC	Type	Data ...

Fig. 4. Base Frame-Format for CAN and Ethernet

4.2 Routing Information Using a Privileged Domain

The DomM needs a scheduling scheme to route information between DomUs and other fieldbuses. Therefore, we integrate a bridging mechanism into DomM to route information ECU internally and externally. DomM implements a bridging functionality (see figure 3) including a Source Address Table (SAT) for Ethernet and a routing table for CAN which hold the routing protocols for incoming messages. A bridge typically acts on layer two of the ISO/OSI-model and routes information. Our VM bridge is divided into a controlling and a forwarding part:

The *controlling part* holds the routing table (see table 1) and the organization of it. In case of routing Ethernet frames there is a SAT (identical to a network switch) containing the MAC addresses which are assigned to connecting ports [5]. In case of CAN communication the routing table contains the CAN IDs. Therefore, we differentiate between a statically (CAN) and a dynamically (Ethernet) construction of our routing table (the SAT). The CAN routing table is configured statically before compile time and holds all routing information in advance. The Ethernet SAT will be setup dynamically during system run-time and assigns MAC addresses to (port) *IDs*.

The *forwarding part* routes messages between VMs or connecting fieldbuses (e.g. CAN or Ethernet). All incoming messages will be accepted, either by polling strategies or retrieved by an Interrupt Service Routine (ISR). We serialize messages and use the given IvmcVDE to exchange information between VMs. To transmit frames to a connected fieldbus, DomM implements needed hardware drivers, which have exclusive peripheral access to needed hardware controllers.

Table 1 lists an exemplary routing protocol for incoming CAN frames. The bridge distinguishes according to the *ID* (the CAN identifier) to which *Port* (the

VM and its core) the message must be routed through (e.g. message ID 0xA2 is routed to $core_1$ and $core_2$). If an incoming frame is assigned for DomM, it will be transferred to the connected fieldbus. All routing information is configured before compile time. In case of incoming Ethernet frames, the bridge distinguishes according to the *ID* (the MAC address) to which *Port* (the VM and its core) the message must be routed through. Similar to the CAN approach, it assigns multiple MAC addresses (*IDs*) to *Ports*.

5   Results and Discussion

We want to evaluate the overhead, which occurs due to paravirtualization of the system and relocating the hardware drivers, with the different approaches mentioned above. Therefore, we compare a paravirtualized system to a native system version. Our measurements are executed on the Infineon AURIX TriCore TC27X [2]. Each calculation core operates at a clock rate of 200 MHz. The focus is on peripheral usage like HighSpeed-CAN (500 kbit/s) and Fast Ethernet (100 Mbit/s) communication controller. For all our measurements, each core is exclusively used for sending or receiving messages. Blocking times due to concurrent accesses are avoided. To be close to real platforms, all measurements are realized multiple times with external clients and include the transmission overheads of peripherals to a connected fieldbus.

Figure 5 and 6 are organized as follows: *Native* systems are not paravirtualized and represent the benchmark for our measurements. For *DomM→ Fieldbus*, frames were transmitted directly from the privileged domain to the connecting fieldbus including all routing efforts. In *DomU→Fieldbus* scenario, frames were transmitted from a DomU to DomM and from this point routed to the fieldbus. In *DomU→DomU* scenario there is no limiting fieldbus involved and frames were exchanged ECU internally from a DomU routed by DomM to another DomU.

5.1   Response Time per Message Size

We want to analyze the response times of single messages for relocated automotive communication drivers. Figure 5 shows the timing measurements to transmit messages over a fieldbus compared by the size of their payload by using interrupt-driven communication mechanisms. After message routing by DomM we use DDA to access peripherals directly and have exclusive access to relevant controller registers. With it, we avoid processing overhead due to the HV for data transmission. For interrupt-driven data reception, there is as static timing overhead of 4 µs to route incoming interrupts to VMs [13]. Thus, for all our measurements the timing gaps between the native and DDA case is minimalistic.

Figure 5a shows the transmission of Ethernet frames using the ICMP protocol to measure echo replies of different sizes (*ping*). The message exchange of bigger frames has more impact on latency compared to CAN. This is reasonable, because copy operations of bigger frame structures are more calculation

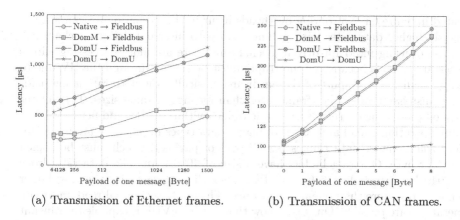

(a) Transmission of Ethernet frames.   (b) Transmission of CAN frames.

Fig. 5. Response time measurements compared by their payload

intensive and cause additional timing overheads. Routing frames from one VM to another need two copy operations, which need more time if the payload size increases. In case of transmitting frames from DomU to DomM, there is firstly additional management overhead for information exchange between VMs using IvmcVDE. Secondly, the calculation effort due to OSI abstraction layers for TCP and message routing (using a SAT) by each VM (compare the gap between *DomM→Fieldbus* and *Native→Fieldbus*). Sending Ethernet frames of 64 byte from any DomU to the fieldbus takes 620 μs. The transmission of 1500 byte of payload takes not even the double amount of transmission time. At around 700 byte of payload, we measured the break-even point of latency to exchange Ethernet frames between DomUs or transmit them over the fieldbus.

The CAN response time analysis is illustrated in figure 5b and shows a similar direct proportional trend for all measurements. Because of small CAN frame sizes, copy operations between VMs are not mentionable which relate to a slightly increasing trend. The management overhead for routing frames in DomM, using a lookup table with a time complexity of $\mathcal{O}(1)$, causes timing overhead around 1 μs. The transmission of frames from any DomU by using IvmcVDE causes additional timing overhead, around 4%. The longest time is required by the CAN controller itself to transmit frames over the fieldbus. The time to instantiate a frame until it is handed over to the controller is less than 5 μs. The remaining time is used for the frame transmission within the CAN controller. Because of small CAN frame sizes the transmission overheads between VMs caused by IvmcVDE are negligible and even faster than the connecting CAN fieldbus. We determine that information routing in an optimal paravirtualized system has nearly no impact on response times and achieves nearly linear measurement results.

5.2   Maximum Throughput Measurements

First, we will analyze the possible bandwidth to transfer data between VMs. Therefore, we will measure the data rates from DomU to DomM, which is presented in figure 6a. No routing overheads incur in this scenario. We can achieve slightly higher data rates with polling than with interrupt-driven mechanisms. In case of using interrupt-driven mechanisms there are more processing efforts necessary. This is because all interrupts must be routed through the HV due to less virtualization support of the hardware. Basically, the data rate is lower for the transmission of smaller frame sizes than for bigger frame sizes. This relates to fixed processing overheads to handle frames within the HV and between VMs. Copy operations (load and store) of bigger data types in sequence are more efficient than smaller data frames (e.g. 7 byte of payload) which must be copied byte per byte. Our ring buffers have a size of 4096 byte. The data rate drops at 2049 byte (including 6 byte of PCI). For this message size the ring buffer cannot store more than one frame at once. Then only sequential read and write operations are possible. Our tests show that the IvmcVDE is capable to transmit data up to 97 Mbit/s, with 2047 byte message size, from one VM to another.

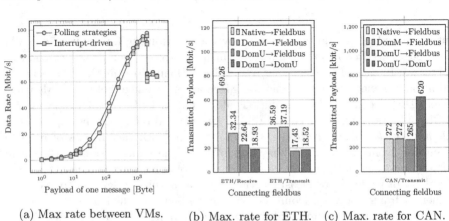

(a) Max rate between VMs.   (b) Max. rate for ETH.   (c) Max. rate for CAN.

Fig. 6. Measured data rates between VMs by using the IvmcVDE

Second, we analyze the maximum data-throughput (interrupt-driven) for CAN and Ethernet. Ethernet measurements (*full-duplex*) are illustrated in figure 6b. Native systems without virtualization (*Native→Fieldbus*) have a doubled reception rate compared by the rate to transmit data. This is reasonable, because no data copies (*zero-copy*) are necessary to receive frames. In addition, incoming frames are allocated per Direct Memory Access (DMA) in the VMs data structures. To transmit frames, each message must be copied once into the data structure of the Ethernet controller individually. In case of *DomM→Fieldbus* the reception rate is nearly cut in half because of an additional copy operation in the bridge of DomM. In case of *DomU→Fieldbus* the data is received by DomM and first copied from IvmcVDE into the ring buffer located in the context of the receiving VM. Here, the data is transmitted to the dedicated DomU which will cause the second data copy. To transmit data to a fieldbus, even a third copy operation into the data structure of the Ethernet controller is necessary. Therefore, to achieve high data-rates with Ethernet, the amount of copy operations by using a DomM has a significant influence on communication performance of smaller embedded controllers. Compared, to native systems we can transfer less data between VMs, either in case of $DomU{\rightarrow}Fieldbus$ or $DomU{\rightarrow}DomU$, due to additional time-consuming copy operations of payload sizes mostly around 1500 byte. Summarized, there are timing penalties to bridge Ethernet frames in a paravirtualized system and using a DomM by using limited hardware.

For CAN, the maximum transmission rates are limited by the speed of the transmitting hardware controller and by the fieldbus bitrate illustrated in figure 6c. There are no maximum reception rates for because we are limited to the bitrate of the CAN fieldbus with only one active transmitter at once. We can receive CAN frames much faster than transmitting them and determined no frame losses. In the *native* case without virtualization, we achieve a maximum transmission data rate of 272 kbit/s with a fixed payload of 8 byte per frame. Including its PCI, a typical CAN frame has a size of 108 bit which now achieves an overall data rate of 459 kbit/s. We obtain the same ratio for $DomM{\rightarrow}Fieldbus$ including all routing efforts. This relates to the much slower transmission time of the CAN controller itself for coping data to any data structures in the MCAL (see section 5.1). In case of $DomU{\rightarrow}Fieldbus$ we achieve similar results. The slight deviation is due to management overhead in the IvmcVDE for message exchange between VMs. To transmit full CAN frames between DomUs by using a managing DomM ($DomU{\rightarrow}DomU$) we measure reception timings around 103 µs which is much faster than sending them over the CAN fieldbus. Therefore, we can obtain higher data rates with a maximum throughput of 620 kbit/s. Summarized, even by usage of a decentralized DomM, software-driven CAN routing within a paravirtualized system has no big impact on the overall performance.

6   Conclusion

In this paper, we showed an approach to relocate hardware drivers of communication controllers like CAN and Ethernet. Our goal was to run them in a safe execution space to decouple safety-related functionality from untrusted software parts. Additionally, the TCB of the HV should be kept as small as possible. Therefore, a privileged VM like DomM is a solution to encapsulate safety-related hardware drivers, isolated from non-qualified software, in coherence of an embedded HV. To achieve real-time and safety requirements, some tradeoffs must be taken into account. If additional communication paths and small timing efforts can be tolerated, we showed a methodology for building virtual gateways to route information between virtualized automotive embedded systems.

Ethernet for automotive environments is mostly used to transfer big data volumes. Due to additional copy operations the transmission rate is reduced between VMs compared to native systems. Achieving higher data rates would require faster hardware controllers with supporting virtualization extensions. CAN is used to transmit small chunks of data within a reasonable timeframe. According to our measurements, these requirements are realizable in our paravirtualized system. Furthermore, the achieved bandwidth between VMs is significant higher compared to any other automotive fieldbuses. If messages are exchanged exclusively by ECUs, the migration to VMs can save bandwidth of connecting fieldbuses. Thus, the system migration to VMs within LSSI platforms could be an intermediate step for communication intensive ECUs. For safety-related systems, our approach, to encapsulate drivers in a safe environment, realizes an already proven method in data centers to separate hardware drivers from VMs.

Acknowledgments. The authors would like to express their gratitude to Michael Scheffer from Infineon Technologies AG for his cooperative work and for supplying the hardware drivers and frameworks. This work was funded within the project ARAMiS by the German Federal Ministry for Education and Research with the funding IDs 01IS11035. The responsibility for the content remains with the authors.

References

1. Barham, P., Dragovic, B., Fraser, K., Hand, S., Harris, T., Ho, A., Neugebauer, R., Pratt, I., Warfield, A.: Xen and the Art of Virtualization. SIGOPS Oper. Syst. Rev. **37**(5), 164–177 (2003)
2. Brewerton, S., Schneider, R.: Hardware based paravirtualization: simplifying the co-hosting of legacy code for mixed criticality applications. In: SAE 2013 World Congress & Exhibition, April 2013
3. Broy, M.: Challenges in automotive software engineering. In: Proc. ACM 28th International Conference on Software Engineering (ICSE 2006), pp. 33–42, Shanghai, May 2006
4. Fürst, S.: Challenges in the design of automotive software. In: Design, Automation Test in Europe Conference Exhibition (DATE), pp. 256–258, March 2010
5. Güntner, M.: Virtualization of Time Critical Communication Interfaces. Bachelor's thesis, University of Applied Sciences Kempten, September 2014
6. Herber, C., Richter, A., Rauchfuss, H., Herkersdorf, A.: Self-virtualized CAN controller for multi-core processors in real-time applications. In: Kubátová, H., Hochberger, C., Daněk, M., Sick, B. (eds.) ARCS 2013. LNCS, vol. 7767, pp. 244–255. Springer, Heidelberg (2013)
7. Intel LAN Access Division. Intel VMDq Technology. White paper, Intel Corporation, March 2008. Revision 1.2
8. ISO 26262. Road vehicles - Functional safety - Part 1–10 (2011)
9. Masmano, M., Ripoll, I., Crespo, A., Metge, J.J.: XtratuM: a hypervisor for safety critical embedded systems. In: Eleventh Real-Time Linux Workshop, Dresden, Germany, September 2009
10. Obermeir, S.: Integration of Virtualized AUTOSAR-Systems on a Multicore-Controller. Master's thesis, University of Applied Sciences Munich, October 2014

11. Rauchfuss, H., Wild, T., Herkersdorf, A.: A network interface card architecture for i/o virtualization in embedded systems. In: Proceedings of the 2Nd Conference on I/O Virtualization, WIOV 2010, p. 2. USENIX Association, Berkeley (2010)

12. Reinhardt, D., Kaule, D., Kucera, M.: Achieving a Scalable E/E-Architecture using AUTOSAR and Virtualization. SAE International Journal of Passenger Cars - Electronic and Electrical Systems **6**(2), 489–497 (2013)

13. Reinhardt, D., Morgan, G.: An embedded hypervisor for safety-relevant automotive E/E-systems. In: 2014 9th IEEE International Symposium on Industrial Embedded Systems (SIES), pp. 189–198, June 2014

14. Schneider, R., Kohn, A., Schmidt, K., Schoenberg, S., Dannebaum, U., Harnisch, J., Zhou, Q.: Efficient virtualization for functional integration on modern microcontrollers in safety-relevant domains. In: SAE 2014 World Congress & Exhibition, April 2014

Network Interface with Task Spawning Support for NoC-Based DSM Architectures

Aurang Zaib[1]([✉]), Jan Heißwolf[2], Andreas Weichslgartner[3], Thomas Wild[1], Jürgen Teich[3], Jürgen Becker[2], and Andreas Herkersdorf[1]

[1] Technical University Munich, Munich, Germany
{aurang.zaib,thomas.wild,herkersdorf}@tum.de
[2] Karlsruhe Institute of Technology, Karlsruhe, Germany
{heisswolf,becker}@kit.edu
[3] University of Erlangen-Nuremberg, Erlangen, Germany
{andreas.weichslgartner,teich}@informatik.uni-erlangen.de

Abstract. Distributed Shared Memory (DSM) architectures are becoming popular to exploit parallelism of architectures while offering flexibility of using both shared and distributed memory paradigms to application developers. At the same time, Networks on Chip (NoC) have become reality to address communication bottlenecks in massively parallel tile-based processor architectures. In NoC-based DSM architectures, the synchronization overhead for spawning a task on a remote network node may lead to high performance penalties. In order to reduce the synchronization delays during remote task spawning, the design of Network Interface (NI) becomes important. In this paper, we present a network interface architecture which supports task spawning between network nodes by employing efficient synchronization mechanisms. The proposed NI internal hardware support offloads the software from handling the synchronization during remote task spawning and hence results in achieving better overall performance. Simulation results highlight that the proposed hardware architecture improves the performance by up to 42 % in comparison to existing state of the art approaches. The FPGA prototype is also used to depict the benefits of the proposed approach for real world applications. Implementation results show the low area footprint of the proposed hardware.

1 Introduction

With the increase in number of transistors which can be integrated on a single chip, systems become more complex and power consuming. This has led to the trend of building many-core systems instead of developing more sophisticated and power hungry single core architectures. Tilera's TilePro [1] and Intel's research chip Single-Chip Cloud Computer (SCC) [2] represent the state of the art examples of existing many-core systems. The trend towards introducing many-core systems on chip has also affected the on-chip communication requirements. Shared bus-based communication infrastructures lack the scalability, which is required in future massively parallel architectures. Distributed

© Springer International Publishing Switzerland 2015
L.M. Pinho et al. (Eds): ARCS 2015, LNCS 9017, pp. 186–198, 2015.
DOI: 10.1007/978-3-319-16086-3_15

interconnects like Networks on Chip [3] are found to be more suitable for many-core systems.

General purpose many-core systems are expected to support the execution of a wide range of applications, each of which may benefit from either a shared memory or message passing based programming style. Researchers have addressed this problem by introducing distributed shared memory architectures which combine the advantages of both shared and distributed memory architectures [4]. Partitioned Global Address Space (PGAS) programming model has emerged as a scalable and productive way for programming DSM architectures [5]. Both shared memory and message passing-based programming models can be efficiently supported on a DSM architecture. DSM architectures enable the shared memory programming paradigm by allowing access to all memories present in the system through a global address space. In addition, the message passing model is supported by distributing the memories in different nodes of architecture which provides scalability by avoiding creation of data access hotspots.

The distributed nature of NoCs brings many challenges for the developers of the parallel on-chip architectures. Communication and synchronization mechanisms between tasks, which are running on different architecture nodes interconnected via NoC, have significant impact on the overall system performance. In order to efficiently exploit the available parallelism on the underlying platform, the delays for synchronizing the application tasks, which are spawned from one node to the other, should be reduced. Efficient mechanisms are thus required in order to enable fast communication and reduce the software overhead involved in task spawning. In the past, both hardware and software based solutions were proposed to support task synchronization in DSM architectures. Software-based solutions are flexible but have higher performance overheads. Hardware-based methods deliver better performance but they require large modifications in architectural building blocks at multiple levels and thus make them less flexible. Along the aforementioned considerations, we propose a hardware-based approach which requires extensions only in the network interface architecture in order to support communication and synchronization for remote task spawning.

We present a NoC interface architecture, which provides hardware-based task spawning support. The proposed support offloads the software and results in delivering higher performance. At the same time, the presented NI enables distributed memory communication through state of the art load/store and remote DMA transfers. The experimental results show better performance and lower overhead offered by our approach compared to other state of the art solutions.

The rest of this paper is organized as follows: In Section 2, background and related work are described. Section 3 gives an overview of the target DSM architecture. Proposed task spawning support in network interface architecture is explained in Section 4. Simulation, prototyping and synthesis results are presented in Section 5. Section 6 gives a conclusion and summarizes our next steps.

2   Related Work

Increasing architecture sizes have encouraged the development of novel methodologies to support synchronization between remote network nodes on a DSM architecture. An approach to support both shared memory and message passing through hardware is presented in [6]. Different components of the hardware architecture are modified to support synchronization between processing elements connected via NoC. Processor pipeline is extended to support custom instructions for shared memory and message passing synchronization. Moreover, the interface between processor and network interface is customized for shared memory and message passing communication. Unfortunately, the work does not present the overhead of the approach which makes the comparison with other concepts difficult.

A mixed hardware-software solution to support a distributed shared memory architecture is presented in [7]. The authors have proposed a Dual Microcoded Controller (DMC) as a core module which contains many sub-modules for supporting operations like core and network interfacing, virtual to physical address translation and synchronization. Synchronization between remote network nodes is supported through test-and-set primitive. The benchmarks which are used as test cases to support shared memory and message passing are quite limited in scope and it is not answered how this approach can be scaled for real-time applications. In addition, the performance improvement or overhead of this approach is not compared with any pure hardware or software-based solution.

Another hardware-software based approach to support communication and synchronization between network nodes is presented in [8]. Distributed communication is enabled through hardware supported remote direct memory access. However, the synchronization is performed through software configured primitives. The synchronization overhead over distributed interconnect while using software-based synchronization is not addressed.

In this paper, we propose an approach which provides architectural support in the network interface for synchronizing remote task spawning. The proposed approach delivers higher performance when compared with hardware-software based approaches because of being a pure hardware implementation. In addition, only an extension of the network interface architecture is required instead of modifying many architectural components in comparison to above-mentioned hardware-based methodology.

3   NoC-Based DSM Architecture

Our concept is based on a many-core DSM architecture in which a NoC is deployed as distributed on-chip interconnect and the memory is physically distributed among the architecture. In contrast to a pure distributed memory system, a DSM architecture enables direct access to each memory in Non-Uniform Memory Access (NUMA) fashion. An example configuration is shown in the Figure 1. However, our concept is not limited to this particular configuration and can be applied to any generic NoC-based DSM architecture.

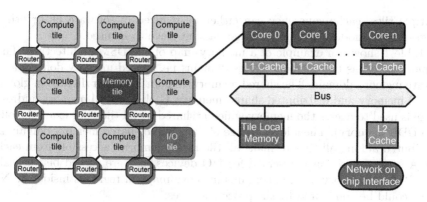

Fig. 1. Network on Chip based DSM architecture

The architecture contains compute, memory and I/O tiles. In compute tiles, several processor cores are connected by a shared bus. Each core has an exclusive L1 cache. The processor cores inside the tile share a common L2 cache. There is also a block of memory named as tile local memory, attached to the bus. Memory tile represents global memory whereas I/O tile enables the interface of architecture with standard external interfaces like UART, Ethernet etc. The network on chip interface enables the communication between different tiles over NoC.

Cache coherence is supported within the tile at the level of L1 caches. The intra-tile cache coherence enables use of shared memory programming model for parallel applications, which can be mapped within a tile. However, no global cache coherence is supported between the caches and tile local memories belonging to different tiles. The reason is the limitation and the overhead of global cache coherence with respect to scalability. Intel's SCC architecture [2] is a prominent representative of an existing architecture, which does not provide global coherence between all caches to ensure scalability. For bigger applications, which use

Table 1. Memory map of considered DSM architecture

Memory access domain		Start Address (MSB)	End Address (MSB)
Shared memory domain	**Private memory domain**		
Global shared memory	-	0x0000	0x7FFF
Distributed shared memory	-		
Tile 0	-	0x8000	0x80FF
Tile 1	-	0x8100	0x81FF
Tile ...	-	...	...
I/O area	-	0xC000	0xDFFF
-	Private range	0xE000	0xFFFF

multiple tiles, cache coherency can either be realized in software [9] or other programming models, such as message passing, have to be used.

Table 1 shows an example of a memory map of the DSM architecture. The memory map has two memory access domains i.e. shared memory domain and private memory domain. The shared memory domain is further divided in global shared memory and distributed shared memory. Global shared memory address range is used to access the memory which is shared by all tiles (for example, off-chip DDR memory). The address range of distributed shared memory domain is distributed among all tiles to make all tile local memories accessible from each tile. A separate section is reserved for I/O devices that are shared between all tiles. Private memory domain contains memory mapped registers inside the NI which could be configured by the processor cores.

4 Remote Task Spawning and Distributed Communication

4.1 Inter-tile Task Spawning Support

For our investigations, we have considered a task spawning model in which the complete code and data associated to the spawned task is copied from the source tile to the destination tile. The software on the source tile initiates the remote direct memory access to transfer the task data. When the data transfer is completed, the task pointer which points to the start address of the code in the destination tile, is sent by the source tile. Afterward, the software clears the memory on the source tile which was allocated for the spawned task. For a NoC-based distributed shared memory architecture, the task spawning between two tiles is represented by a message sequence chart, shown in the Figure 2.

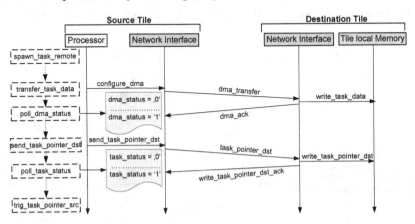

Fig. 2. Message sequence chart showing software managed inter-tile task spawning

As represented in the Figure 2, the remote task spawning could be divided in following three sub-operations:

- **transfer_task_data** relates to the operation in which the task data is moved from the source to the destination tile.
- **send_task_pointer_dst** describes the phase to move the task pointer/object to the destination tile.
- **trig_task_pointer_src** describes the step in which the software releases the memory which was associated to the spawned task on the source tile before spawning the task.

In state of the art approach for remote task spawning [8], the software is involved in performing each of the above steps. Software has to poll the status of the respective sub-operations in order to perform the next subsequent operation. Status polling results in significant overhead on tile-interconnect. In addition, it limits the system performance as the software remains busy with the status polling and can not proceed with the actual application processing.

In NoC-based DSM architectures, network interface plays the role of a gateway between computation elements (tiles) and the distributed communication infrastructure (NoC). Keeping in view this functional significance, we propose hardware support for inter-tile task spawning inside the NI. The proposed support performs the synchronization related to remote task spawning by handling different phases in hardware and thus offloads the software from synchronization overhead. In addition, the presented hardware support handles the synchronization by keeping in view the distributed nature of NoC and thus relieves the tile interconnect from status polling requests. Inter-tile task spawning supported by proposed methodology is presented in Figure 3.

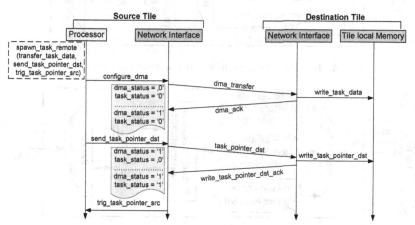

Fig. 3. Message sequence chart showing NI managed inter-tile task spawning

In our approach, software is only required to initiate the task spawning request by configuring task spawning hardware support in the network interface. Afterward, the proposed support initiates the transfer of task data to the destination tile by configuring remote direct memory access. Upon successful completion of the DMA operation, the task pointer is sent to the destination tile. When send_task_pointer_dst operation is completed, trig_task_pointer_src is performed by signaling the software through an interrupt to indicate the completion of task spawning request. The status of sub-operations is monitored inside the NI through the following flags:

- **dma_status** indicates the status of transfer_task_data operation. If the data transfer is completed, it is set to '1', otherwise it is '0'.
- **task_status** indicates the status of send_task_pointer_dst. If the task pointer is transferred, it is set to '1', otherwise it is '0'.

The transmit and receive data-paths of the network interface architecture with proposed task spawning support are shown in the Figures 4 and 5 respectively. Compared to state of the art NI architectures, the presented network interface contains *Inter-tile Task Spawning (ITS)* unit to manage the remote task spawning. ITS unit offloads the software by handling synchronization events related to the remote task spawning in hardware and thus delivers significant improvement in overall performance. The proposed hardware support could be paired with any generic parallel operating system implementation, which is targeted for DSM many-core architectures [10].

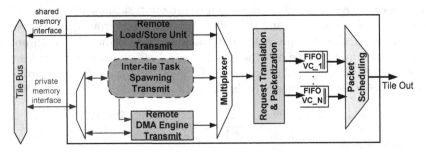

Fig. 4. Transmit data-path of proposed network interface

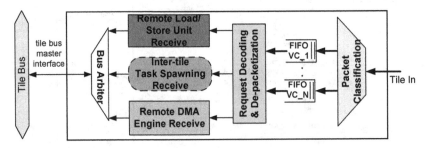

Fig. 5. Receive data-path of proposed network interface

4.2   Distributed Communication Support

The presented network interface architecture consists of many sub-components as shown in the Figures 4 and 5. ITS unit is vital for providing the proposed inter-tile task spawning support as described in Section 4.1. The distributed communication between different tiles is supported via *Remote Direct Memory Access*

(RDMA) and *Remote Load/Store Unit (RLSU)*. Tile to network protocol translation and packet scheduling is realized in transmit data-path through *Request Translation and Packetization* and *Packet Scheduling* units respectively. Whereas receive data-path has *Request Decoding and De-packetization* and *Packet Classification* units for packet decoding and network to tile protocol conversion respectively. For state of the art components in the presented NI architecture, we have only provided the details, which are relevant for our concept.

4.2.1 Remote Direct Memory Access

Remote direct memory access is provided inside the NI through hardware RDMA Engine. RDMA unit can be configured internally via ITS or directly through the processor cores. ITS configures RDMA to transport task data for task spawning. Remote DMA delivers better efficiency while transferring data between distributed memories as compared to state of the art load/store transactions. Remote direct memory access requires following parameters:

- **dma_id** points to the DMA request identifier.
- **dma_len** shows the length (in data words) of the DMA transfer.
- **src_addr** points to the source address in the sender tile from where the data has to be transferred.
- **dst_addr** indicates the destination address where the data has to be copied in the destination tile.

When the DMA operation is completed successfully, the acknowledgment is sent back to the source tile which updates the dma_status flag accordingly.

4.2.2 Remote Load/Store Access

Remote load/store unit supports access to distributed memories in the form of read/write transactions. RLSU supports read/write accesses of configurable size. The tile bus is released during remote load/store operation to prevent blocking of transactions from other tile masters.

To enable distributed communication both via load/stores and DMA, the NI transmit data-path has two different interfaces on the shared bus, which are mapped to the two respective memory access domains in the memory map: the shared memory domain and the private memory domain as illustrated in Table 1. The NI interface in the private memory domain is directly connected to the shared bus and is accessible by the processor cores. The software running on the processor cores can configure the ITS and RDMA units by writing into memory mapped registers of the NI. The shared memory domain interface is mapped through the L2 cache. This interface serves load/store accesses to the shared memory (distributed as well as global) in the architecture. Remote load store unit transparently supports read/write transactions through the L1 and L2 cache hierarchy. As stated before, coherence is not supported between the tiles from hardware perspective.

4.2.3 Request Translation, Packetization and Packet Scheduling

Request Translation and Packetization unit is responsible for translating the requests from RLSU, RDMA and ITS modules and generating the network packets accordingly. For our investigations, we have used a virtual channel based NoC with wormhole switching [11]. Each FIFO in the network interface corresponds to a virtual channel. The communication between the source and destination happens in the form of packets which belong to the particular request type. In each network packet, the corresponding request type i.e. load/store access, DMA or synchronization message is encoded in the packet header. Packet Scheduler is responsible for scheduling transmit FIFOs over the NI output link.

4.2.4 Request Decoding, De-packetization and Packet Classification

The packets arriving at the tile input are placed into the respective FIFOs by the Packet Classifier. In the receive data-path, Request Decoding and De-packetization unit interprets the request type in the packet header and triggers RLSU, RDMA or ITS receive unit to serve the incoming request over tile bus master interface accordingly.

5 Experiments

The experiment section is divided into three subsections. In the first subsection, the evaluations are done in a simulation environment where NoC traffic benchmarks are simulated on the proposed architecture. Then, we have built an FPGA prototype implementing the proposed methodology and executed real-world application on it. Finally, synthesis results show the implementation cost of the proposed architecture on ASIC and FPGA.

5.1 Simulation with NoC Traffic Benchmarks

A cycle accurate tiled architecture model as shown in the Figure 1 including the proposed NI architecture is used for the following investigations. A NoC with mesh topology and XY-routing is used [11]. The size of the platform is configurable. We have applied uniform and hotspot traffic models which are common traffic benchmarks for NoC-based system evaluations [12]. In the uniform case, each tile tries to spawn a number of tasks on every other tile in the architecture in a defined sequence. Task spawning consists of communication between source and destination tile in the form of three steps as mentioned in Section 4.1. All tiles start communicating at the same time. trig_task_pointer_src operation indicates the completion of a task spawning request. For the hotspot scenario, all tiles attempt to spawn tasks on the same destination tile. The corner tile (0, 0) is chosen as the hotspot. The simulation is stopped after all tiles are finished. We have compared our approach with state of the art approach [8] and named it as Reference (Ref). In state of the art approach, the synchronization related to task spawning is managed by software as shown in Figure 2. Our approach in which the task spawning is handled by ITS unit in NI is named as NI_TS. Both the approaches use RDMA to move task data between tiles. The payload which is transferred as task data is kept fixed in these simulation scenarios. Figure 6 shows the comparison of the execution time between two approaches for both the uniform and hotspot scenarios with increasing architecture size. The execution time is further divided in computation time and the

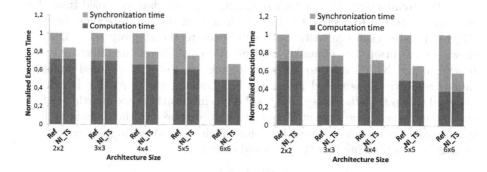

(a) Execution time in uniform scenario   (b) Execution time in hotspot scenario

Fig. 6. Simulation results with NoC traffic benchmarks

synchronization time. The time which is spent for processing and queuing in the architecture is indicated as computation time. Whereas the latency which results from status polling is marked as synchronization time. In the uniform scenario, a linear increase in synchronization time is observed. The results for hotspot scenario show higher increase in synchronization time with the increasing architecture size. Our approach gives a performance improvement of up to 42% in comparison to Reference. The simulation scenarios which have higher degree of parallelism, i.e., more number of tasks are spawned to remote tiles in a bigger architecture configuration, the status polling requests make significant share of traffic on tile interconnect and hence result in higher synchronization time in the Reference configuration. Our approach offloads the software from checking the status of task spawning operation and indicates the completion of spawning process through an interrupt to the software. Hence, the tile interconnect is not loaded with status polling requests which results in the corresponding performance improvement in our configuration.

5.2   FPGA Prototyping with Real World Application

An FPGA prototype of the architecture shown in Figure 1 is realized. A parallel implementation of an integer matrix multiplication application is executed on the prototype to demonstrate the benefits of proposed task spawning support. The *Synopsys CHIPit* system with 6 Virtex-5 VLX330 FPGAs is used for prototyping. A 1 GB DDR memory is used as global shared memory which is present as a memory tile among other compute tiles in the architecture. The global shared memory contains the matrices and code of the parallel application. Each compute tile consists of 4 LEON3 Sparc V8 cores [13]. In addition, each compute tile contains an 8 MB tile local memory in which the respective task data is copied from global shared memory while processing. The proposed NI is used to connect the tiles with the NoC, which is presented in [11].

The memory tile spawns tasks of matrix multiplication application to each tile in the architecture. During task spawning, the task data is copied from the memory tile to the respective tile local memories in the compute tiles through RDMA. Finally, each tile writes its results back to the memory tile. Figure 7 shows the execution time of matrix multiplication for different architecture sizes. Reference and NI_TS refer to the state of the art and the proposed configurations respectively as stated in Section 5.1. Looking at the results, it can be observed that our methodology reduces the synchronization time and thus delivers a performance improvement of up to 19% as compared to the Reference. The synchronization time is reduced by using efficient handshaking and signaling mechanisms as presented by the proposed concept.

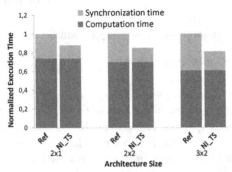

Fig. 7. FPGA prototyping results with Matrix Multiplication Application

5.3   ASIC and FPGA Synthesis for Area Estimation

The HDL representation of the proposed network interface architecture is realized. The implementation cost of the proposed support is measured in terms of area and clock frequency. Table 2 shows the resource utilization of a single NI (without proposed support) and the ITS unit (proposed task spawning support) for both ASIC and FPGA respectively. For ASIC synthesis, a 45 nm standard cell library from TSMC (tcbn45gsbwpwc) with worst case operating conditions is used. Synopsys Design Compiler (F-2011.09-SP4) is taken for synthesis. The target device for the FPGA synthesis is Xilinx Virtex-5 VLX330 which is also used for prototyping. Synopsys Synplify Premier (G-2012.09) is used for FPGA synthesis. After the synthesis, place and route for FPGA is performed by Xilinx P&R tools. The results depict that the proposed hardware support for task spawning offers a low area footprint. The area overhead of ITS unit is around 16% for both ASIC and FPGA implementations in comparison to the NI without the corresponding support. In addition, the proposed hardware can be synthesized at reasonably higher frequency for ASIC implementation which can be compared

Table 2. ASIC TSMC $45\,nm$ and FPGA Virtex-5 VLX330 synthesis Results

Synthesized Entity	ASIC		FPGA		
	Frequency (MHz)	Area (μm^2)	Frequency (MHz)	LUTs	Registers
NI (without ITS unit)	1500	43579	127	4937	1868
ITS unit	1500	7121	130	838	356

to the interconnect frequency of the state of the art many-core architectures like SCC [2].

6   Conclusion and Future Work

In this paper, we have proposed a network on chip interface architecture to support inter-tile task spawning on DSM many-core architectures. The presented hardware architecture offloads the software from the job of handling intermediate synchronization events during remote task spawning. The simulation results illustrate the improvement in performance by up to 42% while comparing with other state of the art approach. The proposed hardware support shows the performance improvement of up to 19%, when real world applications are executed on FPGA prototype. The proposed NI offload is particularly beneficial for applications and benchmarks which have a sizable synchronization overhead. ASIC and FPGA synthesis results depict that the proposed hardware extensions have a small area footprint. In the future, we plan to investigate real world applications with higher degree of parallelism for evaluating our concept.

Acknowledgments. This work was supported by the German Research Foundation (DFG) as part of the Transregional Collaborative Research Center "'Invasive Computing" (SFB/TR 89).

References

1. Agarwal, A.: The tile processor: A 64-core multicore for embedded processing. In: HPEC (2007)
2. Howard, J., Dighe, S., Hoskote, Y., et al.: A 48-Core IA-32 message-passing processor with DVFS in 45nm CMOS. In: ISSCC (2010)
3. Benini, L., Micheli, G.D.: Networks on chips: a new SoC paradigm. Computer (2002)
4. Nitzberg, B., Lo, V.: Distributed shared memory: A survey of issues and algorithms. Computer **24**(8), 52–60 (1991)
5. Yelick, K., Bonachea, D., Chen, W.-Y., Colella, P., Datta, K., Duell, J., Graham, S.L., Hargrove, P., Hilfinger, P., Husbands, P., et al.: Productivity and performance using partitioned global address space languages. In: Proceedings of the 2007 International Workshop on Parallel Symbolic Computation, pp. 24–32. ACM (2007)

6. Tota, S.V., Casu, M.R., Roch, M.R., Rostagno, L., Zamboni, M.: Medea: a hybrid shared-memory/message-passing multiprocessor noc-based architecture. In: Design, Automation & Test in Europe Conference & Exhibition (DATE), pp. 45–50 (2010)

7. Chen, X., Lu, Z., Jantsch, A., Chen, S.: Supporting distributed shared memory on multi-core network-on-chips using a dual microcoded controller. In: Proceedings of the Conference on Design, Automation and Test in Europe, pp. 39–44 (2010)

8. Kavadias, S.G., Katevenis, M.G., Zampetakis, M., Nikolopoulos, D.S.: On-chip communication and synchronization mechanisms with cache-integrated network interfaces. In: Proceedings of the 7th ACM International Conference on Computing Frontiers, ser. CF 2010 (2010)

9. Adve, S.V., Adve, V.S., Hill, M.D., Vernon, M.K.: Comparison of hardware and software cache coherence schemes (1991)

10. Oechslein, B., Schedel, J., Kleinöder, J., Bauer, L., Henkel, J., Lohmann, D., Schröder-Preikschat, W.: Octopos: a parallel operating system for invasive computing. In: Proceedings of the International Workshop on Systems for Future Multi-Core Architectures (SFMA), EuroSys, pp. 9–14 (2011)

11. Heisswolf, J., Koenig, R., Kupper, M., Becker, J.: Providing multiple hard latency and throughput guarantees for packet switching networks on chip. Computers & Electrical Engineering **39**(8), 2603–2622 (2013). http://www.sciencedirect.com/science/article/pii/S0045790613001638

12. Rahmani, A.-M., Afzali-Kusha, A., Pedram, M.: A novel synthetic traffic pattern for power/performance analysis of network-on-chips using negative exponential distribution. Journal of Low Power Electronics **5**(3), 396–405 (2009)

13. Gaiesler, J.: The leon processor user's manual, July 2001. http://www.cs.ucr.edu/~dalton/leon/downloads/leon-2.3.5.pdf

Real-Time Issues

Utility-Based Scheduling of (m, k)-Firm Real-Time Task Sets

Florian Kluge[⊠], Markus Neuerburg, and Theo Ungerer

Department of Computer Science, University of Augsburg, Augsburg, Germany
{kluge,ungerer}@informatik.uni-augsburg.de

Abstract. The concept of a firm real-time task implies the notion of a firm deadline that should not be missed by the jobs of this task. If a deadline miss occurs, the concerned job yields no value to the system. It turns out that for some application domains, this restrictive notion can be relaxed. For example, robust control systems can tolerate that single executions of a control loop miss their deadlines, and still yield an acceptable behaviour. Thus, systems can be developed under more optimistic assumptions, e.g. by allowing overloads. However, care must be taken that deadline misses do not accumulate. This restriction can be expressed by the model of (m, k)-firm real-time tasks that require that within any k successive jobs at least m jobs are executed successfully. This paper presents the heuristic utility-based algorithm MKU for scheduling sets of (m, k)-firm real-time tasks. Therefore, MKU uses history-cognisant utility functions. Simulations show that for moderate overloads, MKU achieves a higher schedulability ratio than other schedulers developed for (m, k)-firm real-time tasks.

1 Introduction

Certain types of real-time systems can tolerate that some jobs miss their deadlines or are not executed at all. Consider, for example, the decoding of a video stream. If single frames are displayed too late, the quality a viewer experiences degrades, but he stills can draw some benefit. Similarly, control systems can also tolerate some job losses due to their robustness. However, in both cases it is necessary that losses do not accumulate. A simple Quality-of-Service (QoS) metric is therefore not sufficient to describe the tolerances, as it can only express the ratio between missed and kept deadlines, but not the distribution of deadline misses over time. Special concepts have been developed in scheduling theory that allow to constrain this distribution, for example the skip-over model [20], (m, k)-firm real-time tasks [14], the dynamic window-constrained scheduler [31], or weakly-hard real-time tasks [3].

In our work, we are especially interested in the scheduling of (m, k)-firm real-time tasks. The (m, k)-firm model describes tasks that require that within any k consecutive jobs at least m jobs are executed successfully. Most works on scheduling of (m, k)-firm real-time tasks use a fixed-priority scheduler for dispatching the single jobs. The only scheduler that we know of that uses dynamic priority scheduling [8] is quite pessimistic in terms of schedulability.

© Springer International Publishing Switzerland 2015
L.M. Pinho et al. (Eds): ARCS 2015, LNCS 9017, pp. 201–211, 2015.
DOI: 10.1007/978-3-319-16086-3_16

In this paper, we present the heuristic MKU algorithm for the scheduling of (m, k)-firm real-time tasks. It is based on the earliest-deadline first (EDF) policy [22]. MKU uses *History-Cognisant Utility Functions (HCUFs)* [18] that are derived from *Time Utility Functions (TUFs)* [15]. A TUF represents a task's utility value depending on the completion time of its current job. Accordingly, a HCUF represents the utility a task has accumulated with respect to the execution of past jobs. In our previous work on HCUFs [18], we have shown that HCUFs can be used to distribute cancellations equally among the tasks in an overloaded task set. However, no guarantees were given about how cancellations are distributed over the life time of a single task. In this work, we investigate, how good HCUFs are apt to give more concrete guarantees to restrict the distribution of cancellations. Therefore, we express the (m, k)-constraints of (m, k)-firm real-time tasks as HCUFs. The scheduling algorithm uses these HCUFs to decide which jobs shall be cancelled in overload situations. This allows for instance to prefer jobs for execution that have been cancelled more often than others in recent history. Experimental evaluations show the performance advantages of MKU over most existing schedulers for (m, k)-firm real-time task sets.

We proceed as follows: In the following section, we review related work on scheduling of (m, k)-firm real-time tasks and scheduling with TUFs. In section 3, the mapping of (m, k)-constraints and the corresponding scheduling algorithm are introduced. Experimental evaluations are presented in section 4. We conclude this paper in section 5.

2   Related Work

2.1 (m, k)-Firm Real-Time Tasks

The concept of (m, k)-firm real-time tasks was introduced by Hamdaoui and Ramanathan [14] as a means to describe acceptable loss rates of streams more precisely. This work also introduces the *Distance-Based Priority (DBP)* assignment technique. Here, a task's distance from a failing state is used as a metric. The distance specifies, how many jobs may consecutively miss their deadlines until the task's (m, k)-constraint will no longer be fulfiled. Each job is assigned a priority that is inversely proportional to its task's distance from a failure state, meaning that jobs of tasks near their failing state get a higher priority. Job dispatching then can be performed in a fixed-priority preemptive (FPP) manner. An exact schedulability test for DBP-scheduled task sets is provided by Goossens [13].

Ramanathan uses the concept of (m, k)-firm real-time tasks for the specific case of control systems [27]. A deterministic classification into mandatory and optional jobs is proposed based on static (m, k)-patterns. Mandatory jobs are scheduled with their original, e.g. rate-monotonic priority, while optional jobs get the lowest possible priority. Due to a peculiarity of the classification technique, the first job of any task is classified as mandatory. Thus, in a synchronous task set the time $t = 0$ is a critical instant where a job from each task gets ready, which introduces a high pessimism into the schedulability analysis. Quan and Hu [26] solve this by calculating rotation values for the (m, k)-patterns to relieve such critical instants. They also point out the NP-hardness of finding a (m, k)-pattern such that a specific task set is schedulable. The rotation values are used by Semprebom et al. [29] for an online admission test of tasks in communication networks. Jia et al. [16] derive a sufficient schedulability condition for (m, k)-firm real-time task sets and present an algorithm that aims to find at least sub-optimal values for m. Flavia et al. [12] present an algorithm that dynamically assigns (m, k)-parameters for plant control. Cho et al. present two schemes for *Guaranteed Dynamic Priority Assignment (GDPA)* [8]. Both schemes are based on EDF scheduling, but additionally take the tasks' distance from a failing state into account. They are aimed at (1) providing a bounded probability of violations of the (m, k)-firm constraints, and (2) maximising the probability of kept deadlines.

2.2 TUF-Based Real-Time Scheduling

The concept of time-utility functions was originally introduced by Jensen et al. [15]. Instead of basing task scheduling solely on the binary notion of a deadline, the use of TUFs allows for a greater flexibility. The benefit of TUFs is demonstrated on EDF scheduling of overloaded task sets. If a high probability for a deadline miss is detected that would render the EDF schedule infeasible, jobs that only contribute with a low utility to the system are selectively cancelled. Thus, schedulability of the system is ensured and accumulated utility is maximised. Locke [23] investigated this technique further for best-effort scheduling. Clark [9] has extended it for tasks with dependent activities.

   Several heuristic scheduling algorithms based on TUFs have been proposed (e.g. [7,21,30]). The notion of time-utility is used in scheduling of real-time systems in general (see [28] for an overview, or e.g. [1,6,10]) and in the special case of overloaded real-time systems (e.g. [4,19,24,25]). Applications of time-value scheduling can be found in dynamic reconfiguration of systems [5], Ethernet packet scheduling [30] and robotics [2].

3   HCUF-Based (m, k)-Firm Real-Time Scheduling

Our work is based on the following task model: A (m, k)-firm real-time task is a tuple $\tau_i = (C_i, T_i, m_i, k_i)$, where C_i denotes the task's worst-case execution time (WCET) and T_i its period. We assume that a task is released initially at time $t = 0$. Thus, jobs $j_{i,l}$ are generated at times $r_{i,l} = lT_i, l = 0, 1, \ldots$ and must be finished until $d_{i,l} = (l + 1)T_i$, i.e. the task's relative deadline equals its period. The completion time of job $j_{i,l}$ is denoted as $f_{i,l}$. The task's (m, k)-constraint is defined by (m_i, k_i), meaning that in any k_i consecutively released jobs at least m_i must be finished before their deadline.

   The aim of this work is to execute a set $\mathcal{T} = \{\tau_1, \tau_2, \ldots, \tau_n\}$ of n independent (m, k)-firm real-time tasks on one processor without violating any task's (m, k)-constraint. In this section, we first define a history cognisant utility function that is able to map a task's current state in terms of its (m, k)-constraint. Then, a scheduler is introduced to schedule $\mathcal{T}$ with the help of the HCUFs.

3.1 Mapping of (m, k)-Constraints as HCUF

The HCUF we introduce is based on a TUF that rates the execution of single jobs. Each job $j_{i,l}$ of a task τ_i is classified by a step-shaped TUF $u_F(j_{i,l})$ that represents a firm real-time requirement. $u_F(j_{i,l})$ is evaluated when job $j_{i,l}$ finishes execution (at time $f_{i,l}$) or is cancelled. If $j_{i,l}$ is completed before its deadline, u_F yields a utility value of 1, and of 0 else:

$$u_F(j_{i,l}) = \begin{cases} 1 & f_{i,l} \leq d_{i,l} \\ 0 & \text{else} \end{cases} \tag{1}$$

For each task τ_i, a sliding window $w_i = (w_i^1, \ldots, w_i^{k_i})$ over k_i consecutive jobs is kept which stores the utility values $u_F(j_{i,l})$ of the last k_i jobs. In the following, w_i^1 shall denote the utility of the most recent job, while w_i^k stands for the utility of the least recent job of τ_i. A task's basic (m, k)-HCUF $H_m(\tau_i)$ is calculated as the mean value of all entries in w_i:

$$H_m(\tau_i) = \frac{1}{k_i} \sum_{j=1}^{k_i} w_i^j \tag{2}$$

Obviously, if all jobs inside the window have kept their deadlines, $H_m(\tau_i) = 1$. Additionally, the (m, k)-constraint of τ_i requires that $H_m(\tau_i)$ never falls below $\frac{m_i}{k_i}$. If $H_m(\tau_i) = \frac{m_i}{k_i}$, the task is in a critical state and must not miss its next deadline. Thus, the HCUF value representing the critical state is very important for scheduling decisions. The HCUF values representing the critical states of tasks with different (m, k)-constraints are not directly comparable. To overcome this drawback and ease scheduler implementation, we scale H_m by $\frac{k_i}{m_i}$ such that the minimally allowed utility for any (m, k)-constraint is 1:

$$\hat{H}_m(\tau_i) = \frac{k_i}{m_i} H_m(\tau_i) = \frac{1}{m_i} \sum_{j=1}^{k_i} w_i^j \tag{3}$$

$\hat{H}_m$ gives a relative measurement of how far a task is away from a violation of its (m, k)-constraint. As long as $\hat{H}_m(\tau_i) \geq 1$, the task's (m, k)-constraint is fulfiled. The maximum value of $\hat{H}_m(\tau_i)$ is $\frac{k_i}{m_i}$, which leads to the following two properties of $\hat{H}_m$ for special (m, k)-parameters:

Property 1. Tasks that have different (m, k)-constraints, but whose constraints have the same ratio $\frac{m}{k}$, can gain the same maximum value. However, for tasks with bigger k, $\hat{H}_m$ has a more fine-grained resolution.

Property 2. Tasks $\tau_i, \tau_j, i \neq j$ with $k_i = k_j$ and $m_i < m_j$ have different maximum values $\max \hat{H}_m(\tau_i) > \max \hat{H}_m(\tau_j)$.

We will discuss how these properties influence scheduling decisions in the following section.

3.2   Scheduling Based on (m, k)-HCUFs

Our scheduling algorithm MKU for (m, k)-tasks is based on the best-effort app-roach by Jensen et al. [15], which in turn is an extension to the EDF algorithm. In the beginning, the entries of the (m, k)-windows w_i of all tasks are initialised to 1. All ready jobs are kept in a list ordered increasingly by their deadlines. Dispatching is performed in EDF manner from the front of the list. If after the insertion of a new job in the ready queue the possibility of a deadline miss is detected for a job j_n, all jobs j_o with deadlines $d_o \leq d_n$ (including j_n) are exam-ined (indices denote position in EDF queue). For each job j_o, its task's possible HCU $\hat{H}_p$ value is calculated, assuming that j_o is cancelled. Assuming that j_o belongs to task τ_i, $\hat{H}_p$ is calculated in accordance with equation (3) as:

$$\hat{H}_p(\tau_i) = \frac{1}{m} \sum_{j=1}^{k_i-1} w_i^j \qquad (4)$$

Note that the sum now only ranges up to w_{k_i-1}, compared to equation (3): If the current job is cancelled, w_i^k will be removed from the window and a new value 0 representing that cancellation will be inserted at the front of w_i. The job with the maximum value of $\hat{H}_p$ is then removed from the schedule. However, only jobs $j_{i,l}$ with $\hat{H}_p(\tau_i) \geq 1$ are considered for cancellation. This procedure is repeated until the overload is resolved. If no candidates for removal can be found, obviously no job can be cancelled without violating its (m, k)-constraint, and therefore the whole task set is not schedulable under MKU with the given (m, k)-constraints.

In the beginning, tasks with equal $\frac{m}{k}$ ratios have the same probability for having their first job cancelled. However, due to the finer granularity of $\hat{H}_m$ of tasks with bigger k values (see property 1 from section 3.1), such tasks also have a higher probability to be chosen for subsequent cancellations, as their $\hat{H}_m$ value decreases more slowly. For tasks τ_i, τ_j with $k_i = k_j$, but $m_i < m_j$ (property 2 from section 3.1), τ_i has a higher probability of cancellation due to its higher $\max \hat{H}_m(\tau_i)$ value, which represents τ_i's higher tolerance towards job losses.

3.3   Complexity

The complexity of the MKU approach can be split in two parts: Concerning regular management of the ready list, MKU inherits the complexity of EDF. A naive implementation using regular lists has a complexity of $O(n)$ for insertion of new jobs. Using balanced trees, the management complexity can be reduced to $O(\log n)$ [11].

Additionally, MKU introduces some overhead for detection and resolution of overload situations. Both operation must only be performed when a new job is added to the ready list. Overload detection, i.e. finding a job that will miss its deadline, takes $O(n)$ steps, as the ready list must be examined from its beginning. To resolve an overload situation, at most n additional walks through the list must be performed, leading to a complexity of $O(n^2)$. The $\hat{H}_m$ value for each task should be initialised once and then be kept in memory. Thus, online calculation/update of $\hat{H}_m$ and $\hat{H}_p$ values can be performed in constant time (regardless of the window size k) by advancing the existing value using the entries of the sliding window w_i of each task τ_i.

4   Experimental Evaluation

We compare the performance of the MKU scheduling policy with that of other scheduling techniques for (m, k)-firm real-time task sets. Therefore, we have performed extensive simulations of randomly generated task sets. The simulations were performed using the `tms-sim` framework developed in our group [17], which is available as open source software[1]. In this section, we discuss the methodology we applied in our evaluations, and subsequently present and discuss the results.

4.1   Methodology

Task Set Generation. Task sets consisting of $n = 5$ tasks are randomly generated in the following manner: The period of the tasks is randomly selected between 5 and 15. The k value of each task is randomly selected from $[2, 10]$, and the m value from $[1, k]$. The execution times of the tasks then is generated such that the task set's utilisation lies inside a given interval $U \pm d_U$. U stands for a target utilisation, d_U represents the maximally allowed deviation from U. For each task τ_i, an execution time weight e_i is randomly selected from $[1, 100]$. Based on the weights e_i and the target utilisation U, a value C_i' is calculated. e_i indicates, how much a task τ_i's utilisation $U_i = \frac{C_i}{T_i}$ contributes to the total utilisation U:

$$\frac{e_i}{\sum_{j=1}^{n} e_j} = \frac{U_i}{U} \tag{5}$$

Solving for C_i' yields:

$$C_i' = \frac{U}{\sum_{j=1}^{n} e_j} T_i e_i \tag{6}$$

A task's actual execution time is retrieved by rounding C_i' to the nearest integer value. If the rounding results in 0, $C_i = 1$ is set. This forced rounding up of C_i leads to slight upward shift of the mean utilisation away from U of the generated task sets within any interval. Task sets with a utilisation outside $U \pm d_U$ are discarded immediately.

Evaluation Environment. We examine utilisations of $U = 1.05, 1.15, \ldots, 1.95$ with a tolerance $d_U = 0.05$. For each utilisation interval, 10.000 task sets are generated. Each task set is executed for 1.000.000 time steps to account at least for the largest possible hyper period of all tasks. In our simulations, we compare the MKU scheduler with several other scheduling policies that have been

---

[1] http://myweb.rz.uni-augsburg.de/~klugeflo/tms-sim/

proposed for (m,k)-firm tasks. An overview of the used models can be found in table 1. The behaviour of the GDPA and GDPA-S schemes [8] is very similar. Therefore, the GDPA-S scheme is omitted. Tasks according to the DBP [14] and MKC/-R [26,27] schemes are dispatched using a fixed priority preemptive (FPP) scheduler. The GDPA scheme uses a modified EDF scheduler according to [8]. The same applies for the MKU scheme presented in this paper (see sect. 3.2). Simulation assumes that the execution time of a task is constant and not subject to any variations. All schedulers cancel jobs as soon as the latest possible starting time of a job $d_{i,j} - c_{i,j}$ elapses without the job being executed, as the job then will not be able to keep its deadline.

Table 1. Task models and schedulers used in the experimental evaluation

Model	Abbr.	Scheduler	Reference
Distance-based priority	DBP	FPP	[14]
(m,k)-firm control tasks	MKC	FPP	[27]
MKC with pattern rotation	MKC-R	FPP	[26]
Guaranteed Dynamic Priority Assignment	GDPA	EDF (modified)	[8]
Utility-based (m,k)-tasks	MKU	EDF (modified)	sect. 3

4.2   Results

First, let us examine the overall success rates that the various schedulers achieve. These are shown in figure 1. Comparing MKC and MKC-R, we can see the improvements that are introduced by the rotation of the (m,k)-patterns in MKC-R. The performance of GDPA lies somewhere between MKC and MKC-R. However, for all three approaches the number of successfully scheduled task sets drops very fast to one percent and below at a target utilisation of 1.45 and beyond. Better results can be achieved with DBP and MKU. Both schemes achieve to schedule at least twice as much task sets as can be scheduled by one of MKC, MKC-R, or GDPA. For moderate overloads with a utilisation $U < 1.5$, MKU even outperforms DBP by being able to schedule 3-17% more task sets. For task sets with high overloads ($U > 1.5$), DBP yields better results. Table 2 lists the absolute numbers of task sets that were schedulable under all schemes. The percentages compare the differences between the MKU and DBP approaches (using DBP as base). A positive percentage indicates that MKU could schedule more task sets than DBP successfully, and vice-versa.

An important parameter is the number of preemptions a job experiences during being executed. In a real implementation, each preemption introduces an additional overhead that delays completion of jobs. Concerning the task sets that were successfully scheduled by any of the scheduling schemes, we present the number of job preemptions that occurred. Table 3 shows the number of preemptions that all task sets that were schedulable under all investigated schedulers incurred. The values for target utilisations $U \geq 1.65$ are omitted due to the low number of overall successful task sets in these intervals. Figure 4.2 shows the average number of preemptions that occurred per task set during simulation.

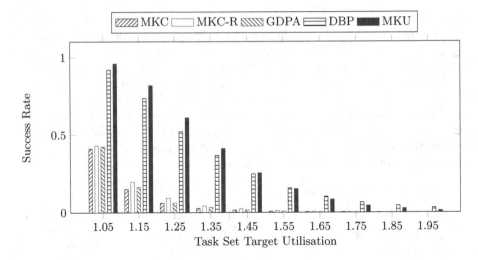

Fig. 1. Overall success rates

Table 2. Absolute number of task sets that were schedulable

Target utilisation	1.05	1.15	1.25	1.35	1.45	1.55	1.65	1.75	1.85	1.95
all Schedulers	2430	661	213	76	32	8	6	0	0	0
MKC	4112	1499	604	268	148	63	36	22	10	1
MKC-S	4305	1974	935	419	219	111	49	20	10	8
GDPA	4240	1635	620	325	154	78	34	18	13	2
DBP	9180	7352	5214	3674	2478	1575	1028	655	452	310
MKU	9572	8164	6111	4109	2540	1525	838	447	250	114
MKU vs. DBP	4%	11%	17%	12%	3%	-3%	-18%	-32%	-45%	-63%

Table 3. Accumulated number of preemptions experienced by all task sets that were schedulable by any scheduler in each utilisation interval

Target utilisation	1.05	1.15	1.25	1.35	1.45	1.55
Schedulable task sets	2430	661	213	76	32	8
MKC	894	180	57	19	10	0
MKC-S	11378	2918	856	294	135	43
GDPA	1688	369	121	41	19	6
DBP	15148	4511	1495	588	241	67
MKU	2089	471	144	48	25	9

Both the table and the figure show that MKU schedules task sets with only a fraction of the preemptions that occur in DBP. Insofar, MKU induces a much lower system overhead than DBP.

Summed up, our results show that for moderate overloads ($U < 1.5$) MKU can outperform the other scheduling schemes for (m, k)-firm tasks. This utilisation region seems also to be the most relevant, as task sets with higher overloads have high probability of being not schedulable at all (see table 2).

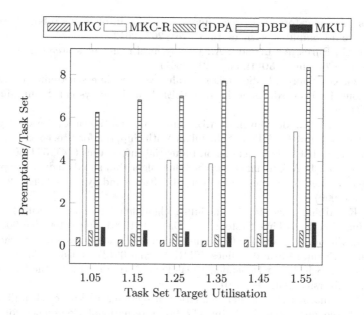

Fig. 2. Average number of preemptions that a task set that was schedulable experienced.

5   Conclusions

We have modeled the (m, k)-constraints of (m, k)-firm real-time tasks as history-cognisant utility functions. The HCUF of a (m, k)-firm real-time task represents the ratio between kept and missed deadlines in the k-window of the task. These HCUFs are used by the heuristic MKU scheduler to decide which jobs to cancel in overload situations. MKU is based on the best effort scheduler by Jensen et al. [15] that uses time-utility functions for these decisions. By looking one step into the future (see $\hat{H}_p(\tau_i)$ in eq. (4)), MKU takes also into account whether a task can tolerate a cancellation at all. Our experimental evaluations show that for moderate overloads with a utilisation $U < 1.5$, MKU can schedule 3-17% more task sets than the DBP approach [14]. Additionally, jobs scheduled with MKU experience much less preemptions than under DBP.

In the future, we are going to analyse MKU formally. A central goal of this analysis is to derive sufficient schedulability conditions. Additionally, we hope to find properties of MKU that explain the tradeoff point against DBP around $U \approx 1.5$ that we found in our simulations. Finally, we plan to apply MKU for scheduling robust control systems.

References

1. Aldarmi, S.A., Burns, A.: Dynamic value-density for scheduling real-time systems. In: Proceedings of the 11th Euromicro Conference on Real-Time Systems, pp. 270–277 (1999)

2. Baums, A.: Indicators of the real time of a mobile autonomous robot. Automatic Control and Computer Sciences **46**(6), 261–267 (2012)
3. Bernat, G., Burns, A., Liamosi, A.: Weakly hard real-time systems. IEEE Transactions on Computers **50**(4), 308–321 (2001)
4. Buttazzo, G., Spuri, M., Sensini, F.: Value vs. deadline scheduling in overload conditions. In: Proceedings of the 16th IEEE Real-Time Systems Symposium, pp. 90–99 (1995)
5. Camponogara, E., de Oliveira, A.B., Lima, G.: Optimization-Based Dynamic Reconfiguration of Real-Time Schedulers With Support for Stochastic Processor Consumption. IEEE Transactions on Industrial Informatics **6**(4), 594–609 (2010)
6. Chen, H., Xia, J.: A real-time task scheduling algorithm based on dynamic priority. In: International Conference on Embedded Software and Systems, ICESS 2009, pp. 431–436 (2009)
7. Chen, K., Muhlethaler, P.: A scheduling algorithm for tasks described by time value function. Real-Time Systems **10**, 293–312 (1996). doi:10.1007/BF00383389
8. Cho, H., Chung, Y., Park, D.: Guaranteed dynamic priority assignment scheme for streams with (m, k)-firm deadlines. ETRI Journal **32**(3), 500–502 (2010)
9. Clark, R.K.: Scheduling Dependent Real-Time Activities. Ph.D. thesis, Carnegie Mellon University (August 1990)
10. Ding, W., Guo, R.: Design and evaluation of sectional real-time scheduling algorithms based on system load. In: The 9th International Conference for Young Computer Scientists, ICYCS 2008, pp. 14–18 (2008)
11. Ekelin, C.: Clairvoyant non-preemptive edf scheduling. In: Proceedings of the 18th Euromicro Conference on Real-Time Systems, ECRTS 2006, Dresden, Germany, July, 5–7, pp. 23–32. IEEE Computer Society (2006)
12. Flavia, F., Ning, J., Simonot-Lion, F., YeQiong, S.: Optimal on-line (m, k)-firm constraint assignment for real-time control tasks based on plant state information. In: IEEE International Conference on Emerging Technologies and Factory Automation, ETFA 2008, pp. 908–915 (2008)
13. Goossens, J.: (m, k)-firm constraints and dbp scheduling: Impact of the initial k-sequence and exact feasibility test. In: 16th International Conference on Real-Time and Network Systems (RTNS 2008), pp. 61–66, October 2008
14. Hamdaoui, M., Ramanathan, P.: A dynamic priority assignment technique for streams with (m, k)-firm deadlines. IEEE Transactions on Computers **44**(12), 1443–1451 (1995)
15. Jensen, E.D., Locke, C.D., Tokuda, H.: A time-driven scheduling model for real-time operating systems. In: 6th Real-Time Systems Symposium (RTSS 1985), San Diego, California, USA, December 3–6, pp. 112–122, December 1985
16. Jia, N., Song, Y.Q., Simonot-Lion, F.: Task handler based on (m, k)-firm constraint model for managing a set of real-time controllers. In: Navet, N., Simonot-Lion, F., Puaut, I. (eds.) 15th International Conference on Real-Time and Network Systems - RTNS 2007, Nancy, France, pp. 183–19 (2007)
17. Kluge, F.: `tms-sim` - timing models scheduling simulation framework - release 2014–12. Tech. Rep. 2014–07, University of Augsburg (December 2014)
18. Kluge, F., Haas, F., Gerdes, M., Ungerer, T.: History-cognisant time-utility-functions for scheduling overloaded real-time control systems. In: Proceedings of the 7th Junior Researcher Workshop on Real-Time Computing (JRWRTC 2013), Sophia Antipolis, France, October 16, October 2013
19. Koren, G., Shasha, D.: Dover; an optimal on-line scheduling algorithm for overloaded real-time systems. In: Real-Time Systems Symposium, pp. 290–299 (1992)

20. Koren, G., Shasha, D.: Skip-over: algorithms and complexity for overloaded systems that allow skips. In: Proceedings of the 16th IEEE Real-Time Systems Symposium, pp. 110–117 (1995)
21. Li, P., Wu, H., Ravindran, B., Jensen, E.D.: A utility accrual scheduling algorithm for real-time activities with mutual exclusion resource constraints. IEEE Transactions on Computers 55(4), 454–469 (2006)
22. Liu, C.L., Layland, J.W.: Scheduling algorithms for multiprogramming in a hard-real-time environment. J. ACM 20(1), 46–61 (1973)
23. Locke, C.D.: Best-effort decision-making for real-time scheduling. Ph.D. thesis, Carnegie Mellon University, Pittsburgh, PA, USA (1986)
24. Mejía-Alvarez, P., Melhem, R., Mossé, D.: An incremental approach to scheduling during overloads in real-time systems. In: Proceedings of the 21st IEEE Real-Time Systems Symposium, pp. 283–293 (2000)
25. Mosse, D., Pollack, M.E., Ronen, Y.: Value-density algorithms to handle transient overloads in scheduling. In: Proceedings of the 11th Euromicro Conference on Real-Time Systems, pp. 278–286 (1999)
26. Quan, G., Hu, X.: Enhanced fixed-priority scheduling with (m, k)-firm guarantee. In: Proceedings of the 21st IEEE Real-Time Systems Symposium, pp. 79–88 (2000)
27. Ramanathan, P.: Overload management in real-time control applications using (m, k)-firm guarantee. IEEE Transactions on Parallel and Distributed Systems 10(6), 549–559 (1999)
28. Ravindran, B., Jensen, E.D., Li, P.: On recent advances in time/utility function real-time scheduling and resource management. In: Eighth IEEE International Symposium on Object-Oriented Real-Time Distributed Computing, ISORC 2005, pp. 55–60 (2005)
29. Semprebom, T., Montez, C., Vasques, F.: (m, k)-firm pattern spinning to improve the gts allocation of periodic messages in ieee 802.15.4 networks. EURASIP Journal on Wireless Communications and Networking 2013(1), 1–15 (2013)
30. Wang, J., Ravindran, B.: Time-utility function-driven switched ethernet: packet scheduling algorithm, implementation, and feasibility analysis. IEEE Transactions on Parallel and Distributed Systems 15(2), 119–133 (2004)
31. West, R., Schwan, K.: Dynamic window-constrained scheduling for multimedia applications. In: IEEE International Conference on Multimedia Computing and Systems, vol. 2, pp. 87–91, July 1999

MESI-Based Cache Coherence for Hard Real-Time Multicore Systems

Sascha Uhrig$^{(\boxtimes)}$, Lillian Tadros, and Arthur Pyka

Technical University of Dortmund, Dortmund, Germany
sascha.uhrig@tu-dortmund.de

Abstract. Demands on computing performance are steadily increasing, also in the domain of embedded hard real-time applications. Accordingly, multicore processors have already entered the hard real-time domain, mainly for execution of multiple applications. Further performance improvements can be gained by executing multithreaded applications on multicores. Since such applications share data between multiple cores, coherent accesses to that data must be guaranteed. To be applied in hard real-time domains, the complete system, including the cache hierarchy, needs to provide a predictable timing behaviour that allows a static estimate of the worst case execution time.

This paper presents an analysis of the well-known MESI (Modified, Exclusive, Shared, Invalid) technique and its drawbacks concerning time predictability. Moreover, we show ways how to implement a MESI technique suitable for hard real-time systems.

Keywords: Hard real-time systems · Timing predictability · Cache coherence · Multicore

1 Introduction

The state of the art in general purpose computing systems is to provide higher performance by multi- and many-core architectures. This trend can also be observed in the embedded systems domain. For example, the Automotive Open System Architecture (AUTOSAR) [1] in its revision 4.0 describes techniques that enable multicore architectures. The Integrated Modular Avionics (IMA) [13] architecture also allows use of multicores if several preconditions are met. Some of these preconditions are defined in the ARINC 653 standard [14].

The major target of using multicores in embedded systems is currently to bundle several applications on the same computing system in order to reduce area, weight, energy as well as profiting from the increased performance. Since different applications require different levels of real-time performance, security and reliability, such systems are called *mixed criticality systems*.

In order to bring certification efforts to a feasible level, all applications must run in total isolation which is the basic idea of the IMA concept [6] and is also included in AUTOSAR 4.0. This means that *freedom from interference* of the

© Springer International Publishing Switzerland 2015
L.M. Pinho et al. (Eds): ARCS 2015, LNCS 9017, pp. 212–223, 2015.
DOI: 10.1007/978-3-319-16086-3_17

applications must be guaranteed by the system. If this is the case, each application can be treated according to its own criticality level. Interferences between applications are eliminated by the system. Freedom from interference means that both the memory regions as well as the timing behaviour of a given application cannot be influenced by any other application. The first problem can be solved by a suitable memory management unit and is not discussed here. The second issue is more problematic since the shared resources of a multicore can be accessed by different applications in parallel. The problem is further aggravated by the execution of multithreaded applications, which frequently share large amounts of data and thus necessitate cache coherence. Parallel hard real-time applications have been researched in the European FP7 project *parMERASA* [12].

Previous examinations of the cache coherence technique of Freescale's P4080 show a significant influence of cache coherence on the execution time [8]. In this work, it is shown that simply enabling cache coherence without actually sharing data decreases performance. Sharing data leads to a further slow-down. Freescale recommends disabling cache coherence if strict time predictable behaviour is required [3]. In view of this, Infineon's AURIX multicore relinquishes cache coherence altogether [4].

The contribution of this paper is a study of different bus-based embodiments of the well-known MESI [5] coherence technique which are examined regarding time predictability, interference, and worst case estimations. Moreover, recommendations for a time predictable implementation are given, which also allow complete freedom from interference.

The paper is organised as follows: Section 2 presents related work addressing isolation of applications on multicores and Section 3 discusses different aspects of MESI variations regarding static timing analysis. In Section 4 we present a possible incarnation of the MESI cache coherence technique that shows predictable timing behaviour. Section 5 concludes the paper.

2 Related Work on Timing Isolation

A basic precondition for timing isolation is that activities of one core cannot affect any other core in an unpredictable way. More precisely, the latency of all accesses to shared resources must be upper-bounded and this upper bound must be known statically. Moreover, the upper bound should be as close as possible to the actual timing to allow a realistic static WCET estimation. The shared resources relevant to cache coherence are the shared bus, the shared memory and the local caches, now that they contain shared data.

Timing isolation on shared buses can be attained by using simple slot-based arbitration schemes like Time Division Multiplexed Access (TDMA) as proposed by Wilhelm et al. [21] or (prioritised) round-robin based arbitration as proposed by Paolieri et al. [10].

Accesses to shared memory can be managed by time predictable memory controllers [2] [11]. These controllers schedule memory accesses in a way that eliminates interferences between accesses. The common idea is to assign cores to memory banks in the style of the multithreaded PRET architecture [18], where the thread slots are assigned to memory banks. The proposed techniques can be extended to allow accesses to the complete memory (instead of private banks) but this comes at the price of even longer (though still bounded) access latencies. One possibility to reduce the worst case latency, where the maximum possible concurrency has to be assumed, is presented by Schlieker et al. [19]. Here, the maximum number of concurrent accesses is determined depending on the behaviour of co-scheduled threads, which requires a statically known schedule and an analysis of all threads. If threads are programmed in a way which makes a static analysis impossible[1], the physical maximum concurrency must be assumed.

Since the price for time predictability is a significantly longer latency of memory accesses caused by the bus and the memory controller, data caches are strongly recommended. Needless to say, these caches must exhibit predictable (timing) behaviour, thus eliminating the possibility of implementing a shared cache [21].

Integrating private caches calls for a technique that keeps accesses to shared data coherent, i.e. the most recently written value must be delivered to the next read access, independent of the cores involved. Current multicores suitable for hard real-time systems either do not comprise any data cache or the caches are used only for private data. Accesses to shared data are performed without the help of a cache, resulting in a long worst case latency for each access. Local caches not holding shared data (and hence, without coherence support) can be analysed by using techniques proposed in [17], [20], and [7].

We expect that future parallel hard real-time applications will need to share larger amounts of data between different cores. Longer latencies because of uncached accesses reducing the overall performance cannot be tolerated in this case. Paolieri et al. [9] proposed a technique that allows software pipelined parallel execution with data cache support. Data that is propagated from one pipeline stage to the next one is stored in separate cache banks (one output bank per pipeline stage). These banks are passed to the next pipeline stage on every pipeline step together with cached data. The cache will be regarded as preloaded by the previous pipeline stage during static timing analysis.

Pyka et al. [15,16] proposed the time predictable *On-demand coherent cache* (ODC[2]) technique which allows sharing data with cache support in special situations. The methodology relies on synchronization using mutexes and barriers. Sharing data outside of synchronized regions is not allowed. Moreover, it must be guaranteed that cache lines with private data are not shared, i.e. private data of different cores must not be located in the same cache line.

Since there is no time predictable technique available that fulfills the need for general cache coherence, we examine the well-know MESI coherence technique for suitability in hard real-time systems. We focus on a bus-based system, given that the number of cores in hard real-time systems is likely to remain comparatively low (2-8) in the near future.

---

[1] In mixed criticality environments, non-critical threads do not need to follow any guidelines or conventions.

3 Analysis of Current Cache Coherence Techniques

All well-known coherence techniques focus on optimising average performance with little attention to providing predictable timing behaviour. We examined the MESI coherence techniques with respect to time predictability. We assume an example system containing multiple cores (the concrete number is irrelevant) connected by a shared bus to a shared memory. The cores are equipped with local first level data caches. Further cache levels are not foreseen because they lack analysability [21]. The bus arbitration follows a homogeneous TDMA scheme as proposed by [21] and [10]. The memory controller is assumed to show predictable timing behaviour as mentioned in Section 2. Instruction caches are not considered in this study given that the read-only nature of these caches alleviates the need for coherence.

The examined cache coherence techniques cover all combinations of the following characteristics and parameters, except for combinations of update-based actualisation with write-back policy[2]:

1. Associativity: Direct mapped and associative caches show different characteristics regarding analysability.
2. Write policy: The timing behaviour of write-back and write-through policies is different. If a write-through technique is applied, write accesses modify both the local cache content (in case of a hit) and the content of memory in parallel. This means the memory is always up-to-date.
3. Write allocation: The chosen write allocation policy defines how a cache deals with write accesses if the corresponding data is not present in the cache. Write-allocate loads the required cache line into the cache and modifies it afterwards. Non-write-allocate does not copy the data, instead the data is written directly to the memory. Note that the latter complicates cache coherence because other caches holding the specific data need to be updated.
4. Actualisation of cache content: We distinguish between invalidation-based and update-based techniques. If one core modifies the content of a memory location held in multiple caches, the corresponding cache lines in other cores can be invalidated or updated to ensure coherent accesses.
5. Data transport: In case of a cache miss on data present in and modified by another core, this data can be sent to the requesting core through the memory (pure bus-snooping) or directly from the source cache to the requesting cache (bus-snarfing). In the first case, the cache holding data interrupts the memory access of the requesting core and writes-back the new data to memory while snarfing means sending the new data directly to the target cache.

For a tight WCET estimation, sufficient knowledge of the cache content and replacement policy (if applicable) is required as well as defined maximum latencies for cache hits and misses (upper bounds must be quantifiable).[3]

---

[2] Sending updates only at the time of evictions would mean that other caches are not aware of remote modifications.

[3] The upper bounds must be reasonably low because otherwise the use of uncached accesses to shared memory would seem preferable over coherent caches.

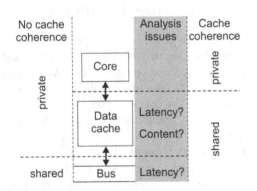

Fig. 1. Nature of local cache (shared, private) with and without cache coherence and questions arising at cache timing analysis

Figure 1 presents three issues that need to be considered in a static analysis of a memory access: the time required to access the local cache, whether the access results in a hit or a miss (depends on cache content), and, in the case of a miss, the latency for loading the cache line from memory.

If no cache coherence is supported, the first two questions can be answered on a local, per-core basis. In this case, other cores can only influence the cache's timing as a result of accesses to the shared bus. In contrast, when cache coherence is applied, there may be communication between a local cache and other cores. Hence, both the cache's contents as well as its timing behaviour w.r.t the local core can be modified by other cores. The cache can therefore not be treated as *private* any more.

The issues affecting cache content are therefore modifications by other cores as well as invalidate/update actions of other caches. These prohibit static prediction of the data stored in a cache line at a given point in time. Additionally, the access latencies of cache hits and misses can vary depending on the states and actions of other caches. These timing variations can be caused by:

- invalidate/update requests from the local cache that need to be sent to other caches,
- memory requests that are interrupted by other caches (e.g. if another core needs to write-back modified data),
- requests of other caches that need to be handled by the local cache (e.g. an interruption of memory accesses of other caches).

We consolidated these issues and identified the following four topics that are influenced by the presence of cache coherence: (A) Unpredictable invalidation, (B) Cache access latency, (C) Shared data miss latency and (D) Write hit latency. Here, (A) addresses individual cache lines or cache sets, (B) affects all cache accesses independent from the state and the nature (private or shared) of the accessed data, (C) is relevant only for cache misses if a shared cache line is accessed, and (D) for writes on shared cache lines.

Since each can lead to uncertainties during timing analysis or even to an unpredictable timing behaviour, we discuss them individually in the following sections.

3.1   A: Unpredictable Invalidation

In case of an invalidation-based coherence technique, the availability of a specific piece of data is hard to predict. This applies primarily to cache lines with shared data but also to private data in associative caches:

1. A cache line containing data which is shared with other cores can become invalid if another core intends to write to that data.
2. Even though the lifetime of any private cache line is not directly affected by shared data, the state of the replacement policy can be modified by invalidations of shared cache lines. This problem does not exist for direct-mapped caches since there is no replacement policy.

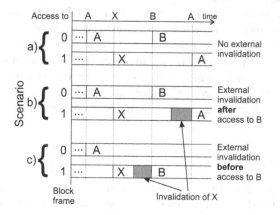

A simple example (see Figure 2) illustrates a situation where private data is affected by a coherence message: We assume a 2-way set-associative cache with a Least-Recently-Used (LRU) replacement policy and the cache line access order A, X, B, A, where the cache lines A and B hold private and X holds shared data. All accesses occur within the same set. If X is

Fig. 2. Different scenarios of shared data invalidation can lead to eviction or preservation of private data A

invalidated before the access to B (scenario c), the free cache line can be used for B. In the case X is not invalidated before (scenario a and b), B will evict A and the next access to A will lead to a cache miss.

Hence, the lifetime of any cache line within a set that can hold shared data can be influenced by unpredictable invalidations of other cores if an associative cache is used. This makes the prediction of the cache content practically impossible.

In contrast, direct-mapped caches do not exhibit the problem of unpredictable replacement status and are thus candidates for hard real-time multicore systems.

3.2   B: Cache Access Latency

Snooping- and snarfing-based coherence techniques require that all cores listen to the activities of the bus. The cache control logic has to check at each activity if the local cache is affected. This is done by comparing the address on the bus with the cache tags stored locally. If the addressed cache line is available in the local cache, the type of the bus transaction together with the local state of the cache line is checked. Depending on the outcome of this check further actions may be required by the cache controller.

In general purpose systems, all these steps can be done by the same logic that controls the accesses of the local core. If an internal and an external access occur at the same time, one of the requests can be delayed, preferably the internal one. With respect to hard real-time systems, delaying either of the requests is problematic: Delaying the external request means affecting the timing of the requesting core by local activities, while delaying the internal request means, at first glance, an unpredictable influence on the local timing.

Whereas delaying external accesses is not an option, delaying internal accesses has an upper bound, given a TDMA bus arbitration, and can therefore be analysed thus: During the TDMA slot assigned to the local core no external request can occur. Hence, there will be no conflict at that time and the local access to the cache can be performed.

Unfortunately, this solution brings a high overhead to the WCET because, even for cache hits, a maximum latency of the length of one TDMA period must be assumed (i. e. external disruptions in all other slots). One possible solution is to implement the cache as dual-ported cache resulting in higher hardware complexity. The cache controller would then be able to deal with two requests simultaneously: the internal read access from the local core and the external invalidation or update request from another core. Write accesses are not an issue because of (D).

3.3   C: Shared Data Miss Latency

A cache miss typically generates a read burst from main memory. Since data in the main memory could be outdated with modified data present in another core's cache, a previous write back of the cache line possessing the data is necessary. This topic is relevant only for write-back policy or if a write buffer is integrated. If a simple write-through policy (i.e., no write buffers) is applied, this problem does not occur. The use of bus-snarfing can also mitigate the problem.

The issue of data write-back leads to the following questions: Is the required data modified by another core and not yet written back to memory? If so, when will the other core be able to respond to the request and, if necessary, write back the current data?

Since we are assuming a time predictable TDMA bus arbitration, the timing of both issues must fit into the slots of the bus. In both cases, the remote core (if any) can use the slot of the local core to respond to the read request. This is possible because, at that instance, the remote core is not allowed to send its own request to the bus anyway. Figure 3 shows an example timing of a TDMA-based quad-core system in combination with bus-snooping and bus-snarfing, respectively.

As can be seen in the figure, a snooping-based technique with write-back policy does not meet the requirements of hard real-time systems: In the first step, a core (core 1) issues a read request for a cache line present in another core (core 2). Core 2 has to write-back that data first which cannot be performed in the current time slot because this slot is already occupied by the read request aborted by core 2. Since it is not allowed for core 2 to use its own slot

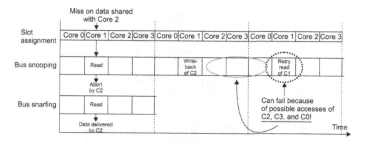

Fig. 3. Example timing of a cache miss when accessing shared data that is modified and available in another cache (write-back policy). An unpredictable and possibly unbounded waiting time can occur in case of a bus-snooping technique.

(which is reserved for core 2's own memory accesses), the write-back has to take place during the next slot of core 1. Now, the cores 2, 3, and 0 could access that particular data in the following slots with intention to write (write-allocate technique assumed, read accesses are no problem here). If this is the case, the new request is handled immediately since the memory is up-to-date and the requesting core (2,3, or 0) afterwards holds again a modified copy of the data originally requested by core 1.

This circumstance results in the original starting situation from core 1's point of view. In this case, the next attempt of core 1 to read the data will again fail. We conclude that the access latency to shared data cannot be bounded if a snooping-based write-back technique with write-allocate is used since starvation can occur.

With bus-snarfing, the data required by core 1 is delivered by core 2 directly, given that core 2 is able to handle the request immediately (see Section 3.2). Since the read is now an atomic action, it cannot be interrupted or harmed by any other core. The latency of a cache miss can be bounded independently of the availability of the corresponding data in other caches.

Alternatively, a non-write-allocated write technique can be applied. In this case, no core will ask for the specific cache line with intention to write within the critical phase (between write-back and second trial of core 1). Instead the intended write will be performed on the memory directly without copying the data to the cache.

3.4 D: Write Hit Latency

If a core wants to write on a cache line that is present in the local cache as well as in other cores (i.e. in MESI *shared* state), the write cannot be executed immediately even if a write-back policy is applied. Figure 4 demonstrates the following situation: The local caches of two cores hold the same cache line and both cores want to write on that line in the same cycle. Both cores recognise a hit which means that each one has to announce the write to the other cores in order to get the line in *exclusive* state. In general purpose systems, both cores

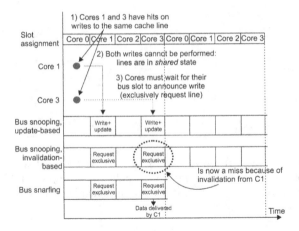

Fig. 4. Two cores perform writes to the same cache line which is present in both caches. The writes cannot be performed immediately since the cores do not know about each others' activity.

will compete for the bus. The winner will perform the write first and the second core will follow.

In case of a TDMA-based bus arbitration scheme, each core has to wait until its own time slot has arrived before making the announcement. This means that in the worst case a core has to wait for one TDMA period before performing a write on a cache hit. Moreover, this is valid only for bus-snarfing or update-based techniques. For invalidation-based bus-snooping, a similar starvation situation as described in paragraph 3.3 can occur, resulting in an indefinite delay. Since the cache lines are already available in the cache, there is no difference between write-allocate and non-write-allocate.

Note that with write-through policy every core has to wait for its TDMA slot anyway. Accordingly, there is no difference between write hits and misses to shared data or to private data.

4   Cache Coherence for Hard Real-time Systems

Figure 5 shows a summary of the issues concerning time predictability of MESI-based cache coherence techniques. The figure targets single-ported direct-mapped caches since associative caches generally suffer from the problem of external modifications of the replacement state with all invalidation-based techniques (left sub-figure). The combination of *update-based* and *write-back* is not useful and not considered here. The labels refer to the issues mentioned in the preceding paragraphs. *(CU)* and *(DU)* represent the unbounded delays of *(C)* and *(D)*, respectively.

The snooping-based write-invalidate techniques are probably the most frequently implemented techniques in general purpose and high performance

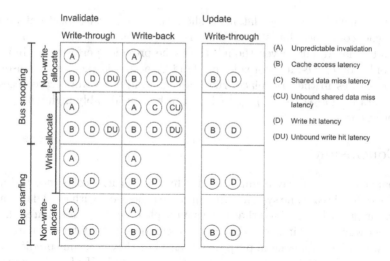

Fig. 5. Summary of issues concerning time predictability of different cache coherence techniques. The summary focuses on single-ported direct-mapped caches.

systems. As can be seen, these techniques suffer from all the above mentioned issues complicating or even impeding (unbounded delays *CU* and *DU*) a static WCET analysis.

In contrast, update-based caches with write-through policy allow a static WCET analysis in principle. Moreover, if several preconditions are fulfilled, overestimation can be reduced to a minimum: Since *(B)* is based on the implementation of a single-ported cache, it is not relevant anymore with a dual-ported cache. Hence, only *(D)* affects the WCET analysis of update-based caches, independently of the used write-allocate and data transportation techniques. Fortunately, *(D)* does not impede a WCET analysis but rather just slightly increases pessimism.

In the following equations 1-4, we present worst-case bound estimations for the accesses *read hit* (t_{rd_hit}), *read miss* (t_{rd_miss}), *write hit* (t_{wr_hit}), and *write miss* (t_{wr_miss}) if an update-based dual-ported cache with write-through (WT) policy is used. T_{TDMA} represents the period of the TDMA arbitration scheme in processor clock cycles and $T_{Lat_{mem}}$ indicates the latency of the memory and the bus for data delivery of read requests.

$$t_{rd\_hit} - immediate processing \tag{1}$$

$$t_{rd\_miss} = T_{TDMA} + T_{Lat_{mem}} \tag{2}$$

$$t_{wr\_hit} = \begin{cases} T_{TDMA}, \text{ if } exclusive \text{ because of } write\text{-}trough \\ T_{TDMA}, \text{ if } shared \text{ because of (D)} \end{cases} \tag{3}$$

$$t_{wr\_miss} = \begin{cases} T_{TDMA}, & \text{for } non\text{-}write\text{-}allocate \\ 2 * T_{TDMA} + T_{Lat_{mem}}, & \text{for } write\text{-}allocate \end{cases} \tag{4}$$

The presented worst-case latencies show that integrating local data caches with cache coherence for shared data is reasonable compared to uncached accesses to shared data. Even though the cache provides performance improvements only for cache-hits-on-read, this kind of access is the major reason for applying caches in the first place. Here, a cache improves worst-case access to shared data by $T_{TDMA} + T_{Lat_{mem}}$ [4] which can be considerably high with a large number of cores.

5 Conclusion

This paper presents a way to implement a hardware cache coherence technique suitable for hard real-time systems. In multicore processors with local data caches a technique must be provided that allows multiple cores to access shared data in a coherent way. A multiplicity of coherence techniques with different characteristics are well-known for general purpose systems but they lack time predictability.

After a study of different embodiments of bus-based MESI cache coherence methods with respect to timing analysis, we found out that time predictable cache coherence is possible with well-known MESI techniques. Together with a time predictable TDMA bus interconnect and an analysable memory controller, an update-based dual-ported direct-mapped cache using bus-snarfing can provide statically predictable timing behaviour. Moreover, the worst-case latencies are in the range of the timing given by the TDMA bus and need to be assumed even if no cache is applied.

References

1. AUTOSAR: AUTomotive open system architecture. http://www.autosar.org/
2. Akesson, B., Goossens, K., Ringhofer, M.: Predator: A predictable sdram memory controller. In: Proceedings of the 5th IEEE/ACM International Conference on Hardware/Software Codesign and System Synthesis, CODES+ISSS 2007, pp. 251–256. ACM, New York (2007). http://doi.acm.org/10.1145/1289816.1289877
3. Bost, E.: Hardware support for robust partitioning in freescale qoriq multicore socs (p4080 and derivatives) p. 35, May 2013. http://cache.freescale.com/files/32bit/doc/white_paper/QORIQHSRPWP.pdf
4. Harnisch, J.: Predictable hardware: The aurix microcontroller family. In: Workshop on Worst-Case Execution Time Analysis, WCET 2013, Paris, France, July 2013. http://wcet2013.imag.fr/program.php
5. Hennessy, J., Patterson, D.: Computer Architecture - A Quantitative Approach. Morgan Kaufmann (2003)
6. Lewis, J., Rierson, L.: Certification concerns with integrated modular avionics (ima) projects. In: The 22nd Digital Avionics Systems Conference, DASC 2003, vol. 1, pp. 1.A.3–1.1-9, October 2003
7. Liu, Y., Zhang, W.: Exploiting stack distance to estimate worst-case data cache performance. In: Shin, S.Y., Ossowski, S. (eds.) Proceedings of the 2009 ACM Symposium on Applied Computing (SAC), Honolulu, Hawaii, USA, March 9–12, 2009, pp. 1979–1983. ACM (2009)

---

[4] Latency in case of uncached accesses.

8. Nowotsch, J., Paulitsch, M.: Leveraging multi-core computing architectures in avionics. In: 2012 Ninth European Dependable Computing Conference (EDCC), pp. 132–143, May 2012
9. Paolieri, M., Quiñones, E., Cazorla, F., Wolf, J., Ungerer, T., Uhrig, S., Petrov, Z.: A software-pipelined approach to multicore execution of timing predictable multi-threaded hard real-time tasks. In: 2011 14th IEEE International Symposium on Object/Component/Service-Oriented Real-Time Distributed Computing (ISORC), pp. 233–240 (2011)
10. Paolieri, M., Quiñones, E., Cazorla, F.J., Bernat, G., Valero, M.: Hardware support for wcet analysis of hard real-time multicore systems. In: Proceedings of the 36th Annual International Symposium on Computer Architecture, ISCA 2009, pp. 57–68. ACM, New York (2009). http://doi.acm.org/10.1145/1555754.1555764
11. Paolieri, M., Quiñones, E., Cazorla, F.J., Valero, M.: An Analyzable Memory Controller for Hard Real-Time CMPs. IEEE Embedded Systems Letters 1(4), 86–90 (2009)
12. parMERASA - Multi-Core Execution of Parallelised Hard Real-Time Applications Supporting Analysability, EU FP7 Project. http://www.parmerasa.eu/
13. Prisaznuk, P.: Integrated modular avionics. In: Proceedings of the IEEE 1992 National Aerospace and Electronics Conference, NAECON 1992, vol. 1, pp. 39–45, May 1992
14. Prisaznuk, P.: Arinc 653 role in integrated modular avionics (ima). In: IEEE/AIAA 27th Digital Avionics Systems Conference, DASC 2008, pp. 1.E.5-1–1.E.5-10, October 2008
15. Pyka, A., Rohde, M., Uhrig, S.: Performance evaluation of the time analysable on-demand coherent cache. In: TrustCom/ISPA/IUCC, pp. 1887–1892 (2013)
16. Pyka, A., Rohde, M., Uhrig, S.: A real-time capable coherent data cache for multicores. Concurrency and Computation: Practice and Experience 26(6), 1342–1354 (2014). http://dx.doi.org/10.1002/cpe.3172
17. Ramaprasad, H., Mueller, F.: Bounding worst-case data cache behavior by analytically deriving cache reference patterns. In: Proceedings of the 11th IEEE Real Time on Embedded Technology and Applications Symposium, RTAS 2005, pp. 148–157. IEEE Computer Society, Washington, DC (2005). http://dx.doi.org/10.1109/RTAS.2005.12
18. Reineke, J., Liu, I., Patel, H.D., Kim, S., Lee, E.A.: PRET DRAM controller: bank privatization for predictability and temporal isolation. In: CODES+ISSS 2011: Proceedings of the Seventh IEEE/ACM/IFIP International Conference on Hardware/Software Codesign and System Synthesis, pp. 99–108. ACM, October 2011
19. Schliecker, S., Ivers, M., Ernst, R.: Integrated analysis of communicating tasks in mpsocs. In: Proceedings of the 4th International Conference on Hardware/Software Codesign and System Synthesis, CODES+ISSS 2006, pp. 288–293. ACM, New York (2006). http://doi.acm.org/10.1145/1176254.1176325
20. Sen, R., Srikant, Y.N.: Wcet estimation for executables in the presence of data caches. In: Kirsch, C.M., Wilhelm, R. (eds.) Proceedings of the 7th ACM & IEEE International Conference on Embedded Software, EMSOFT 2007, Salzburg, Austria, September 30 - October 3, 2007, pp. 203–212. ACM (2007)
21. Wilhelm, R., Grund, D., Reineke, J., Schlickling, M., Pister, M., Ferdinand, C.: Memory hierarchies, pipelines, and buses for future architectures in time-critical embedded systems. Trans. Comp. Aided Des. Integ. Cir. Sys. 28(7), 966–978 (2009)

Allocation of Parallel Real-Time Tasks in Distributed Multi-core Architectures Supported by an FTT-SE Network

Ricardo Garibay-Martínez[(✉)], Geoffrey Nelissen,
Luis Lino Ferreira, and Luís Miguel Pinho

CISTER/INESC-TEC Research Centre, ISEP/IPP,
Rua Dr. António Bernardino de Almeida 431, 4200-072 Porto, Portugal
{rgmaz,grrpn,llf,lmp}@isep.ipp.pt

Abstract. Distributed real-time systems such as automotive applications are becoming larger and more complex, thus, requiring the use of more powerful hardware and software architectures. Furthermore, those distributed applications commonly have stringent real-time constraints. This implies that such applications would gain in flexibility if they were parallelized and distributed over the system. In this paper, we consider the problem of allocating *fixed-priority fork-join Parallel/Distributed real-time tasks* onto distributed multi-core nodes connected through a Flexible Time Triggered Switched Ethernet network. We analyze the system requirements and present a set of formulations based on a *constraint programming* approach. Constraint programming allows us to express the relations between variables in the form of constraints. Our approach is guaranteed to find a feasible solution, if one exists, in contrast to other approaches based on heuristics. Furthermore, approaches based on constraint programming have shown to obtain solutions for these type of formulations in reasonable time.

Keywords: Constraint programming · Real-time · Parallel tasks · Distributed multi-core architectures

1 Introduction

Modern cars are a good example of time-constrained distributed systems. They are composed of tens of computing nodes, some of them based on multi-core architectures interconnected by various types of communication networks. The complexity of their workload never stops increasing, therefore, many of their applications would gain in flexibility if they were parallelized and distributed over the system.

The fork-join Parallel/Distributed real-time model (P/D tasks) [1], was designed to consider such execution pattern. In this paper, we consider P/D tasks and a distributed computing platform composed of multi-core nodes, and interconnected by a Flexible Time Triggered - Switched Ethernet (FTT-SE) network [2].

© Springer International Publishing Switzerland 2015
L.M. Pinho et al. (Eds): ARCS 2015, LNCS 9017, pp. 224–235, 2015.
DOI: 10.1007/978-3-319-16086-3_18

A P/D task starts with a master thread executing sequentially, which may then fork to be executed in parallel on local and remote nodes. When the parallel execution is completed on the local and remote nodes, the partial results are transmitted using messages, and aggregated by the master thread. The master thread then resumes its execution until the next fork. Since the threads are potentially distributed over the different nodes composing the platform, we call these operations Distributed-Fork (D-Fork) and Distributed-Join (D-Join).

Furthermore, for a given task set and a given computing platform, the main challenge is to find a feasible allocation for the tasks in a way that all the tasks meet their associated end-to-end deadlines. An end-to-end deadline represents the longest elapsed time that a sequence of threads and messages composing a task is permitted to take from the time instant at which it is activated, and the instant at which the last thread of the task completes its execution.

Contribution. In this paper, we present a set of formulations for modeling the allocation of P/D tasks in a distributed multi-core architecture by using a constraint programming approach. Constraint programming approach expresses the relations between variables in the form of constraints. Our constraint programming formulation is guaranteed to find a feasible allocation, if one exists, in contrast to other approaches based on heuristic techniques. Our work is close to the one presented in [4], but with the main difference: (i) that we model fork-join Parallel/Distributed real-time tasks executing over a distributed multi-core architecture, and (ii) that we consider messages being transmitted through a Flexible Time Triggered Switched Ethernet (FTT-SE) network. Furthermore, similar approaches based on constraint programming have shown that it is possible to obtain solutions for these type of formulations in reasonable time [3,4].

Structure of the Paper. Section 2 presents the related work. In Section 3 we introduce the system model. We introduce the constraint programming formulation in Section 4. Finally, our conclusions are drawn in Section 5.

2   Related Work

In this section, we briefly review work related to: (i) scheduling of fixed-priority parallel real-time tasks, and (ii) the problem of allocating tasks and messages in distributed systems. Nevertheless, we restrain our attention to the case of real-time pre-emptive fixed-priority scheduling.

Research related to the scheduling of fixed-priority parallel real-time tasks has essentially targeted multi-core architectures. In [5], the authors introduced the *Task Stretch Transformation* (TST) model for parallel synchronous tasks that follow a fork-join structure. The TST considers preemptive fixed-priority periodic tasks with implicit deadlines partitioned according to the *Fisher-Baruah-Baker First-Fit-Decreasing* (FBB-FFD) [6] algorithm. Similarly, the *Segment Stretch Transformation* (SST) model was introduced in [7]. The authors converted the parallel threads of a fork-join task into sequential tasks by creating a master thread, but with the difference (when compared to [5]) that no thread is ever allowed to migrate between cores. That work was generalized in [8], by allowing an arbitrary number of threads per parallel segment, and in [9] for the scheduling of tasks represented by a *Directed Acyclic Graph* (DAG).

The problem of allocating sequential task in distributed systems has been intensively studied. Related works can be divided into: (i) heuristic based, and (ii) optimal strategies.

Related to heuristics based research, Tindell *et al.* [10] addressed these issues as an optimization problem, solving it with the general purpose Simulated Annealing algorithm. In [11] the authors assume a set of tasks and messages that are statically allocated to processors and networks (therefore no partitioning phase is considered), focusing on assigning the priorities to tasks and messages. Azketa *et al.* [12], addressed this problem by using the general purpose genetic algorithms. The authors initiate their genetic algorithm by assigning priorities using the HOPA heuristic [11], which is based on Deadline Monotonic (DM) priority assignment [13], and iterate over different solutions. To test schedulability they use the holistic analysis presented in Tindell *et al.* [14] and Palencia *et al.* [15,16] schedulability tests. In [17] we proposed the DOPA heuristic, which simultaneously solves the problem of assigning tasks to processors and assigning priorities to tasks. DOPA is based on Audsleys Optimal Priority Assignment (OPA) algorithm [18] to assign priorities to tasks and messages.

Regarding optimal strategies, in [19] a solution based on branch-and-bound was proposed, enumerating the possible paths that can lead to an allocation, and cutting the path whenever a feasible schedule cannot be reached by following such task assignment. The bounding step is performed by checking the schedulability of each branch, based on the schedulability analysis derived by Tindell *et al.* [14]. In [3] the authors propose to solve the problem of allocation of tasks by formulating a mixed integer linear programming framework. Similarly to this work, in [4], the authors model the task partitioning problem as a constraint optimization programming problem. Both works assume that each thread has its own period and deadline.

In the previous work [1] we studied the problem of scheduling fork-join tasks on a distributed system composed of single-processor nodes and a shared bus communication network. Distributed systems have the particularity that the transmission delay of messages communicating threads within a task, cannot be deemed negligible as in the case of multi-core systems [5,7,8]. In here, we extend the problem of task allocation of fork-join real-time tasks presented in [1], by considering (i) a distributed multi-core architecture, and (ii) using a FTT-SE network for message transmission.

3   System Model

We consider a distributed computing platform composed of a set $N = \{\nu_1, \ldots, \nu_m\}$ of m multi-core nodes to execute tasks. Each node ν_r ($r \in \{1, \ldots, m\}$) is composed of m_r identical cores $\pi_{r,s}$ ($s \in \{1, \ldots, m_r\}$). The total number of cores in the system is therefore equal to $m_{tot} = \sum_{\nu_i \in N} m_r$. The processing nodes are interconnected by an FTT-SE network $\rho = \{SW_1, \ldots, SW_w\}$ of w Ethernet switches. The switches and distributed nodes are interconnected through full-duplex links.

Also, we consider a set $T = \{\tau_1, \ldots, \tau_n\}$ of n periodic P/D tasks. Figure 1 shows an example of a P/D task τ_i. A task τ_i is activated with a period T_i, and is characterized by an implicit end-to-end deadline D_i. A P/D task τ_i ($i \in \{1, \ldots, n\}$) is composed of a sequence of n_i sequential and parallel distributed segments $\sigma_{i,j}$ ($j \in \{1, \ldots, n_i\}$). n_i is assumed to be an odd integer, since a P/D task should always start and finish with a sequential segment. Therefore, odd segments $\sigma_{i,2j+1}$ identify sequential segments and even segments $\sigma_{i,2j}$ identify P/D segments. Each segment $\sigma_{i,j}$ is composed of a set of threads $\theta_{i,j,k}$ with $k \in \{1, \ldots, n_{i,j}\}$, where $n_{i,j} = 1$ for sequential segments.

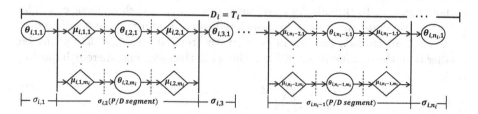

Fig. 1. The fork-join parallel distributed periodic real-time task (P/D task) model.

All sequential segments of a P/D task τ_i belong to the master thread, therefore, they are assumed to execute on the same core. This means that the core that performs a D-Fork operation (invoker core) is in charge of aggregating the result by performing a D-Join operation. Some threads within a P/D segment may be executed on remote node ν_l. Consequently, for each thread $\theta_{i,j,k}$ belonging to a P/D segment, two messages $\mu_{i,j-1,k}$ and $\mu_{i,j,k}$ are transmitted between the invoker and remote core. That is, P/D threads and messages that belong to a P/D segment and execute on a remote core, have a precedence relation: $\mu_{i,j-1,k} \rightarrow \theta_{i,j,k} \rightarrow \mu_{i,j,k}$. We call this sequence a *distributed execution path* (denoted as $DP_{i,j,k}$). If a P/D thread executes on the same node ν_l than the master thread, the transmission time of $\mu_{i,j-1,k}$ and $\mu_{i,j,k}$ are equal to zero, since the transfer of data through a shared memory can be considered negligible.

For each P/D segment, there exists a *synchronization point* at the end of the segment, indicating that no thread that belongs to the segment after the synchronization point can start executing before all threads of the current segment have completed their execution. Threads are preemptive, but messages are non-preemptive. Each thread $\theta_{i,j,k}$ has a Worst-Case Execution Time (WCET) of $C_{i,j,k}$, and each message $\mu_{i,j,k}$ has a Worst-Case Message Length (WCML) $M_{i,j,k}$.

4   Constraint Programming Formulation

The problem of task allocation can be seen as a two-sided problem: (i) finding the partitioning of threads and messages onto the processing elements of the distributed system, and (ii) finding the priority assignment for the threads and messages in that partition so that the real-time tasks and messages complete their execution before reaching their respective end-to-end deadlines.

In this section we analyze the system requirements and provide a formulation based on a constraint programming approach similar to [4].

4.1 Parallel/Distributed Tasks

In a similar manner as in [1], we transform threads composing a P/D task into a set of *independent sequential* tasks with constrained deadlines. This transformation is based on the imposition of a set of *artificial intermediate deadlines* (denoted as $d_{i,j}$), to threads $\theta_{i,j,k}$ and messages $\mu_{i,j,k}$, in each segment $\sigma_{i,j}$. The following two constraints must be associated to each intermediate deadline $d_{i,j}$.

Even if all threads execute in parallel, the relative deadline $d_{i,j}$ cannot be smaller than the maximum WCET of a thread in that segment, thereby imposing that:

$$\bigwedge_{\forall \tau_i \in T} \bigwedge_{\forall \sigma_{i,j} \in \tau_i} d_{i,j} \geq \max_{k=1,\ldots,n_{i,j}} \{C_{i,j,k}\}. \tag{1}$$

Also, the total execution granted to all segments constituting a task τ_i must be smaller or equal than the relative deadline of τ_i, that is:

$$\bigwedge_{\forall \tau_i \in T} \sum_{\forall \sigma_{i,j} \in \tau_i} d_{i,j} \leq D_i. \tag{2}$$

Thus, the artificial deadline $d_{i,j}$ is the maximum time that threads of a segment $\sigma_{i,j}$ are permitted to take, from the moment they are released, to the moment they complete their execution. Therefore, the problem can be formulated as to find the artificial deadlines $d_{i,j}$ for every segment $\sigma_{i,j}$, in a way that the Worst-Case Response Time (WCRT) of threads $\theta_{i,j,k}$ (and messages $\mu_{i,j,k}$) is smaller or equal to the end-to-end deadline D_i. More constraints are presented in Sections 4.2 and 4.3.

4.2 Fully-Partitioned Distributed Multi-core Systems

In this work, we assume a fixed-priority fully-partitioned scheduling algorithm. Let us assume that each core in the system (regardless the processing node they are part of) is assigned a unique identifier in the interval $[1, m_{tot}]$. Then we define the integer variable $\Pi_{\theta_{i,j,k}}$, indicating the identifier of the core on which the thread $\theta_{i,j,k}$ is mapped. By definition of the core identifier, the following constraints apply:

$$\Pi_{\theta_{i,j,k}} > 0, \tag{3}$$

$$\Pi_{\theta_{i,j,k}} \leq m_{tot}. \tag{4}$$

A constraint of the P/D task model is that all sequential segments of a task τ_i must execute on the same core $\pi_{r,s}$. This is imposed by (5):

$$\bigwedge_{\forall \theta_{i,2j+1,1} \in T} \bigwedge_{\forall \theta_{i,2b+1,1} \in T} \Pi_{\theta_{i,2j+1,1}} = \Pi_{\theta_{i,2b+1,1}}. \tag{5}$$

Let us define the variable $p_{i,j,k}$ as the priority of a thread $\theta_{i,j,k}$. Although $p_{i,j,k}$ could be an integer variable of the problem for which the solver finds a valid value in its proposed solution, in a concern of drastically reducing the number of variables and therefore the complexity of the problem, one may also assume that priorities are assigned using DM [13], in which case $p_{i,j,k} = d_{i,j}$, and $p_{i,j,k}$ can be omitted in the description of the problem. Yet, it is necessary to evaluate if a certain partitioning leads to a valid solution. We know from [20], that the worst-case response time $r_{i,j,k}$ of an independent thread $\theta_{i,j,k}$ scheduled with a preemptive fixed-priority scheduling algorithm, is given by (6):

$$r_{i,j,k} = C_{i,j,k} + \sum_{\theta_{a,b,c} \in \mathsf{HP}_{i,j,k}} \left\lceil \frac{r_{i,j,k}}{T_a} \right\rceil C_{a,b,c}, \tag{6}$$

where $\mathsf{HP}_{i,j,k}$ is the set of threads with higher or equal priority than $\theta_{i,j,k}$, and executing on the same core than $\theta_{i,j,k}$.

This can be modeled in the constraint problem as:

$$\bigwedge_{\forall \theta_{i,j,k} \in T} r_{i,j,k} = C_{i,j,k} + \sum_{\forall \theta_{a,b,c} \in T} \mathsf{IHP}_{i,j,k}^{a,b,c}, \tag{7}$$

where $\mathsf{IHP}_{i,j,k}^{a,b,c}$ is the interference caused by a thread $\theta_{a,b,c}$ on $\theta_{i,j,k}$.

Higher priority relation is represented by the following boolean variable:

$$p_{i,j,k}^{a,b,c} = \begin{cases} 1 & \text{if } \theta_{a,b,c} \text{ has higher priority than } \theta_{i,j,k} \ (p_{i,j,k} \leq p_{a,b,c}), \\ 0 & \text{otherwise.} \end{cases}$$

Because $\Pi_{\theta_{i,j,k}} = \Pi_{\theta_{a,b,c}}$ indicates that the $\theta_{i,j,k}$ and $\theta_{a,b,c}$ threads execute on the same core, the total interference over a thread $\theta_{i,j,k}$ is expressed as:

$$\bigwedge_{\forall \theta_{i,j,k} \in T} \bigwedge_{\forall \theta_{a,b,c} \in T} \mathsf{IHP}_{i,j,k}^{a,b,c} = \begin{cases} \mathsf{I}_{i,j,k}^{a,b,c} \times C_{a,b,c} & \text{if } \left((p_{i,j,k}^{a,b,c} = 1) \wedge (\Pi_{\theta_{i,j,k}} = \Pi_{\theta_{a,b,c}}) \right), \\ 0 & \text{otherwise,} \end{cases} \tag{8}$$

where $\mathsf{I}_{i,j,k}^{a,b,c}$ is the number of preemptions a thread $\theta_{i,j,k}$ suffers from a thread $\theta_{a,b,c}$. Since $\mathsf{I}_{i,j,k}^{a,b,c}$ is an integer, the ceiling operator can be rewritten as follows:

$$\left\lceil \frac{r_{i,j,k}}{T_a} \right\rceil = \mathsf{I}_{i,j,k}^{a,b,c} \quad \Longrightarrow \quad \frac{r_{i,j,k}}{T_a} \leq \mathsf{I}_{i,j,k}^{a,b,c} < \frac{r_{i,j,k}}{T_a} + 1, \tag{9}$$

thereby, leading to the following constraints:

$$\bigwedge_{\forall \theta_{i,j,k} \in T} \bigwedge_{\forall \theta_{a,b,c} \in T} (\Pi_{\theta_{i,j,k}} = \Pi_{\theta_{a,b,c}}) \ \rightarrow \ (\mathsf{I}_{i,j,k}^{a,b,c} \times T_a \geq r_{i,j,k})$$

$$\wedge \left((\mathsf{I}_{i,j,k}^{a,b,c} - 1) \times T_a < r_{i,j,k} \right), \tag{10}$$

$$\bigwedge_{\forall \theta_{i,j,k} \in T} \bigwedge_{\forall \theta_{a,b,c} \in T} (\Pi_{\theta_{i,j,k}} \neq \Pi_{\theta_{i,j,k}}) \quad \rightarrow \quad |_{i,j,k}^{a,b,c} = 0. \tag{11}$$

Furthermore, in the P/D task model, some threads within a P/D segment may be executed on remote nodes. Consequently, for each such thread $\theta_{i,j,k}$, two messages $\mu_{i,j-1,k}$ and $\mu_{i,j,k}$ are transmitted between the invoker and remote node. That is, a distributed execution path is generated ($\mu_{i,j-1,k} \rightarrow \theta_{i,j,k} \rightarrow \mu_{i,j,k}$).

$NV(\theta_{i,j,k})$ is a function denoting to which node ν_q a thread $\theta_{i,j,k}$ has been assigned. Then, $NV(\theta_{i,j,k}) = NV(\theta_{a,b,c})$ indicates that the threads $\theta_{i,j,k}$ and $\theta_{a,b,c}$ execute on the same node, in which case no message is transmitted through the network. However, if $NV(\theta_{i,j,k}) \neq NV(\theta_{a,b,c})$, the WCRT $r_{DP_{i,j,k}}$ of a distributed execution path $DP_{i,j,k}$ must be as follows:

$$\bigwedge_{\forall \mu_{i,j,k} \in T} \bigwedge_{\forall \theta_{i,j,k} \in T} r_{DP_{i,j,k}} = \begin{cases} r_{i,j-1,k}^{msg} + r_{i,j,k} + r_{i,j,k}^{msg} & \text{if } NV(\theta_{i,j,k}) \neq NV(\theta_{a,b,c}), \\ r_{i,j,k} & \text{otherwise,} \end{cases} \tag{12}$$

where $r_{i,j,k}$ is the WCRT of thread $\theta_{i,j,k}$ obtained with (7), and $r_{i,j-1,k}^{msg}$ and $r_{i,j,k}^{msg}$ are the WCRTs of messages $\mu_{i,j-1,k}$ and $\mu_{i,j,k}$ respectively, obtained with a network dependent analysis. In this paper, we assume the network analysis presented in [21] for FTT-SE networks. Thus, for a partition of tasks τ_i to be considered a valid solution (all deadlines are met), the following condition has to be respected:

$$\bigwedge_{\forall \theta_{i,j,k} \in T} r_{DP_{i,j,k}} \leq d_{i,j}. \tag{13}$$

4.3   FTT-SE Network

The communications within a FTT-SE network are done based on fixed duration slots called *Elementary Cycles* (ECs). The construction of the EC schedule is done by keeping updated tables for synchronous (i.e., periodic) and asynchronous (i.e., sporadic) messages. The scheduler applies a scheduling policy (e.g., Deadline Monotonic) over these tables, generating the ready queues for transmission for that EC. This process is repeated until no other message fits in its respective scheduling window for that EC (i.e., considering all messages from higher to lower priority). For building the ECs it is important to consider:

i. the architecture of the distributed system. The architectural model must include the full-duplex transmission links. We represent the architecture as an *adjacency-matrix* of a graph $G = (V, E)$. The set $V = \{v_1, \ldots, v_{|V|}\}$ of vertices v_i represents the set of switches ρ and the set of nodes N, and the set $E = \{(v_1, v_2), \ldots, (v_{|V|-1}, v_{|V|})\}$ of edges (v_i, v_j), represent the communication links, from nodes to switches, from switches to nodes or between switches. Note that: (i) direct links between nodes do not exist, (ii) links are directed; that is, (v_i, v_j) and (v_j, v_i) represent two different links, and (iii) the network is full-duplex; that is, if (v_i, v_j) is part of the graph, then (v_j, v_i)

is too. Thus, the adjacency matrix representation of a graph G consists of a $|V| \times |V|$ matrix $A = (a_{i,j})$ such that:

$$a_{i,j} = \begin{cases} 1 & \text{if } (v_i, v_j) \in E, \\ 0 & \text{otherwise,} \end{cases}$$

depending of the partitioning of threads onto the nodes ν_l of the system, there exists a set $\mathsf{PN}_{\mu_{i,j,k}} \subseteq V$ containing the vertices (i.e., switches) that a message $\mu_{i,j,k}$ traverses during a D-fork or a D-join operation. For determining $\mathsf{PN}_{\mu_{i,j,k}}$, we use the Breadth-First Search (BFS) Algorithm [22] for each message $\mu_{i,j,k}$. The BFS inputs are: the matrix A (representing the system architecture), the origin vertex (invoker core/remote core), and the destination vertex (the remote core/invoker core). The BFS finds the shortest path from the origin node to the destination node. Therefore, the BFS algorithm finds the switches that a message $\mu_{i,j,k}$ crosses during a D-fork or a D-join operation. The set $\mathsf{PN}_{\mu_{i,j,k}}$ is required for computing the WCRT of a message $\mu_{i,j,k}$ in the FTT-SE network.

ii. the switching delays. In this paper, we consider a switching delay (denoted as $\mathsf{SD}_{i,j,k}$) when a message $\mu_{i,j,k}$ crosses a switch SW_z. $\mathsf{SD}_{i,j,k}$ has two components, the switch relaying latency (denoted as Δ), which has a constant value related to the specifications of the switch, and the Store-and-Forward Delay (denoted as $\mathsf{SFD}_{i,j,k}$), i.e., $\mathsf{SD}_{i,j,k} = \mathsf{SFD}_{i,j,k} + \Delta$. However, for each EC, only the maximum switching delay $\mathsf{SD}_{i,j,k}$ is considered.

iii. the EC is subdivided into time slots for transmitting different types of traffic (e.g. synchronous window, asynchronous window, etc.). Thus, one must consider the length of the specific transmission window for each type of traffic (denoted as LW). The length of such a window is the reserved bandwidth for transmission in that EC, and cannot be exceeded when transmitting messages within the FTT-SE protocol. This is modeled by the *request bound function* in (14), and the *supply bound function* (19), presented in the following.

Response Time Analysis for FTT-SE Networks. Depending on a given partition, we have to find the WCRT of the messages in the network to verify if the condition in (13) is respected. We consider the work presented in [21] for the computation of the WCRT of messages within the FTT-SE protocol, with a slight modification.

The **request bound function** $\mathsf{rbf}_{i,j,k}(t)$ represents the maximum transmission requirements generated by a message $\mu_{i,j,k}$ and all its higher priority messages during an interval $[0, t]$. The $\mathsf{rbf}_{i,j,k}(t)$ is computed as:

$$\bigwedge_{\forall \mu_{i,j,k} \in T} \mathsf{rbf}_{i,j,k}(t) = M_{i,j,k} + \mathsf{sn}_{i,j,k} \times \mathsf{SFD}_{i,j,k} + \mathsf{WI}_{i,j,k}(t) + \mathsf{Wr}_{i,j,k}(t), \qquad (14)$$

where, $\mathsf{sn}_{i,j,k}$ is the number of switches that a message $\mu_{i,j,k}$ traverses from the origin node to its destination node, $\mathsf{WI}_{i,j,k}(t)$ is the *"Shared Link Delay"*, and $\mathsf{Wr}_{i,j,k}(t)$ is the *"Remote Link Delay"*, which are explained below.

Shared Link Delay. The transmission of a message $\mu_{i,j,k}$ may be delayed by all the higher priority messages that share a link with $\mu_{i,j,k}$. However, such interference occurs only once, so messages that caused such interference on a previous link are excluded from the analysis for the next links. Also, when building the schedule for each EC, the scheduler considers the maximum switching delay $\mathsf{SD_z}$ (see (16)), only once. Therefore, $\mathsf{Wl_{i,j,k}(t)}$ is computed by separating the interference of messages from the *switching-delay-effect* (denoted as $\mathsf{Is_{i,j,k}(t)}$) for each EC. The shared link delay is computed in (15):

$$\mathsf{Wl_{i,j,k}(t)} = \sum_{\forall \mu_{a,b,c} \in \mathsf{SLD}_{i,j,k}} \left\lceil \frac{t}{T_a} \right\rceil M_{a,b,c} + \mathsf{Is_{i,j,k}(t)}, \tag{15}$$

where $\mathsf{SLD}_{i,j,k} = \{\forall \mu_{a,b,c} : \mu_{a,b,c} \neq \mu_{i,j,k} \wedge (\mathsf{PN}_{\mu_{i,j,k}} \cap \mathsf{PN}_{\mu_{a,b,c}} \neq 0) \wedge \mu_{a,b,c} \in \mathsf{hp}(\mu_{i,j,k}) \wedge \mu_{a,b,c} \in WT(\mu_{i,j,k})\}$, where, $\mathsf{hp}(\mu_{i,j,k})$ is the set of messages with priority higher or equal than $\mu_{a,b,c}$ and $WT(\mu_{i,j,k})$ is the set of messages that are scheduled in the same window as $\mu_{a,b,c}$ (i.e. the synchronous or the asynchronous window). The set $\mathsf{hp}(\mu_{i,j,k})$ for messages $\mu_{i,j,k}$ in (15), as well as the ceiling function, can be formulated in a similar manner as in Section 4.2.

For computing the switching-delay-effect $\mathsf{Is_{i,j,k}(t)}$, it is needed to compute an upper bound on the number of switching delays ($\mathsf{SD}_{i,j,k}$) from each message that contributes to (15), at time t. In [21], depending on time t, a number of switching delays are inserted into an array whenever a message crosses a switch in the network. The array is sorted in order to consider the maximum switching delays only. A sorting operation is not amenable to optimization solvers. Therefore, we introduce a simpler upper bound with the cost of slightly increment the pessimism.

The number of ECs in an interval $[0, t]$ is given by: $\mathsf{z(t)} = \left\lceil \frac{t}{EC} \right\rceil$ (the ceiling function, can be formulated as in Section 4.2), thus, in order to consider the worst-case scenario for the computation of the WCRT, we consider the maximum switching delay ($\mathsf{SD}_{i,j,k}^{\max}$) for each message that contributes to (15), and computed as:

$$\mathsf{SD}_{i,j,k}^{\max} = \max_{\forall \mu_{a,b,c} \in \mathsf{SLD}_{i,j,k}} \{\mathsf{SFD}_{i,j,k} + \Delta\}. \tag{16}$$

Then, the maximum switching delay is multiplied by the number of ECs at time t (given by $\mathsf{z(t)}$). Thus, the switching-delay-effect is computed as:

$$\mathsf{Is_{i,j,k}} = \mathsf{SD}_{i,j,k}^{\max} \times \mathsf{z(t)}. \tag{17}$$

Remote Link Delay. A message $\mu_{i,j,k}$ can be blocked by other higher priority messages even if they do not share a transmission link. Thus, a higher priority message can delay a lower priority message even though they do not share a transmission link [21]. Therefore, to compute the worst-case remote link delay, it is needed to consider all messages that share links with the messages that contributed to the shared link delay (see (15)), excluding all messages that are already considered in (15). Hence, we have:

$$\mathsf{Wr_{i,j,k}(t)} = \sum_{\forall \mu_{p,q,r} \in \mathsf{RLD}_{i,j,k}} \left\lceil \frac{t}{T_p} \right\rceil M_{p,q,r} \tag{18}$$

where, $\mathsf{RLD}_{i,j,k} = \{\forall \mu_{p,q,r} : \mu_{p,q,r} \neq \mu_{a,b,c} \neq \mu_{i,j,k} \wedge (\mathsf{PN}_{\mu_{p,q,r}} \cap \mathsf{PN}_{\mu_{a,b,c}} \neq 0) \wedge$
$(\mathsf{PN}_{\mu_{p,q,r}} \cap \mathsf{PN}_{\mu_{i,j,k}} = 0)(\mathsf{PN}_{\mu_{a,b,c}} \cap \mathsf{PN}_{\mu_{i,j,k}} \neq 0) \wedge \mu_{p,q,r} \in hp(\mu_{a,b,c}) \wedge \mu_{p,q,r} \in$
$WT(\mu_{a,b,c})\}$.

The demand bound function is then compared with the **supply bound function** $\mathsf{sbf}_{i,j,k}(t)$, which represents the minimum effective communication capacity that the network supplies during the time interval $[0, t]$ to a message $\mu_{i,j,k}$. In each EC, the bandwidth provided for transmitting each type of traffic (e.g., synchronous or asynchronous traffic) is equal to $\frac{(LW-I)}{EC}$, where LW is an input and represents the length of the specific transmission window and I is the maximum inserted idle time of such window. The inserted idle time results from the fact that the maximum window duration cannot be exceeded.

$$\bigwedge_{\forall \mu_{i,j,k} \in T} \mathsf{sbf}_{i,j,k}(t) = (\frac{LW - I}{EC}) \times t. \tag{19}$$

Then, the response time of a message $\mu_{i,j,k}$ is computed by introducing a new variable $t_{i,j,k}$ such that:

$$\bigwedge_{\forall \mu_{i,j,k} \in T} t_{i,j,k} > 0, \tag{20}$$

$$\bigwedge_{\forall \mu_{i,j,k} \in T} \mathsf{sbf}_{i,j,k}(t_{i,j,k}) \geq \mathsf{rbf}_{i,j,k}(t_{i,j,k}). \tag{21}$$

Since it is not possible to determine the specific time of transmission of messages inside an EC, the computation of the WCRT for a message $\mu_{i,j,k}$ is in terms of a number of ECs, thus the WCRT of a message $\mu_{i,j,k}$ is given by:

$$\bigwedge_{\forall \mu_{i,j,k} \in T} r_{i,j,k}^{msg} = \left\lceil \frac{t_{i,j,k}}{EC} \right\rceil \times EC. \tag{22}$$

4.4   Constraint Satisfiability

The constraints sketched above are a combination of linear and non-linear constraints over a set of integer and boolean variables. This implies the use of extremely powerful optimization methods. It has been shown (e.g., [4]) that such type of optimization problems are not amenable for conventional numerical optimization solvers. However, for real-time purposes, a correct solution is obtained by guaranteeing that all the constraints are satisfied, regardless of the value of a given objective function. Thus, the optimization problem gets reduced to a Satisfiability (SAT) problem, in which solutions can be obtained in reasonable time [4]. The constrains and optimization variables are summarized in the following.

Summary. We convert a set of P/D tasks τ_i into a set of independent sequential tasks, by imposing a set of artificial intermediate deadlines. The constraints for intermediate deadline are: (1) and (2). A valid partition, in which all threads respect their intermediate deadlines $d_{i,j}$, is constrained with (5) and (7). The WCRT of a distributed execution path $(DP_{i,j,k})$ depends on where the threads in a P/D segment are executed (i.e., locally or remotely), that is modeled in (12). If threads $\theta_{i,j,k}$ are executed remotely, the WCRT of messages transmitted through an FTT-SE network has to be considered. That is modeled with (20)-(21). Finally, all tasks have to respect the condition in (13).

5   Conclusions

In this paper we presented the formulations for modeling the allocation of P/D tasks in a distributed multi-core architecture supported by an FTT-SE network, by using a constraint programming approach. Our constraint programming approach is guaranteed to find a feasible allocation, if one exists, in contrast to other approaches based on heuristic techniques. Furthermore, similar approaches based on constraint program have shown that it is possible to obtain solutions for these formulations in reasonable time.

Acknowledgments. The authors would like to thank the anonymous reviewers for their helpful comments. This work was partially supported by National Funds through FCT (Portuguese Foundation for Science and Technology) and by ERDF (European Regional Development Fund) through COMPETE (Operational Programme 'Thematic Factors of Competitiveness'), within project FCOMP-01-0124-FEDER-037281 (CIS-TER); by FCT and the EU ARTEMIS JU funding, ARROWHEAD (ARTEMIS/0001/2012, JU grant nr. 332987), CONCERTO (ARTEMIS/0003/2012, JU grant nr. 333053); by FCT and ESF (European Social Fund) through POPH (Portuguese Human Potential Operational Program), under PhD grant SFRH/BD/71562/2010.

References

1. Garibay-Martínez, R., Nelissen, G., Ferreira, L.L., Pinho, L.M.: On the scheduling of fork-join parallel/distributed real-time tasks. In: 9th IEEE International Symposium on Industrial Embedded Systems, pp. 31–40, June 2014
2. Marau, R., Almeida, L., Pedreiras, P.: Enhancing real-time communication over cots ethernet switches. In: IEEE International Workshop on Factory Communication Systems, pp. 295–302 (2006)
3. Zhu, Q., Zeng, H., Zheng, W., Natale, M.D., Sangiovanni-Vincentelli, A.: Optimization of task allocation and priority assignment in hard real-time distributed systems. ACM Transactions on Embedded Computing Systems **11**(4), 85 (2012)
4. Metzner, A., Herde, C.: Rtsat-an optimal and efficient approach to the task allocation problem in distributed architectures. In: 27th IEEE Real-Time Systems Symposium, pp. 147–158, December 2006
5. Lakshmanan, K., Kato, S., Rajkumar, R.: Scheduling parallel real-time tasks on multi-core processors. In: 31st IEEE Real-Time Systems Symposium, pp. 259–268, November 2010

6. Fisher, N., Baruah, S., Baker, T.P.: The partitioned scheduling of sporadic tasks according to static-priorities. In: 18th Euromicro Conference on Real-Time Systems, p. 10 (2006)
7. Fauberteau, F., Midonnet, S., Qamhieh, M.: Partitioned scheduling of parallel real-time tasks on multiprocessor systems. ACM SIGBED Review **8**(3), 28–31 (2011)
8. Saifullah, A., Li, J., Agrawal, K., Lu, C., Gill, C.: Multi-core real-time scheduling for generalized parallel task models. Real-Time Systems **49**(4), 404–435 (2013)
9. Qamhieh, M., George, L., Midonnet, S.: A Stretching algorithm for parallel real-time DAG tasks on multiprocessor systems. In: 22nd International Conference on Real-Time Networks and Systems, p. 13, October 2014
10. Tindell, K.W., Burns, A., Wellings, A.J.: Allocating hard real-time tasks: an NP-hard problem made easy. Real-Time Systems **4**(2), 145–165 (1992)
11. García, J.G., Harbour, M.G.: Optimized priority assignment for tasks and messages in distributed hard real-time systems. In: Third IEEE Workshop on Parallel and Distributed Real-Time Systems, pp. 124–132, April 1995
12. Azketa, E., Uribe, J.P., Gutiérrez, J.J., Marcos, M., Almeida, L.: Permutational genetic algorithm for the optimized mapping and scheduling of tasks and messages in distributed real-time systems. In: 10th International Conference on Trust, Security and Privacy in Computing and Communications (2011)
13. Leung, J.Y.T., Whitehead, J.: On the complexity of fixed-priority scheduling of periodic, real-time tasks. Performance Evaluation **2**(4), 237–250 (1982)
14. Tindell, K., Clark, J.: Holistic schedulability analysis for distributed hard real-time systems. Microprocessing and Microprogramming **40**(2), 117–134 (1994)
15. Palencia, J.C., Gonzalez Harbour, M.: Schedulability analysis for tasks with static and dynamic offsets. In: 19th IEEE Real-Time Systems Symposium, pp. 26–37, December 1998
16. Palencia, J.C., Gonzalez Harbour, M.: Exploiting precedence relations in the schedulability analysis of distributed real-time systems. In: 20th IEEE Real-Time Systems Symposium, pp. 328–339 (1999)
17. Garibay-Martínez, R., Nelissen G., Ferreira L.L., Pinho L.M.: Task partitioning and priority assignment for hard real-time distributed systems. In: International Workshop on Real-Time and Distributed Computing in Emerging Applications (2013)
18. Audsley, N.C.: Optimal priority assignment and feasibility of static priority tasks with arbitrary start times. University of York, Dep. of Computer Science (1991)
19. Richard, M., Richard, P., Cottet, F.: Allocating and scheduling tasks in multiple fieldbus real-time systems. In: IEEE Conference on Emerging Technologies and Factory Automation, pp. 137–144, September 2003
20. Joseph, M., Pandya, P.: Finding response times in a real-time system. The Computer Journal **29**(5), 390–395 (1986)
21. Ashjaei, M., Behnam, M., Nolte, T., Almeida, L.: Performance analysis of master-slave multi-hop switched ethernet networks. In: 8th IEEE International Symposium Industrial Embedded Systems, pp. 280–289, June 2013
22. Cormen, T.H., Leiserson, C.E., Rivest, R.L., Stein, C.: Introduction to algorithms, vol. 2, pp. 531–549. MIT Press, Cambridge (2001)

Speeding up Static Probabilistic Timing Analysis

Suzana Milutinovic[1,2](✉), Jaume Abella[2], Damien Hardy[3],
Eduardo Quiñones[2], Isabelle Puaut[3], and Francisco J. Cazorla[2,4]

[1] Universitat Politecnica de Catalunya (UPC), Barcelona, Spain
[2] Barcelona Supercomputing Center (BSC-CNS), Barcelona, Spain
[3] IRISA, Rennes, France
[4] Spanish National Research Council (IIIA-CSIC), Barcelona, Spain
suzana.milutinovic@bsc.es

Abstract. Probabilistic Timing Analysis (PTA) has emerged recently
to derive trustworthy and tight WCET estimates. Computational costs
due to the use of the mathematical operator called *convolution* used by
SPTA – the static variant of PTA – and also deployed in many domains
including signal and image processing, jeopardize the scalability of SPTA
to real-size programs. We evaluate, qualitatively and quantitatively, optimizations to reduce convlution's computational costs when it is applied
to SPTA. We showthat SPTA specific optimizations provide the largest
execution time reductions, at the cost of a small loss of precision.

1 Introduction

Probabilistic Timing Analysis (PTA) [2,3,5,7,9,16] has emerged recently as a
powerful family of techniques to estimate the worst-case execution time (WCET)
of programs. Recent PTA techniques advocate for hardware and software designs
that either have fixed latency or randomized timing behavior [5,7,10,11], to
produce WCET estimates that can be exceeded with a given – arbitrarily low –
probability, which are typically referred to as probabilistic WCET (pWCET)
estimates. Using those hardware and software designs increases coverage (and
so usefulness) of pWCET estimates [6]. Examples of time-randomized hardware
elements are caches with random placement and/or replacement [5,11,13].

The static variant of PTA, called SPTA, has recently been object of intense
study [2,5,8,14]. In this paper we contribute to SPTA development by identifying
and mitigating one of the major bottlenecks for SPTA to scale to industrial-size
programs: its execution time requirements.

Under SPTA, each instruction has a probabilistic timing behavior represented with an Execution Time Profile (ETP). An ETP is expressed by a timing vector that enumerates all the possible latencies that the instruction may
incur, and a probability vector, which for each latency in the timing vector,
lists the associated probability of occurrence. Hence, for an instruction $\mathcal{I}_i$ we
have $ETP(\mathcal{I}_i) = <\vec{t_i}, \vec{p_i}>$ where $\vec{t_i} = (t_i^1, t_i^2, ..., t_i^{N_i})$ and $\vec{p_i} = (p_i^1, p_i^2, ..., p_i^{N_i})$, with
$\sum_{j=1}^{N_i} p_i^j = 1$. The *convolution* function, $\otimes$, is used to combine ETPs, such that
a new ETP is obtained representing the execution time distribution of the execution of all the instructions convolved.

© Springer International Publishing Switzerland 2015
L.M. Pinho et al. (Eds): ARCS 2015, LNCS 9017, pp. 236–247, 2015.
DOI: 10.1007/978-3-319-16086-3_19

With real-time programs growing in size, the need to carry out a convolution operation for every instruction in the object code may incur high computation time requirements. Hence, efficient ways to perform convolutions in the context of SPTA are needed. In this paper we analyze a number of optimizations of the convolution operation. Some optimizations keep precision, whereas some others sacrifice some precision to reduce computational cost, while preserving WCET trustworthiness.

– Among precision-preserving optimizations we consider convolution parallelization, as largely studied previously in the literature [15,17], in 2 forms: (1) *inter-convolution parallelization*, where ETPs to be convolved are split into several groups that are convolved in parallel and (2) *intra-convolution parallelization* where one (or both) of the ETPs to be convolved is split into sub-ETPs so that each sub-ETP is convolved with the other ETP in parallel.
– Among optimizations that sacrifice some precision to reduce convolution cost, we consider (3) *discretization*, such that few different forms of ETPs exist and convolutions across identical ETPs need not be carried out too often. We also consider (4) *sampling* where several elements in the ETP are collapsed into one [12], thus reducing the length of the ETPs to be convolved and so the number of operations.

Our results show that discretization and sampling – the SPTA specific optimizations – lead to the highest reductions in execution time, whereas the combination of intra- and inter-convolution parallelization provides second order reductions in execution time. In particular, discretization and sampling reduce execution time by a factor of 10 whereas precision-preserving optimizations reduce it by a factor of 2. This execution time reduction comes at the expense of a pWCET increase around 3%.

Another approach to speed-up convolutions is to use Fourier Transformation, and in particular its discrete fast version (DFT). This approach needs first to convert the distribution from the time domain to the frequency domain using DFT. Then, according to the convolution theorem, a point-wise multiplication is applied, which is equivalent to the convolution in the time domain. Finally, inverse DFT is performed to obtain the distribution in the time domain. Evaluating DFT to speed up convolutions is left for future work.

The rest of the paper is organized as follows. Section 2 provides background on PTA and convolutions. Section 3 presents issues challenging SPTA scalability and optimizations to reduce its computational cost. Optimizations are evaluated in Section 4. Finally, Section 5 concludes the paper.

2 Background: PTA and Convolutions

Along a given path, assuming that the probabilities for the execution times of each instruction are independent, SPTA is performed by deploying the discrete convolution ($\otimes$) of the ETPs that describe the execution time for each instruction along that path. The final outcome is a probability distribution representing the

Algorithm 1. Convolution canonical implementation

```
1:  c ← 1
2:  for i = 1 to N do
3:     for j = 1 to N do
4:        etpr.lat[c] ← etp1.lat[i] + etp2.lat[j]
5:        etpr.prob[c] ← etp1.prob[i] * etp2.prob[j]
6:        c ← c + 1
7:     end for
8:  end for
```

timing behavior of the entire execution path. For the sake of clarity we keep the discussion at the level of a single execution path.

More formally, if $\mathcal{X}$ and $\mathcal{Y}$ denote the random variables that describe the execution time of two instructions x and y, the convolution $\mathcal{Z} = \mathcal{X} \otimes \mathcal{Y}$ is defined as follows: $P\{\mathcal{Z} = z\} = \sum_{k=0}^{k=+\infty} P\{\mathcal{X} = k\}P\{\mathcal{Y} = z - k\}$. For instance if an instruction x is known to execute in 1 cycle with a probability of 0.9 and to execute in 10 cycles with a probability of 0.1 and an instruction y has an equal probability of 0.5 to execute in 2 or 10 cycles, we have:

$$\mathcal{Z} = \mathcal{X} \otimes \mathcal{Y} = (\{1, 10\}, \{0.9, 0.1\}) \otimes (\{2, 10\}, \{0.5, 0.5\})$$
$$= (\{3, 11, 12, 20\}, \{0.45, 0.45, 0.05, 0.05\})$$

For every static instruction, i.e. instruction in the executable of the program, SPTA requires that their ETPs are not affected by the execution of previous instructions. When time-randomized caches are used, there is an intrinsic dependence among the hit probability of an access (P_{hit}) and the outcome of previous cache accesses [5,8]. Existing techniques to break this dependence create a lower bound function to P_{hit} (so an upper bound to P_{miss}) of every instruction to make it independent – for WCET estimation purposes – from previous accesses [2,5,8]. Given that those methods are orthogonal to the cost of convolutions, we omit details and refer the interested reader to the original works.

3   SPTA: Performance Issues and Optimizations

When implementing ETP convolution it is convenient to operate normalized ETPs (ETPs whose latencies are sorted from lowest to highest). Canonical convolution of normalized ETPs then consists of three steps: *convolution, sorting* and *normalization*. *Convolution* per se, shown in Algorithm 1, consists of multiplying each pair of probabilities from both ETPs and adding their latencies. After convolution, latencies in the result ETP are not sorted anymore, which is corrected by the *sorting step*. *Normalization*, shown in Algorithm 2, then removes repeated latencies in ETPs; it combines consecutive repeated latencies by adding up their probabilities.

Given two normalized ETPs of N elements each, convolution per se, has a complexity of $\mathcal{O}(N^2)$, and the resulting ETP contains N^2 elements. The complexity of sorting the N^2 elements is $\mathcal{O}(N^2 \log N^2)$. However, the resulting ETP

Algorithm 2. Normalizing function

```
1: c ← 0
2: etp_out.lat[0] ← etp_in.lat[0]
3: for i = 1 to N do
4:     if etp_in.lat[i] = etp_in.lat[i − 1] then
5:         etp_out.prob[c] ← etp_out.prob[c] + etp_in.prob[i]
6:     else
7:         c ← c + 1
8:         etp_out.lat[c] ← etp_in.lat[i]
9:         etp_out.prob[c] ← etp_in.prob[i]
10:    end if
11: end for
```

contains N blocks of N elements, each block sorted internally, which reduces computational cost in practice down to $\mathcal{O}(N^2)$. The cost of normalization is linear with the number of elements in the ETP.

Starting from the canonical convolution, we survey optimizations related to (i) the cost of each individual operation, (ii) parallelization, (iii) sampling and (iv) discretization. Experimental results are shown in Section 4.

3.1   Cost of Each Operation

The main particularity when convolution is applied to SPTA is that SPTA works with very small probabilities (e.g. 10^{-30}) due to the fact that multiplication of probabilities during convolution leads to lower values for probabilities with an increased number of decimal digits. Operating with such low values makes IEEE 754 standard floating-point (FP) representations inaccurate. For instance, 64-bit double precision FP IEEE 754 numbers use 52 binary digits for the fraction, which allows representing up to 15 decimal digits approximately. To avoid issues with precision, arbitrary-precision FP (*apfp*) numbers can be used. *apfp* precision is not limited by fixed-precision arithmetic implemented in hardware. This increase in precision is provided at the cost of significant longer latency to carry out each operation, as each operation may require dozens of assembly instructions. The impact of the *apfp* precision on the execution time of convolutions will be studied in Section 4.

3.2   Parallelization

Parallelization can be applied across different convolution operations on different ETPs (inter-convolution parallelism) or in the convolution of a pair of ETPs (intra-convolution parallelism).

Intra-convolution Parallelism. Given two ETPs with N and M elements respectively, convolution requires adding the latencies and multiplying the probabilities for the $N \times M$ different pairs of elements from both ETPs. Dividing such work into T parts to be performed in parallel can be done in many different ways. In our case, we divide the N-point ETP_1 (or ETP_2) into T subETPs of N/T points each, ETP_1^{part} where T is the number of cores/processors used. Each such ETP_1^{part} can be convolved with ETP_2 in parallel. The result of this step are T different ETPs. Those have to be concatenated and normalized to become the final outcome of the convolution of ETP_1 and ETP_2.

Inter-convolution Parallelism. In the case of SPTA, typically each instruction has its own ETP. Programs may have easily thousands if not hundreds of thousands of instructions. Hence, convolutions can be performed in parallel. Given a list of M ETPs to be convolved, our approach consists in splitting the list into T chunks of $Mc = M/T$ ETPs each. Each chunk to be convolved is assigned to a different core or processor. Two approaches can be followed to convolve the ETPs in each chunk:

Sequential Order within a Chunk. The first two ETPs (e.g., of N elements each) are convolved, which requires N^2 operations if sorting and normalization of the resulting ETP are omitted, and generates an ETP with up to N^2 elements, which in a following step is convolved with the third ETP requiring up to N^3 operations. Equation 1 shows the maximum number of operations carried out with this approach.

$$OpCount_{seq}^{Mc} = \sum_{i=2}^{Mc} \left(N^i\right) \tag{1}$$

Tree Reduction within a Chunk. In a first step, the Mc ETPs (each of N elements) are convolved in pairs, so each convolution requires N^2 operations. In a second step, the resulting $Mc/2$ ETPs, each of up to N^2 elements, are convolved in pairs requiring up to N^4 operations each and resulting in $Mc/4$ ETPs. Equation 2 shows in the general case the maximum number of operations carried out with this approach.

$$OpCount_{tree}^{Mc} = \sum_{i=1}^{\lceil \log_2 Mc \rceil} \left(\frac{Mc}{2^i} \times N^{2^i}\right) \tag{2}$$

If the number of ETPs is not a power-of-two, the tree reduction approach requires an adjustment phase. Given M ETPs, we convolve as many pairs as needed so that we obtain M' ETPs where M' is a power-of-two.

3.3 Sampling

When two ETPs of N elements are convolved the resulting ETP may have up to N^2 elements. Hence, there is an exponential increase in the number of elements in the result ETP as the number of convolutions increases. In order to limit the number of elements in the ETP, sampling techniques can be used [12].

The principle of sampling, largely used in the literature, is reducing the number of points in the ETPs. In a real-time context, an additional requirement is to ensure that the new ETP is an upper-bound of the original one, so that pWCETs are never underestimated. This is done by collapsing probabilities to the right [12]. For instance, $ETP1 =< (1,2,3,4), (0.2,0.1,0.5,0.2) >$ could be sampled as $ETP1' =< (2,4), (0.3,0.7) >$ or $ETP1' =< (3,4), (0.8,0.2) >$.

There are several ways of sampling an ETP such that, while ensuring it is a safe upper-bound of the original one, the pessimism introduced is kept low [12]. As shown in [12], sampling makes convolution cost to flatten asymptotically so that it does not grow exponentially.

3.4 Discretization of Probabilities

In order to introduce discretization we use an example. Let us assume an architecture in which each instruction can take exactly two latencies (e.g., cache hit and cache miss [11]). Discretization consists in rounding probabilities such that the probability of the highest latency is rounded up and the one of the lowest latency is rounded down. For instance, given $ETP =< (1,20), (0.24,0.76) >$, if we round to a given fraction, e.g. 0.1, this would result in $ETP_{rounded} =< (1,20), (0.2,0.8) >$. Overall, rounding consists in adding ϵ to the probability of the high latency (and subtracting ϵ from the probability of low latency) such that it becomes a multiple of a given rounding value rv, where $rv \leq 1$ and $1 \bmod rv = 0$, so that $(p_{high\ lat} + \epsilon) \bmod rv = 0$.

Rounding has two effects. On the one hand, the resulting ETP can have only $1/rv + 1$ different forms. On the other hand, the probability of high latencies is increased, thus inducing higher pessimism. Similarly to sampling, discretization reduces precision. However, those optimizations sacrifice precision in a controlled and trustworthy way from a WCET estimation perspective (the resulting ETP always upper-bounds the exact one).

In the presence of an M-element vector of ETPs, in a first pass all the probabilities of the ETPs are rounded as explained resulting in g different forms of ETP, with $g = 1/rv + 1$. The convolution of N copies of the same ETP can be done much faster than the normal convolution. This is explained later in this section.

After the first step, there are up to g ETPs to convolve, with g being typically a relatively low value (e.g., $g = 101$ if $rv = 0.01$). Those ETPs can be convolved in parallel applying any of the techniques explained before.

Convolution of E Copies of the Same ETP. Convolving E times an ETP consists, in essence, of applying the power operation. In order to reduce the execution time of the power operation of convolutions we need to decompose E into an addition of power-of-two values. For instance, $E = 7$ can be decomposed into 4, 2 and 1. In this case we convolve $ETP_1^{pow(2)} = ETP_1 \otimes ETP_1$. In a second step we convolve $ETP_1^{pow(4)} = ETP_1^{pow(2)} \otimes ETP_1^{pow(2)}$. The final ETP can be obtained by convolving at most all those ETPs as shown in Equation 3.

$$ETP_1^{pow(7)} = ETP_1^{pow(4)} \otimes ETP_1^{pow(2)} \otimes ETP_1^{pow(1)} \qquad (3)$$

In general, generating the power-of-two ETPs requires performing $\lceil log_2 E \rceil - 1$ convolutions. Then, at most each such ETP (including the original one, ETP_1)

needs to be convolved once, thus requiring up to $\lceil log_2 E \rceil - 1$ extra convolutions. Overall, with this approach the power of a given ETP can be carried out with at most $2 \times (\lceil log_2 E \rceil - 1)$ convolutions, whereas the sequential approach requires $E - 1$ convolutions.

4   Experimental Results

In this section we evaluate the execution time reduction and pessimism increase of the techniques presented when applied in isolation and in a combined manner. The number of configurations and results presented is limited due to space constraints. All these optimizations have been integrated into an ETP management library, developed in C++.

4.1   Experimental Conditions

Platform and *apfp* Library. We use a quad-core AMD Opteron^{TM} processor connected to a 32GB DDR2 667 MHz SDRAM. We run a standard Linux distribution on top of it. For arbitrary-precision FP computations we use the GNU *mpfr* (multiple-precision FP) Library, http://www.mpfr.org/.

The precision of the *mpfr* library was selected according to the criticality level of the target applications. Obviously, the higher the precision the longer takes each operation to execute and the higher are the memory requirements of the library. As an example, for commercial airborne systems at the highest integrity level, called DAL-A, the maximum allowed failure rate per hour of operation [1] in a system component is 10^{-9}. Thus, if a task is fired up to 10^2 times per second, it can be run up to 3.6×10^5 times per hour, and so its probability of timing failure per activation, TPF_{act} should not exceed 3.6×10^{-14}. Therefore, an exceedance probability threshold of 10^{-15} ($TPF_{act} \leq 10^{-15}$) suffices to achieve the highest integrity level. Similarly, exceedance probability thresholds can be derived for other domains and safety levels. We have observed empirically that even if millions of multiplications are performed, a precision of 20 decimal digits suffices to keep accurate results for the 15th decimal digit (and beyond). This means that when enforcing the 20th decimal digit to be rounded up or down for trustworthiness reasons, such pessimism does not propagate up to the 15th decimal digit. Thus, we regard 20 decimal digits as enough for our needs, and select this value as a default value in the experiments. The impact of this parameter in terms of computation cost is studied later in this section. A sensitivity study of the impact of this parameter on pessimism has not been performed due to space constraints, but our choice limits such pessimism to much less than 0.01% in practice in all our experiments.

Optimization Parameters. When applying inter-convolution parallelism, one has to choose between *tree reduction* and *sequential order* when convolving the ETPs within each parallel chunk. Tree reduction typically requires fewer operations than those required with sequential processing ETPs (up to 50% fewer operations). However, it makes ETP size grow faster until their maximum size, which is limited by calling the *sampling* function. Hence with tree reduction most operations require working with two ETPs of E elements. Instead, sequential order also make intermediate ETPs grow up to E elements, but keeps convolving them with N-elements ETPs, with $N \ll E$. Overall, sequential order works faster than tree reduction so it is our default choice in the rest of the paper.

As far as sampling is concerned, many sampling methods have been defined and compared in [12]. Among those, we use *uniform space sampling*, as it provides a good balance among execution time requirements and pessimism introduced. In the experiments, unless otherwise stated, sampling will be systematically applied, and the size of ETPs will be limited to 1,024 elements. If larger ETPs are explicitly used (i.e. 2,048 or 4,096 elements) and sampling is applied, the size of the original ETPs determines the size of the output ETPs.

Test-case Generation and Metrics. In each experiment we use several ETPs with different number of elements. These input ETPs have been generated randomly. To measure the improvement brought by each optimization, we use the execution time reduction, typically w.r.t. non-optimized execution in a single core. Optimizations studied are orthogonal to other methods for convolution optimization [4] whose analysis is beyond the scope of this paper. Pessimism resulting from some optimizations (sampling and discretization) is also computed w.r.t. to the non-optimized results. Pessimism is measured in terms of weight of the ETP, which is obtained as $W = \sum_{i=1}^{N} p_i \times l_i$ where N is the number of elements in the ETP, and p_i and l_i are the probability and latency at position i respectively [12]. Then, the weight of the ETP after optimizations (W_{optim}) is compared w.r.t. to the ETP without optimizations ($W_{baseline}$).

4.2 Impact of *apfp* and *mpfr* Precision on the Cost of Each Operation

To evaluate the price to pay for having sufficient precision in the ETPs, we first evaluate the execution time of each basic operation used by convolutions (comparison, assignment, addition, multiplication, division). All values are normalized to the execution time of the native FP addition operation, i.e. the operation to add FP numbers in the ISA. Results have been obtained by running

ISA					apfp				
$\geq$	$=$	$+$	$*$	$/$	$\geq$	$=$	$+$	$*$	$/$
1	1	1	2	3	5	22	17	36	75

Fig. 1. Cost of each operation normalized to native ISA FP add operation

on our processor a set of micro-benchmarks that exercise the same number of operations of each type.

The results are given in Fig. 1, with the precision of the *apfp* library set to a high value, 300 digits. We observe that the impact of the *apfp* library is significant. The *apfp* operation with lower overhead, the comparison, has an execution time 5x higher than an ISA regular FP comparison. We attribute this to the fact that it is often completed after comparing only a subset of the digits. Addition and assignment have a similar slowdown around 20x while

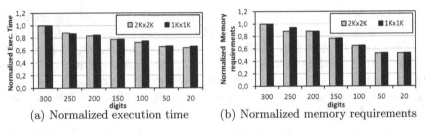

(a) Normalized execution time   (b) Normalized memory requirements

Fig. 2. Execution time and memory requirements for different *mpfr* library precisions

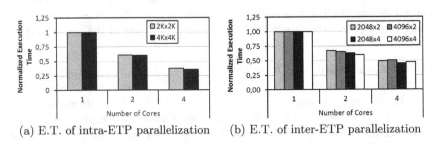

(a) E.T. of intra-ETP parallelization   (b) E.T. of inter-ETP parallelization

Fig. 3. Impact of parallelization on execution time

multiplication and division have a latency 36x and 75x higher than the ISA addition respectively. This represents an increment of more than 22x and 26x w.r.t. their ISA counterparts.

To further evaluate the impact of the *apfp* library precision, we run a single-threaded version of the convolution varying the precision of *mpfr* from 300 digits down to 20, which is considered reasonable for SPTA as explained earlier. Fig. 2(a) and Fig. 2(b) respectively show the reduction in execution time and memory requirements as the number of digits decreases from 300 to 20 when convolving two ETPs. Two ETP sizes are evaluated: 2,048 (i.e *2K*) and 1,024 (i.e. *1K*), and sampling is applied. We observe significant reductions of more than 35% and 45% in execution time and memory respectively when moving from 300 to 20 digits, for both ETP sizes.

4.3   Parallelization

Intra-ETP Parallelization. In this experiment we carry out the convolution of 2 ETPs in parallel, with sorting, sampling and normalization turned off. Only the first step of canonical convolution (see Section 3) is executed in parallel and measured. In this way, we obtain an upper-bound of the execution time reduction (scalability) of intra-convolution parallelism. Two different ETP sizes are evaluated: 2,048 (2K) and 4,096 (4K).

Fig. 3(a) shows the execution time results when running the convolution on 1, 2 and 4 cores. We observe good scalability: execution time reduces by 40% with 2 cores and by 65% with 4 cores. The size of the ETPs has a marginal impact.

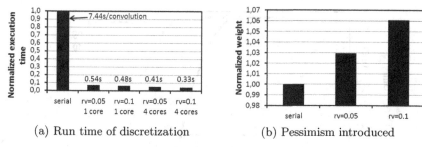

(a) Run time of discretization   (b) Pessimism introduced

Fig. 4. Evaluation of the *Discretization* optimization

Inter-ETP Parallelization. In contrast to intra-ETP parallelization, inter-ETP parallelization does not parallelize one convolution, but instead splits a sequence of convolutions into chunks to be processed in parallel. In this experiment, given a vector of M ETPs to convolve, we measure the benefit of dividing it into $T \in [1, 4]$ chunks, which are processed in parallel (each chunk in one core). The ETPs in each chunk are processed in sequential order.

Fig. 3(b) shows the execution time reduction of inter-ETP parallelization when convolving vectors of 2,048 and 4,096 ETPs (e.g., 4096x2 in the legend stands for 4,096 ETPs of 2K elements each). Results are also shown across different numbers of elements per ETP, namely, 2 and 4. Results do not reach optimal scaling due to: (i) the intrinsic overhead of parallelization (e.g., spawning and synchronizing threads) and (ii) because eventually the number of ETPs to convolve is lower than the core count, thus leaving some cores idle. As it can be observed in Fig. 3(b), the number and size of the ETPs has marginal impact on execution time.

4.4 Probability Discretization

In this experiment, we assess the execution time benefits and impact on pessimism introduced by probability discretization. For this experiment we carry out the convolution of a vector of 4,096 ETPs of 2 elements each[1]. Probabilities of those ETPs are randomly generated, latencies are $l_{hit} = 1$ and $l_{miss} = 60$. We carry out the evaluation for two different rv values: 0.05 and 0.1.

Fig. 4 shows the results, obtained by averaging the ETP weight and execution times on 1,000 runs. When run on one single core (two leftmost bars in Fig. 4(a)), we observe that with $rv = 0.05$, we obtain an execution time reduction of more than 93% (from 7.44s/convolution down to 0.54). With $rv = 0.1$ there is an additional slight reduction in the execution time. However, in terms of pessimism (ETP weight, shown in Fig. 4(b)), $rv = 0.05$ shows to have low pessimism. The increase in pessimism of $rv = 0.1$ does not pay off its additional small reduction in execution time.

Fig. 5 compares the pWCET estimates obtained after convolving 4,096 random ETPs when discretization is not applied, and when it is applied with

---

[1] A two-point ETP represents an architecture with a single level of cache, e.g. the instruction cache, where each ETP takes the form: $< (l_{hit}, l_{miss}), (p_{hit}, p_{miss}) >$

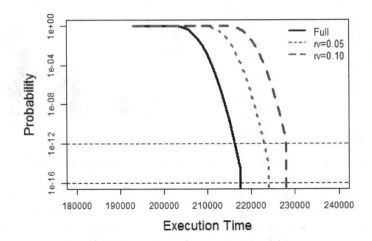

Fig. 5. pWCET estimates with and without discretization

$rv = 0.05$ and $rv = 0.1$. We observe that with discretization pWCET estimates obtained are more pessimistic than when not using discretization. However, the pessimism introduced is relatively small. For instance, for a cutoff probability of 10^{-12} the overestimation is 3.1% for $rv = 0.05$ and 5.5% for $rv = 0.1$.

4.5   Combination of Techniques

The two rightmost bars in Fig. 4(a) show the result of combining discretization and hybrid parallelization. We observe that the combination of both reduces the cost of convolutions to less than 5% of the cost of the non-optimized convolution method, thus showing that benefits of optimizations increase when combined. In terms of absolute execution time, the cost of one convolution reduces from 7.44s down to 0.33s. Thus, if a program has 100,000 instructions, those optimizations reduce convolution cost from 8.6 days down to 9.2 hours. While such cost is still high, we regard it as affordable and it can be further reduced if other optimizations are applied [4] (e.g., fast-fourier transformation).

5   Conclusions

PTA has been regarded as a powerful approach to obtain trustworthy and tight WCET estimates. The static variant of PTA, SPTA, requires the use of convolutions, whose computational cost is high. In this paper we have identified some features of convolutions that require a large number of computations and provide a set of optimizations to reduce their cost. Those optimizations, integrated into a software library, include precision-preserving optimizations (e.g., parallelization), as well as optimizations that trade off some accuracy for some computational cost reduction while preserving trustworthiness. Among those, discretization shows to be the most effective solution. Our results prove the effectiveness of the different optimizations and a small subset of them show a combined execution time reduction down to less than 5% of that of the non-optimized version.

All in all, SPTA specific optimizations trading off execution time reduction and accuracy show to be the most effective ones and they can be combined straightforwardly with non-specific ones.

Acknowledgments. The research leading to these results has received funding from the European Community's FP7 under the PROXIMA Project, grant agreement no 611085. This work has also been partially supported by the Spanish Ministry of Science and Innovation under grant TIN2012-34557, the HiPEAC Network of Excellence, and COST Action IC1202: Timing Analysis On Code-Level (TACLe).

References

1. Guidelines and methods for conducting the safety assessment process on civil airborne systems and equipment. ARP4761 (2001)
2. Altmeyer, S., Davis, R.I.: On the correctness, optimality and precision of static probabilistic timing analysis. In: DATE (2014)
3. Bernat, G., et al.: WCET analysis of probabilistic hard real-time systems. In: RTSS (2002)
4. Breitzman, A.F.: Automatic Derivation and Implementation of Fast Convolution Algorithms. PhD thesis, Drexel University (2003)
5. Cazorla, F.J., et al.: PROARTIS: Probabilistically analyzable real-time systems. ACM Transactions on Embedded Computing Systems $12(2s)$ (2013)
6. Cazorla, F.J., et al.: Upper-bounding program execution time with extreme value theory. In: WCET Workshop (2013)
7. Cucu, L., et al.: Measurement-based probabilistic timing analysis for multi-path programs. In: ECRTS (2012)
8. Davis, R.I., et al.: Analysis of probabilistic cache related pre-emption delays. In: ECRTS (2013)
9. Hansen, J., et al.: Statistical-based WCET estimation and validation. In: WCET Workshop (2009)
10. Kosmidis, L., Quiñones, E., Abella, J., Vardanega, T., Broster, I., Cazorla, F.J.: Measurement-based probabilistic timing analysis and its impact on processor architecture. In: 17th DSD (2014)
11. Kosmidis, L., et al.: A cache design for probabilistically analysable real-time systems. In: DATE (2013)
12. Maxim, D., Houston, M., Santinelli, L., Bernat, G., Davis, R.I., Cucu, L.: Re-sampling for statistical timing analysis of real-time systems. In: RTNS (2012)
13. Quinones, E., et al.: Using randomized caches in probabilistic real-time systems. In: ECRTS (2009)
14. Reineke, J.: Randomized caches considered harmful in hard real-time systems. Leibniz Transactions on Embedded Systems $1(1)$ (2014)
15. Turner, C.J., et al.: Parallel implementations of convolution and moments algorithms on a multi-transputer system. Microprocessors and Microsystems $19(5)$ (1995)
16. Wartel, F., et al.: Measurement-based probabilistic timing analysis: Lessons from an integrated-modular avionics case study. In: SIES (2013)
17. Yip, H.-M., et al.: An efficient parallel algorithm for computing the gaussian convolution of multi-dimensional image data. J. Supercomput. $14(3)$ (1999)

Author Index

Printed in the United States
By Bookmasters